MEDIA PROMOTION AND MARKETING FOR
BROADCASTING, CABLE, AND THE INTERNET

Media Promotion and Marketing for Broadcasting, Cable, and the Internet

FIFTH EDITION

Edited by

SUSAN TYLER EASTMAN
DOUGLAS A. FERGUSON
ROBERT A. KLEIN

ELSEVIER

AMSTERDAM • BOSTON • HEIDELBERG • LONDON
NEW YORK • OXFORD • PARIS • SAN DIEGO
SAN FRANCISCO • SINGAPORE • SYDNEY • TOKYO

Focal Press is an imprint of Elsevier

Focal
Press

Acquisitions Editor: Amy Jollymore
Project Manager: Dawnmarie Simpson
Assistant Editor: Cara Anderson
Marketing Manager: Christine Degon
Cover Design: Cate Barr

Focal Press is an imprint of Elsevier
30 Corporate Drive, Suite 400, Burlington, MA 01803, USA
Linacre House, Jordan Hill, Oxford OX2 8DP, UK

∞ Recognizing the importance of preserving what has been written, Elsevier prints its books on acid-free paper whenever possible.

Library of Congress Cataloging-in-Publication Data
Media promotion and marketing for broadcasting, cable, and the Internet / [edited by] Susan Tyler Eastman, Douglas A. Ferguson, Robert A. Klein.
    p. cm.
Rev. ed. of: Promotion and marketing for broadcasting, cable, and the web. 4th ed. c2002.
Includes bibliographical references and index.
ISBN-13: 978-0-240-80762-1 (pbk. : alk. paper)
ISBN-10: 0-240-80762-6 (alk. paper)
    1. Television broadcasting—Marketing.   2. Radio broadcasting—Marketing.   3. Cable television—Marketing.   I. Eastman, Susan Tyler.   II. Ferguson, Douglas A.   III. Klein, Robert A., 1928–   IV. Promotion and marketing for broadcasting, cable, and the web.
HE8689.7.M37P76 2006
384.55068'8—dc22

                                                                    2005027692

British Library Cataloguing-in-Publication Data
A catalogue record for this book is available from the British Library.

ISBN 13: 978-0-240-80762-1
ISBN 10: 0-240-80762-6

For information on all Focal Press publications
visit our website at www.books.elsevier.com

05 06 07 08 09 10   10 9 8 7 6 5 4 3 2 1

Printed in the United States of America

Working together to grow
libraries in developing countries

www.elsevier.com | www.bookaid.org | www.sabre.org

ELSEVIER   BOOK AID
            International   Sabre Foundation

Contents

Foreword

Welcome to the freshly updated, and painstakingly prepared fifth edition of *Media Promotion and Marketing*. When PROMAX agreed to support the efforts of the publisher, our overriding goal was to make certain that each edition of this book was the most relevant, up-to-date, and practical book of its kind anywhere.

Thousands of hours have been committed by the authors, with the support of scores of television organizations worldwide, to ensure that when you review this book's contents, you'll be getting the most valuable learning experience available in print about promotion and marketing in the television, radio, cable, and news media fields.

It isn't easy. The pace at which the industry sheds old technologies for breathtaking new ones is staggering. New consumer applications of entertainment technology are now sweeping the globe quickly, as our industry races to keep up with viewers. We'd like to acknowledge the generosity of the many television and media organizations that have so enthusiastically provided materials for this work.

So, welcome to your new guidebook to our world of television and the challenges of finding viewers and drawing them to channels, programs, and technologies. We hope that as you read, you'll begin to feel a passion for this global world of television and be inspired to contribute your gifts to its future.

Jim Chabin
President & CEO
PROMAX&BDA

Acknowledgments

We have many people to thank for their help in preparing this book. One group consists of previous authors whose work has been incorporated in this edition. We especially want to thank recent contributors Joseph G. Buchman of Capella University in Utah; Randy D. Jacobs of the University of Hartford; Bradley A. Moses now of WFLA in Tampa; and Suzann Mitten Owen, formerly of WTIU-TV in Bloomington, Indiana. And we welcome new contributors Mary Dickson of KUED in Salt Lake City and Gregory D. Newton of Ohio University. We also thank our reviewers Carl "Bud" Carey of Syracuse University, J. Steven Smethers of Kansas State University, Patricia Williamson of Central Michigan University, and Robert Affe of Indiana University for their practical ideas for improving this edition. We have tried to incorporate as many of their suggestions as possible — especially that the book include more illustrations.

Another group we are grateful to are those who assisted with providing insights, illustrations, and exemplars for this edition. In particular, John Miller and Andee Rosen of NBC Universal, Gloria Lee of ABC, and Steve King of CBS were enormously helpful in providing illustrations of network promotion (and getting the language for them just right). We also warmly thank Milton Hamburger of Radio-TV Services at Indiana University for his invaluable help with artwork and the technology of computer illustrations. For other illustrations (and insights), we especially thank Tom Conner of T.A.G, Dave Devlin of Devlin Design, Robert Dillon of here! Networks, Bryan Flores of Time Warner Cable, Rick Grossman of Woods TV in Paris, Melissa Herr of PBS, John Hite of Discovery, Gregg Jablonski of Oxygen, James Krause of Indiana University, Kathleen Leonard of Sci-Fi Channel, Martin MacAlpine of Disney Latino, Chris Moseley of the Hallmark Channel, Mary-Jo Osborn of CBC, Dave Perry of VH1, Julie Sbuttoni of Oxygen, Leslie Rivera of Telemundo, David Salinger of Starz, Kurt Tovey of WXIN Fox59, Julie Willis of Discovery, and many others. Although wonderful examples of promotional materials appear daily on the air, in print, and online, finding stills of items that are effective when reduced to small size in black-and-white and obtaining formal permissions is an enormous task — fit for Sisyphus and his uphill rock-rolling.

We especially could not have managed without the aid and support of Jim Chabin and Roz McLean of PROMAX and several past and present members of the PROMAX Board of Directors. Indeed, the association's endorsement of several editions of this book has opened the doors to industry insiders and surmounted many legal barriers, enabling the multiplicity of illustrations in this edition. Moreover, PROMAX makes available the annual "State of Our Art" tapes and DVDs that are so valuable to teachers and professionals as supplements to this book. We truly appreciate everyone who helped us illustrate this edition with examples of current media promotion.

We also give especial thanks to our publisher, Amy Jollymore of Focal Press, our production editor, Dawnmarie Simpson, and our copyeditor, Terri Morris, all of whom worked hard to put this edition together. And we thank the many students, teachers, and practitioners who use this book.

Susan Tyler Eastman
Douglas A. Ferguson
Robert A. Klein

Detailed Contents

CHAPTER 1

Promoting the Media: Scope and Goals

Susan Tyler Eastman, Douglas A. Ferguson, and Robert A. Klein

Although the field of promotion is part of the larger field of marketing, promotion of electronic media content differs strikingly from marketing of other products. Many excellent textbooks about marketing exist, but most focus on consumer products for sale. They talk about how to use coupons, direct mail, point-of-purchase displays, ties-ins, games and contests, and premiums and incentives to get consumers to buy products — all topics that come up in this book. The key distinction, illustrated in 1.1, is that a particular tube of toothpaste or box of cereal is identical to thousands of other tubes or boxes, whereas, in contrast, every program is unique. *Every program is at least slightly different from every other program.* Consequently, the promotion of programs differs in a crucial way from the marketing of other products: *To be effective, promotion must be specific to that program and even to a series' individual episodes.*

THE SCOPE OF THE BOOK

This book is primarily about *promoting programs*, including television series and specials. It's also about promoting radio shows and formats. It's about how cable systems and cable networks market programs and niche formats to television viewers and advertisers. It's about promoting the content of streaming media on the Internet and even about promoting video blogs and podcasts.

Promotion of television programs is so important that the commercial media industry forfeits billions of dollars in potential advertising revenue each

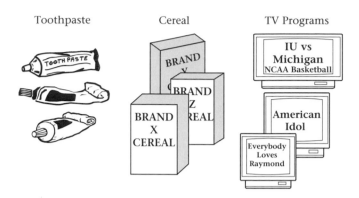

1.1 *Products versus programs.*

year to carry promotional messages (**promos**). Instead of selling every bit of their limited — and oh so very expensive — airtime to advertisers, the hundreds of broadcast and cable networks and the thousands of radio and television stations, as well as groups of local cable systems, give up some of their airtime to put on promos. They also pay other companies to run advertising for their programs (such as in newspapers) and devote the bulk of their websites to promotion of their content. They pay people to create the spots, pages, and advertising, and they lose time and space that could have produced income, merely to invite audiences to watch or listen to their programs. These practices are evidence of program promotion's indispensable role in retaining and increasing audiences.

THE SPECIAL NATURE OF MEDIA CONTENT

The word *programs* is commonly associated with television, and the singular nature of most broadcast and cable network programs certainly stands out (or with copycat programs, their lack of specialness stands out). But all electronic media have unique content, and if the media content is preproduced (recorded or prepared in fixed units for live distribution) and intended for large audiences, we can call all such content "media programming." It is the uniqueness of the individual programs (and separate formats in any single market and of program sites on the web) that gives rise to separate identities for specific content and media companies and thus the need for individualized promotion — both of the program and its source — a network, station, system, or site.

Kinds of Program Content

In the case of television programs, the words used to describe programs signal the amount of uniqueness a viewer should expect. A program can be a **series**, meaning the characters stay generally the same but the plot varies. Or a program can be a **special** or an annual special, which means the show is either truly one of a kind or appears on television only once every year (for instance, the Academy Awards or the Super Bowl). Words such as **clone**, **spinoff**, and **rerun** convey the amount of duplication viewers should expect.

In radio — whether the signal is aired by a broadcast station, comes from a satellite program service, or is streamed on the Internet — usually only one station in each market has a particular program **format** (arrangement of content elements), thus that format is unique to that market.[1] At a minimum, small differences always exist between, say, two rock, or two hip-hop, or two country stations in a market, and only larger markets have several stations of the same general format. Nonetheless, even if two or more have the same format, some differences exist in the exact type and proportions of music, local and network news, syndicated shorts, advertising spots, and announcing content. These elements make up the unique identity of a station (or channel), and *effective promotion must exploit that uniqueness of identity by creating and maintaining its image.*

In media, identity promotion is the same as product branding. When HBO heralds "It's not TV. It's HBO," that represents an effort to establish an identity for the pay network distinct from that of all other entertainment and information services. NBC's familiar peacock logo, a brand identifier known around the world, appears in 1.2. The niche cable services automatically brand their identities as they promote their individual niches (and woe to the national cable network that can't communicate its distinctiveness). Individual broadcast stations and local cable channels also identify themselves in ways that show off their uniqueness, which may be a channel's association with a particular place. For example, the frames from the on-air logo sequence for the Vegas TV Channel in 1.2 explicitly associate the channel with Las Vegas, Nevada.

Unique content appears on the Internet, too. Identity for portals to the Internet has become a function of name and service. GOOGLE is a brand name that *is* what

1.2   *NBC peacock and two Vegas TV Channel logos. Used with permission.*

it *does*, and widespread use of phrases like "Let's Google it" is firm evidence of its enormous success (an example of a brand identity becoming a verb). At a lower level, distinct from portals and search engines, and alongside the seemingly infinite variety of nonprogram-related content, the Internet also carries "programs" — channels of streamed audio or video — comparable to radio formats and television programs. Some channels repeat content from other media, such as reruns of old movies or TV shows, live streaming of a radio station, or encores of sporting events. In addition, producers are developing programs wholly original to the Internet, such as local-only sports, experimental shorts of video/audio, and made-for-online movies, some of which make use of the web's potential for interactivity, others of which — such as video blogging and podcasting — provide opportunities for thousands of amateur voices. New channels and new content need promotion on the air and online to gain large numbers of viewers or listeners.

Moreover, each of the broadcast and cable networks and the big television and radio stations has its own website that promotes its current schedule, with links to specific program sub-sites that combine streamed video and audio with biographies of stars, plot summaries, activities, and so on. Such long-established hits as *ER, CSI*, and the most current *Survivor* series, as well as newer ensemble series like *Lost*, have especially dedicated fans, as do soap operas and sports. Such programs spawn multiple websites, some maintained by media organizations, others by individuals and small groups. Chats and picture sites provide supplements and enhancements for viewers of over-the-air and cable television shows. Such sites are themselves promotion for programs.

In summary, *every program on broadcast and cable television requires individual promotion, every format in a radio market requires promotion; every website with original content requires promotion.* What appears on the Internet may be promotion for cable or broadcast programming, or it may be unique programming that requires its own promotion. Moreover, radio and television stations and cable networks **cross-promote** each other (if co-owned) as well as occasionally carry paid advertising that promotes programs on other channels. Indeed, it is sometimes hard to draw a line between these two kinds of messages. Distinction is needed because one costs the carrier money (self-promotion) and one makes money (paid advertising), although promoting a rival may, in the long run, cost more than it makes.

What Promotion Does

Effective promotion draws on the special identity of a program or format to find listeners or viewers. Ultimately, each program must die (get canceled) or live (get renewed) on its own merits, but strategic tools such as advantageous scheduling and large promotional budgets usually boost audience size.

Promotion serves a wide range of functions. It is a tool for attracting new listeners and viewers to programs, extending their listening or viewing, and retaining their listening or viewing over time — from day to day or week to week. It includes talk about new programs and stars on such programs as *Entertainment Tonight* and on such cable networks as *E! Entertainment*. Promotion includes on-screen **logo-bugs** and elaborate radio **signatures** that remind audiences of the name of the channel being watched or listened to. Frequent reminders are crucial for two reasons: because programs establish a medium's identity, and in ratings, the right name must be used when audience members fill out diaries so the right channel gets credit for their viewing or listening.

Promotion also comes as topical **spots, tickers, bumpers**, and **next-up** titles that encourage viewing or listening to an upcoming program ("Next . . ."). Considerations in designing such promotional materials are discussed in Chapter 5. Generic information about programs can also function as promotion, which has led all the broadcast and cable networks to create websites intended to amplify fans' involvement with their on-screen viewing experience. Magazine advertisements, outdoor billboards, and on-air spot promotion are primary tools for drawing attention to a new or improved broadcast or cable or online offering.

Promotion is the way the audience hears about new and ongoing programs, and it influences audience size. *The best program in the world will have no audience unless, somehow, people hear about it and learn when and where to hear/see it.* Promotion is about that "somehow."

PROMOTION'S TARGETS

The three main groups for which marketing messages are created are *audiences, advertisers*, and *affiliates*, as shown in 1.3. Of these, audiences get the overwhelming portion of attention from promoters of programming and are the focus of this book. Audiences may be either *current* viewers, listeners, or subscribers or *potential*

1.3 *Marketing message targets.*

viewers, listeners, or subscribers. They may be children, teens, or adults; they may be English-speaking or Spanish-speaking; they may be primarily female or primarily male; they may be green aliens or upside-down-viewing nightworkers!

Audience Messages

Audiences come in as many **demographic** groups and **psychographic** (lifestyle) combinations of interests and attitudes as one can imagine. And they may be people who consume mostly one type of music or many formats, watch mostly sitcoms or many kinds of television programming, or want mostly news or mostly entertainment on screen and online. What is important is that the designers of promotion know which subgroup is being targeted in particular pieces of promotion and whole marketing campaigns.

As Chapter 5 points out, one little piece of promotion cannot convey multiple messages and successfully reach very different people.

- At the network level in broadcasting, the most attention goes to audience promotion over-the-air, online, and in print to potential new viewers.
- At the premium cable networks, national audience promotion to retain current subscribers is the current focus.
- At the headquarters of groups of broadcast television and radio stations, local viewers and listeners in a region are the centers of attention.
- At satellite distributors, going after new subscribers remains the primary goal.
- At cable system groups, however, the main goal at present is to convince subscribers to upgrade to digital and broadband services.

All these are different kinds of audiences, and promotion must be designed with different messages that appeal to these different groups of people. The ad for White Sox fans in 1.4 is a generic message from WFLD that both creates and maintains the station's sports image (using increasingly dirtier socks) while reminding fans where the games can be seen.

Advertiser Messages

In addition to audiences, all entities have to promote to the people that supply the money that supports them. Both commercial and noncommercial media entities promote to their funding sources.

- Commercial media companies devote considerable attention to preparing materials for businesses to sell them advertising time or space. This is called **sales promotion**.

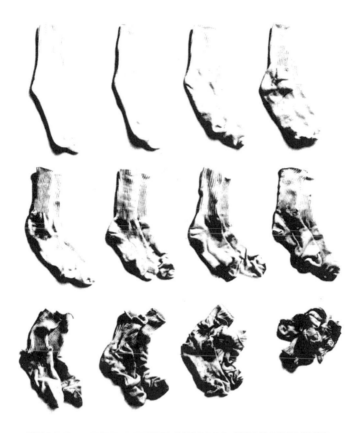

FOLLOW THE WHITE SOX ALL SEASON LONG.

WFLD is carrying seventy White Sox games this year. We suggest you tune in as often as possible. After all, you should never go too long without watching your Sox. **32** WFLD

1.4   *WFLD's ad for the White Sox games. Used with permission.*

- In noncommercial television, the corporations supplying grants for producing or airing programs (called **underwriters**) are the equivalent of advertising targets for promotional messages.

The ad for the Military Channel in 1.5 targets advertisers by pointing out how many millions of households can see the channel and consequently will see the advertising messages it carries.

Similarly, **studios** and **syndicators** (distributors of programs) have to prepare promotional materials to aid in the selling of movies and programs to

1.5 *Military Channel ad targeting advertisers. Used with permission.*

1.6 *Syndicator's ad for* Maury *targeting television stations. Used with permission.*

potential affiliates, either in broadcasting or cable. Figure 1.6 illustrates one of the usual ways syndicators commonly appeal to potential program buyers: They compare the ratings performance of a series to similar competing syndicated shows (the buyers' other choices), and they also explain when the program does best (4 p.m. for *Maury*) and how much larger an audience it averages over a popular lead-in series.

Although the faces and voices of stars may appear briefly in video, print, and online communications about time/space sales, series buys, or underwriting grants, the key attribute of advertiser and syndicator messages is factual information *about* audiences, taken from ratings or other research, that responds to the concerns of potential program buyers.

Affiliate Messages

Finally, there are other industry groups (loosely called affiliates) who are targets of promotion. The term affiliates here refers to program outlets (the stations and the cable systems) that are connected to a program source such as a broadcast network or a cable network). Broadcast networks have to prepare materials especially for their affiliated stations to keep them informed and satisfied. Affiliation is no longer a permanent condition. Similarly, cable networks have to supply materials to local cable systems and satellite distributors for their use in promotion, and all but the very largest try to convince additional systems to carry them (for an example, look ahead at 7.11). Today, the media world feels upheaval at all levels, and relationships that have endured for decades are now open to change.

ATTRIBUTES OF PROMOTIONAL MEDIA

The attributes of promotion differ by the medium of promotion. Each mass-market medium has special characteristics that influence what can be communicated, and each has its own combination of limitations and advantages.

First, the successful message designer separates the *persuasion* media from the *informational* media. On-air promos for programs, radio spots, billboards, and ads in magazines and newspapers are messages that try to persuade potential viewers to watch, listen, or subscribe. In contrast, Internet websites (at least the pages for television and radio programs, which are the topic of this book) must be sought out by web users, and those users want some kind of information. Designers of web pages have the initial task of providing whatever users want, and on television program sites, for example, users typically want such things as actor bios, plot summaries, feedback and chat options, and pictures to print. At the same time, page designers also try to persuade people into other behaviors, such as watching other shows, listening longer to a station, subscribing to a digital service, and so on. But the first requirement is to supply the wanted information.

Another way to describe this key difference is that some media messages *approach the viewer* (listener or user), whether that person is interested or not, while others are *purposively sought by the user* (or viewer or listener) to serve that person's needs — the push/pull distinction. Approach messages *push themselves* at audiences; sought messages require audience members to individually *pull them from* a larger context (click on icons or bookmarks, go to splash page, and so on). In other words, is the user or the media company the primary agent?

These distinctions do not minimize the role of being entertaining. Both persuasive and informative promotional messages have to be visually and auditorily intriguing to get users to do as they ask or to come back again.

Second, *the media vary in physical attributes affecting promotional messages.* On-air and print have attributes of environment and time and space. A promo can be located in a popular or unpopular program; it can be surrounded by many other messages or be relatively isolated. A promo has a fixed length in time (seconds), and normally, viewers cannot extend that or repeat the spot — except by using **TiVo**-like (**DVR**) storage controls. In print media, an ad may be buried on a highly cluttered page, or at the other extreme, stand out visually from its environment. Each ad occupies a fixed amount of space that cannot be immediately manipulated.

In contrast, a program promoted on a web page may have an entire **splash page** to itself, although other commercial matter in **banners** and **pop-ups** can clutter it up. More crucially, sites promoting programs are continuously there at the user's convenience and can be instantly printed and otherwise manipulated by most computers. When accessed on a cell phone, however, the *manipulation* characteristic is minimal, while *redistribution* — by forwarding to other phones — becomes simple, as it is on computers. Cell phones are a mobile technology like wireless computing, which means messages become portable. *The consequences for promotional messages are that they must communicate successfully in all kinds of environments and cannot depend on readability or audibility.*

INDUSTRY CHANGES

The most sweeping change in promotional strategy in recent years has been the widespread adoption of *cross-promotion in multiple media.* When a single company owns many media, then each of the company's programs and properties can readily be marketed on all the other programs and properties. Although cross-promotion has been around for a long time as paid and traded advertising, it has only recently become a major thrust of marketing because of four changes in the industry.

Looser Limits

The relaxation of Federal Communications Commission (FCC) regulations affected both programs and promotion of those programs. Promotion is governed by the legal restrictions on advertising when it is paid but falls into a special classification when it is unpaid (and not traded between companies with different owners). The Federal Trade Commission (FTC) and FCC have gradually lifted dozens of irritating restrictions on break content, quantities of messages separating program segments, program lengths, and station name changes.

Of all changes, the end of most FCC restrictions on *ownership of programs* by the broadcast networks most profoundly affected promotion. Owners of programs now have a much greater interest invested in the success of their owned programs than they ever had in the past when virtually all programs were purchased from some other company. In the latter case, the prevailing attitude when a program failed was "Get another program." But when programs are owned by the distributor itself (the network or station), a greater effort goes into finding the right time periods for scheduling them and using extensive promotion (and research) to find the right audience. Several changes in federal law have removed restrictions on what broadcasters can do in their program promotion, whereas cable and the Internet have always been free of these restrictions.

Tighter Controls

A second change was that the largest media companies became increasingly **vertically integrated** with regard to the programming process. Most of the big companies now control all the stages from production through distribution for programs. They make many of the television series and movies they carry; they own some of the teams and sporting events they carry; and they own many of the stations, cable systems, and satellite services that distribute their programming. This situation gives their key programs enormous importance as potential sources of revenue, which makes this content worth promoting heavily. The top-five major players — Time Warner, Disney, Viacom, Fox, and NBC Universal (owned in turn by GE) — appear in 1.7, along with some of their largest media possessions.

Multiple Interests

A third change is that the largest media companies have now become *media conglomerates*. Most own or have major interests in all kinds of media properties — domestic and foreign — including broadcast networks, cable networks (pay and basic), television stations and cable systems, radio stations and recording companies, major production studios, syndication companies, websites, book publishers, newspapers and magazines, sports rights, and maybe theme parks and theaters. Figure 1.7 also illustrates the wide variety of properties owned by these five giant media companies. Promotion can thus go both ways, not only between co-owned cable and broadcast properties, but also between amusement parks and books, between CDs and magazines, and between movie theaters and television series.

Fewer Competitors

A fourth change is that there are fewer competitors in the media business nowadays. The media have *consolidated*, so that just five companies dominate the entire media business. The Big Five (seen in 1.7) control between 80 and 90 percent of the media industry.

At the same time, the intensity of competition continues to increase. Indeed, the fewer the competitors, the more directly they can compete. For example, this occurs when two or three companies take over the majority of radio or television stations in a market. The formats that go head-to-head in competition for both audiences and advertisers operate at a constant intense level of rivalry, just as contending early-evening television newscasts have traditionally done.

Time Warner:
The WB • CNN • Headline News • AOL • TBS • TNT • SI TV • HBO • The Movie Channel • Cartoon Network • T W Cable Systems • • Warner Bros. Studio • Warner China Films. • New Line Cinema • Time Inc. (magazines and books)

Viacom:
CBS • UPN • MTV • VH1 • Nickelodeon • SBS • CMTV • BET • Infinity Radio Stations • Comedy Central • Showtime • TV Land • Viacom Outdoor • Viacom Cable Systems • Spelling Entertainment • King World Productions • Paramount Pictures • National Amusement parks and movie theaters • Simon & Schuster Publishers

Disney:
ABC • ESPN • ESPN II • ESPN Classic • ESPNU • ESPN Radio • A&E • The History Channel • Lifetime • ABC Radio Networks • The Disney Channel • ABC Family • Disney Theme Parks • Radio Disney • Buena Vista Television • CBS Records • Walt Disney Imagineering • NHL's Mighty Ducks • Disney Theatrical Productions • The Walt Disney, Miramax, and Touchstone Studios • Resorts • Disney Cruise Line • Disney Consumer Products (toys, books, software)

News Corporation (Fox):
FOX • FOX Sports • FOX News • FX • DirecTV • SKY • STAR • Sky Italia • The Speed Channel • TV Guide • FOX Searchlight • Foxtel Digital • 20th Century Fox Studios • Harper Collins Publishers • hundreds of newspapers and magazines

NBC Universal:
NBC • CNBC • MSNBC • USA • PAX • Bravo • Telemundo • The Sci Fi Channel • CANAL + • Universal Studios • NBC Studios • Universal Pictures • Universal Theme Parks

1.7 *The dominant media players.*

Over the very long haul, however, when there are few but powerful peer competitors, the danger is that they will carve up the market with each seeking different portions of the audience (and advertisers). Although it is illegal to do so by conspiring (an anti-trust violation), market forces quite naturally lead companies away from expensive head-on confrontation toward distinct markets. All of a subgroup of, say, radio stations targeting young men, may be larger (or more appealing to some advertisers) than merely a narrow slice of one main pie. Both the increasing strength of competition and the trend toward market segmentation have led to new attitudes toward program promotion.

On the cable front, companies proliferate line extensions (**subniche channels**) to hang onto segments of the market. The Discovery Channel, for example, comes in Discovery Health, Discovery Home, Discovery Times, Discovery Kids, Discovery HD Theater, and Discovery en Espanol, as well as Animal Planet, the Science Channel, the Travel Channel, the Military Channel, TLC, Fit TV, and maybe other subniche channels. Besides the main ESPN channel, the brand has been extended to ESPN 2, ESPN Classic, ESPN Radio, ESPN Online, and the newest entry, ESPNU (all college sports). Each of these programming channels needs separate as well as collective promotion — a big task when most airtime has a very high monetary value.

SHIFTING GOALS AND TACTICS

As the structure and economics of the companies controlling media in the United States changed, their perspective on programs and, concomitantly, their sense of the essential purposes for promotion changed. Because promotion usually costs money (expense) rather than makes money (revenue), tight-fisted managers seek the best use of their expenditure.

The Multi-Platform Vantage

The combination of an ownership interest in specific programs, combined with vertical integration, conglomeration, and consolidation, has led to a new *multiplatform perspective* that in turn has led to development of cross-promotional strategies and tactics. The media giants think of each property as an extension of their other properties as well as a separate revenue stream.

For instance, when a program service such as Viacom owns all or part of three broadcast networks (CBS, UPN, and SBS — Spanish Broadcasting Service); owns upwards of a dozen cable networks (MTV, VH1, Comedy Central, BET, Showtime, and others); owns a large number of major radio stations (Infinity Radio) and an outdoor company; and has websites, theaters, and amusement parks, it possesses multiple **platforms** for reaching audiences. In addition to the network itself and a movie studio (Paramount), Viacom owns a major independent producer (Spelling) and a major television syndicator (King World). Controlling multiple platforms means that Viacom can make a television show that can be aired (and promoted) on several different television channels, distributed to others by one arm of the corporation while the show is talked about on radio programs, and can appear on billboards and other signage — all at little actual cost in dollars. Simultaneously, a radio star from an Infinity station can appear on CBS or UPN television talk programs. Moreover, the CBS website can have acres of material about the stars, plots, and productions of owned programs, and its site can readily include activities interacting with stars or producers and contests that necessitate viewing of owned programs. Lead actors from programs can be treated as celebrities in media appearances, web fan clubs can be started, and representations of the actors (in cutouts, costumed look-alikes) can appear in advertising and theater promotional displays and become adjuncts of amusement rides and theme parks. Books can be quickly published about the making of an owned program or the life of one of its stars. A television program can be turned into a movie, as well as the other way around. A program can become a computer game. Its stars can appear at halftime in sporting events and concerts. Indeed, an owned program can be fuel for dozens of cross-promotional efforts among owned properties.

The multi-platform perspective is driven by both *availability* and *cost*. Owners can tell their employees what to do, what to air, what to carry, what to focus on, and thus require the promotion of owned programs in the most valuable time on its networks and stations and in the best positions in its newspapers and magazines. They can require the hosts of owned shows to talk about other owned programs and the stars that are important to the owners, thus attracting public and media attention to their owned properties. (Consider, for example, who appears on Leno and Letterman and other entertainment talk programs.) A lot of talk leads to more audience interest and more audience interest to higher ratings (or greater sales) and that, in turn, leads to increased advertising and sales revenue. And an owner can bump other advertising messages in favor of the company's own. No longer must the company *ask* for advertising time on other channels in the hope that an ideal time period is available.

All this self-advertising is free, or in a practical sense, low cost. When a company doesn't own other media, the cost of paid advertising can be high and thus the amount of paid promotion that is practical will be limited. If a company owns many other media outlets, however, the price of touting a key program falls, and the variety of kinds of promotion that are possible leaps upward. Although an owner can no longer sell time to others that is dedicated to promotion, at least it is the company's and not someone else's programs that are being promoted, and thus the benefit redounds to the company.

Repurposing Programs

Programs have become reusable across platforms, and thus promotion of them touts their availability in multiple forms. A television "property" can be shown to audiences not just once or twice, but on both broadcasting and cable channels and perhaps streamed on the Internet. A hit program is no longer just a show for, say, NBC on Tuesdays at 9 p.m. It might also air on co-owned USA, Bravo, PAX, and Telemundo, and if suitable, on CNBC and MSNBC or Sci-Fi Channel, as well as get streamed on the Internet. In recent years, NBC has spread its Olympic coverage across most of these platforms.

Cross-Promotion's Benefits

As an outgrowth of the industry's structural and economic changes, cross-promotion became the hot new strategy in the early 2000s, more or less replacing the emphasis on **branding** in the industry of the preceding years. More than a decade ago, the term *cross-promotion* usually meant cross-program hyping — promoting one show in preceding programs on that same channel. Then, it came to be applied to advertising a show on other channels in the same medium, such as in paid advertising spots for a broadcast prime-time show on a cable channel. Moreover, public television has long cross-promoted from public television to and from public radio, exchanging time for messages about the other medium's content. Thus, the term also became a way of referring to traded airtime between commercial television and radio stations. Nowadays, the new element is that cross-promotion has exploded across all media, with the emphasis on co-owned media.

News Corporation (FOX), for example, is able to use its control of hundreds of newspapers and magazines to generate interest in 20th Century Fox movies and FOX television programs. Its print empire includes such giants as *The New York Post, The Times of London, The Sun, The Australian*, and *TV Guide* magazine, as well as hundreds of small papers and dozens of magazines. Its video empire includes FX and The Speed Channel as well as FOX Sports, FOX News, FOX Searchlight, and the satellite services, DirecTV, SKY, and STAR, and all these entities can cross-promote each other and other News Corporation properties.

Building **buzz** for programs (especially movies) has become a key element of promotional strategy, and it is particularly evident in the way information about co-owned programs has infiltrated radio and morning television talk programming and magazine article topics in a big way. And for the hit programs, the potential exists for animated cartoon characters and computer games, as well as toys and clothing to merchandise to the public. Thus, cross-promotion boosts revenues in all directions for owners of hot media properties.

Changing Resource Allocations

One recently intensified aspect of media economics has been a further shift of resources away from conventional television into cable and the Internet. Although radio remains strong as an industry and active in self-branding and promotion (and as a place for jobs for new graduates), domestic television has markedly retrenched its self-promotion, because the industry's large corporate owners focus almost solely on the bottom line.

Owners now see promotion as an expense that must result in direct, not indirect, benefits on the profit side of the ledger. In consequence, the industry has moved away from promotion as a domestic branding tool to emphasize short-term profits. At the same time, however, global promotion of brand names remains a crucial part of extending audience size and advertising revenue on the world stage.

PERSISTENT CONSTRAINTS ON PROMOTION

Certain legal constraints on promotion, described in 1.8, continue to affect what promotional practitioners can and can't do. These include limits on lotteries and contest construction and frequency. Lotteries are particularly knotty problems. Because lotteries operate under prohibitions in some states, and because those contests deemed to be lotteries are restricted by the FCC, broadcasters must analyze what they put on the air to keep themselves free of FCC inquiries. In addition, some sales practices related to advertising are legally forbidden, and reuse of program content in promotional materials is limited by copyrights and requirements for releases.

Finally, there are major ethical and legal questions associated with artificially inflating ratings, using phony testimonials, and taking money surreptitiously to advertise another business (such as a restaurant or a song) without declaring the income on taxes. Hiding such a sales relationship from audiences is either **payola** or **plugola** and punished by fines (and firing). The negative effects of **pay-for-play** have long been a drag on the music industry, hindering effective station promotion based on audience preferences in favor of playlists influenced by bribery.[2]

MODELS OF PROMOTIONAL STRATEGIES AND TACTICS

Models are ways of picturing relationships between the parts of something, in this case, the promotional process. Two kinds of promotional models coexist at different levels of strategy. The first model relates to the strategies and tactics that

1.8 Legal Concerns: Promotional and Marketing

Lotteries

Few legal issues affect only promotion practices; most are shared by all producers (copyright) or other businesses (fraud). One area of unique legal concern to broadcasters is that of lotteries, because many states continue to prohibit the advertising of privately run or charity lotteries but have declared lotteries otherwise legal. Indeed, a special law had to be passed by Congress to permit the reporting of state lottery results on television and radio in the states where they are permitted. Each state determines whether (1) lotteries are legal within state boundaries and (2) whether they can be advertised.

Broadcasting information about a lottery is legal under federal law if the lottery is not prohibited by state law and if either (1) the lottery is conducted by a charitable organization (charitable organizations are those that qualify as tax-exempt under Section 501 of the Internal Revenue Code) or (2) the lottery is conducted by a business where the lottery is "a promotional activity and is clearly occasional and ancillary to the primary business of that organization." Lotteries are legal in most but not all states, but advertising them is more restricted, leaving stations in states permitting lotteries and advertising able to air some contests that are lotteries without penalty and leaving other stations under strong prohibitions.

The manager of a contemporary music format radio station needs to be an expert in what constitutes a lottery. Specifically, any game involving a valuable prize, a just-above-minimal cost for entering the contest (called *consideration*), and random chance (not skill) is a lottery. Deciding whether a contest activity requires skill or random chance is sometimes difficult, as is deciding if an effort reaches the level called consideration. Promotion managers should consult station management or legal staff about potential lotteries to learn which laws and station policies apply.

Contests

A *contest* is simply a lottery with one of the three elements missing. Contests may be freely promoted and advertised by all broadcast stations. Common contests are those that involve a valuable prize and chance but no consideration (as in giving concert tickets to the tenth caller) or involve a valuable prize and consideration but require an element of skill rather than chance to win.

Whenever contests are conducted by broadcast stations, care should be taken to assure that the contest is not false, deceptive, or misleading. For example, a contest to win "the keys to a brand-new car" should include the car (unless it's clearly stated that only the keys are being awarded as a prize). Specific elements of all contests that should be disclosed to potential contestants include (1) how to enter, (2) entry deadlines, (3) when the prize will be awarded, (4) how the winner will be selected, and (5) tie-breaking procedures. Station contests that are not broadcast to the public are not covered by these rules. For example, sales department contests among account executives or clients may be pure lotteries and are restricted only by fair practices and station policies. Finally, whenever a winner of a contest (listener, viewer, salesperson, or client) is awarded more than $600 in prizes, the station must file a form 1099 with the IRS, on which the station reports the prize as income for the winner.

Sales Practices

Any practice that is illegal or unethical in selling goods or services — such as systematically discounting for certain buyers among competing companies — also is illegal in selling broadcast time. Federal laws relating to sales practices can be enforced by the FTC and the FCC.

Federal law explicitly enjoins broadcasters and networks from unfair trading practices in the sale of time. The shift from prepublished station rate cards to flexible patterns of time pricing (since there now are several ratings books from which to choose audience estimates) has blurred time sales transactions. However, many broadcast network discounting practices that traditionally favored major advertisers such as Procter & Gamble (and tended to create monopolies) have been eliminated in recent years due to investigative efforts by the FCC and FTC and the networks' pressing need for increased revenue.

Another sales practice that occasionally affects promotion staffs is that of cooperative advertising in which a manufacturer and a retailer share advertising costs. FTC guidelines on co-op advertising now prohibit a wide variety of practices. Although these regulations apply more directly to sales efforts rather than to promotion, an employee seeking cooperative contracts for public service efforts, for example, should consult the station or system's legal advisor to see if the arrangement falls within the FTC's guidelines.

Copyright

Two other areas of legality relating to promotion are *trademark* protection and *copyright*. Network and station logos, wordmarks, and slogans can be registered as trademarks to receive protection within the United States. Moreover, many attention-getting symbols, characteristic sounds, original program titles, call letters, and distinct personalities may be protected. Advice on what a station can protect is available from the National Association of Broadcasters.

Copyright looms as an important concern to all producers of local materials. Contracts for materials produced by production resource companies spell out the limitations on a station's use of the materials supplied. Generally, the station licensing a program, jingle, or copyrighted slogan may make unrestricted use of it for a designated period of time (such as one year). After that time, the station loses the right to air the materials except under a renewed contract.

All music registered with the American Society of Composers, Authors, and Publishers (ASCAP), Broadcast Music Incorporated (BMI), and the Society of European Stage Authors and Composers (SESAC) is protected from use without payment of fees. Similarly, photographs and drawings not created by station employees must be purchased (or leased) from the copyright holders before they can be incorporated in promotional productions. However, the fair use provision of the Copyright Act allows a station to use a creator's work (a book cover, for example) as illustration in a promotion that advertises that person's presence on a program (a talk show), without seeking explicit permission. Moreover, syndicators of movies and series conditionally incorporate in licensing contracts permission for the stations or networks to use clips and stills in on-air and print promotion to audiences.

Release Forms

Release forms permitting the use of someone's face or voice are required before the likeness may be broadcast in programs or promotional spots. This stipulation applies to both hired actors and members of the public; it does not apply to news footage, celebrities, or public officials. Shots of people participating in large-scale public activities, such as rallies, parades, or fairs, are exempted from the need for releases. Recognizability is the criterion determining when a signed release must be obtained from a casually recorded member of the public (who did not seek recording and was not participating in a mass activity). In producing promotional spots, it must be assumed by management that payment may be required if members of the public are asked to be on camera or to take direction of any kind. Certainly, a release form must be signed, and it is best to check with the company's legal counsel, the Screen Actors Guild (SAG), or the American Federation of Television and Radio Artists (AFTRA).

Hypoing, Phony Testimonials, and Payola

Promotion departments always share ethical responsibility with other employees for the social effects of both the broadcast programs and the commercial advertising messages. Quantities and types of violence and sexual content on program promotions are issues of broad social concern that reach far beyond quibbles about good taste or puffery. They have resulted in loss of audience and sales for media companies. Another fundamental social concern is the long-term effect of mass consumerism projected in broadcast programming when many people in the world do not possess even the necessities of life.

Four practices relating to audience promotion should be considered unethical despite their frequent occurrence: (1) the use of excessive hypoing to boost audience ratings; (2) the creation of erroneous impressions of program content or the conditions for winning prizes; (3) the airing of phony testimonials by celebrities, actors, or members of the general public; and (4) the toleration of payola or plugola.

The rating services that measure audiences actively discourage practices classified as *hypoing*, which constitutes flagrant artificial inflation of the viewing or listening audience to maintain audience allegiance and drive up the measures on which advertising rates are based. Prohibited are on-air mentions of diaries or ratings (particularly in connection with the station's call letters) and the conduct of field surveys (about programming, news, or viewing preferences) during a rating period or the preceding four weeks. Scheduling documentaries or news interviews about ratings during this period is especially discouraged by the rating services. Unfortunately, such prohibitions have little effective force. Creating an erroneous impression in on-air promotion also is unethical. Promotional spots sometimes make misleading suggestions regarding the importance of roles played by celebrities or use titillation as a come-on to series episodes. Using an actor to pose as a celebrity or a public figure is obviously misleading, as is false testimony solicited by producers of spots; both practices may violate FTC regulations. These practices may not harm the public, but they can minimize the effectiveness of other promotional efforts. A more serious concern, for radio stations especially, is misleading information about on-air contests. The FCC requires broadcasters to disclose periodically all the terms of a contest on the air.

Other practices may not be so obvious, however. Public display of microphones and television cameras influence people's responses in subtle ways in "man-on-the-street" interviews, a common means of gaining content for local promotional spots. Most people tend to give positive responses if they anticipate some reward, such as a giveaway. Also such interviews are prone to bias arising from the subject's assumption that any negative responses will be edited out of the broadcast material. Thinking that the wool can be pulled over the public's eyes is generally unproductive; the audience usually sees through contrived testimonies.

The dividing line between promotion and advertising becomes blurred when stations join with advertisers (for example, in a promotion for a rock concert) in any fashion that promotes the interests of both the advertiser and the station. Both radio and television management must be watchful for instances of staff payola and plugola. *Payola* refers to illegal payment for promoting a recording or song on the air. DJs who accept free merchandise or other bribes for playing particular songs are guilty of taking payola. *Plugola* is the variant in which material is included in a program for the purpose of covertly promoting or advertising a product without disclosing that payment of some kind was made. For example, mentioning the name of a restaurant as if it were a personal favorite of the DJ, instead of something he or she has been secretly paid to do, constitutes plugola. The penalties for violating payola or plugola regulations include fines up to $10,000 or a year in jail or both for each offense, and ethical managers will promptly fire DJs when there is evidence that payola or plugola occurred.

The subject of ethics for promotion usually involves questions of personal and social values rather than purely legal issues. Ethics are a matter of concern throughout the industry. Many articles in PROMAX publications have addressed borderline promotional practices and exhorted promotion managers to adopt high standards.

associate with particular media, such as broadcast television networks or cable television networks or local radio stations. The second model relates to the efficacy of particular kinds of mediated messages.

Strategic Goals

Strategies depend on goals. The overarching strategic goal of most prime-time television, for example, is to capture the largest possible audience, especially those viewers aged 18 to 49. As the diagram in 1.9 shows, a company can have three goals in relation to *audience ratings*: It can seek to capture new viewers (or listeners or subscribers or users), the **acquisitive goal**; it can strive to move audiences

1.9 *A model of audience strategies and tactics.*

from one time period into another time period, the **recycling goal**; or it can focus on keeping its current audience, the **retentive goal**. Although a company may have all three aims at different times, any single piece of promotion (an ad or even a campaign) should ideally concentrate on just one goal. Alternatively or concurrently, a company's overarching purpose may be to increase *revenue in another property*, such as a different channel, a theme park, or a movie studio. In that case, the company may focus on achieving wide positive recognition of parent name in association with its programming, the **brand positioning goal**. Seeking to improve ratings and build cross-media revenue are not mutually exclusive, but the most effective promotion doesn't try to do more than one thing.

Another goal for promotion shows up occasionally. Some spots or ads have the overriding purpose of denigrating or interfering with another entity's promotional efforts. Called **competitive promotion**, it is clearly seen when one company names another company (or its programs) in promotional messages for the purpose of claiming how much better or newer or something the first company's programs are. Radio stations of the same format sometimes undercut direct competitors on the air by saying, in effect, "our music is better than WXXX's music." The phenomenon has even appeared in network television promotion, catching attention because it is so counter to normal practice — as for example, when NBC said "[CBS's] *CSI-Miami* is a repeat, so here's your chance to watch [NBC's] *Medium*" (Feb. 26, 2005).

Strategic Targets

A strategy also needs to have a **target group**. Although the major broadcast networks and some cable networks go after the largest possible audiences, in fact they are concentrating on reaching certain large subgroups in different time periods and for different programs. The viewers of late-night talk/comedy may not be the same as the viewers of a particular daytime or prime-time show. Generally, audiences for television and radio are defined by age and gender — their *demographic groups* — because age and gender are what the ratings companies measure. They can also be defined by common interests or hobbies, and by *psychographic groups*, such as viewers of gardening or house redecoration or users of the Internet. Finally, audiences can be distinguished by their subscriber groups — such as whether they pay for newspapers or premium movie channels.

The ideal medium for reaching adults 18 to 49 years is network television itself (and reaching this demographic group is the networks' **strategic goal**). In every hour of prime time, ABC, CBS, FOX, or NBC competes ferociously by airing eight or more promos for its other prime-time shows or subsequent episodes of the current program. Indeed, the networks promote their hits and almost-hit shows the hardest to keep and raise ratings (an example of a **tactical goal**). In addition, as the evening progresses, they air additional promos for their late-night Leno and Letterman shows, and may include other promos for the next day's morning talk/news and afternoon soaps.

Telemundo and Univision target a broad age-range of Spanish-speaking viewers and provide full day and night schedules of programs, including news. They target also adults 18 to 49 years because they are desirable to advertisers, but in addition, Telemundo and Univision provide some programs for children, teens, and older viewers in order to be full-service networks. In contrast, UPN and the WB seek more narrowly defined audiences for their programs, such as teen/young adult males or females, and they provide only limited schedules of programming to their affiliates (just 2 hours most nights in prime time and less than 7 days a week — no daytime or late-night programs). Their shorter schedules generate fewer programs to promote but less time to schedule the on-air promos. Thus they make deals with their affiliates to get them to air network promos in what might normally be "local time." PAX, at the present time, consists largely of rerun programming and has not been actively competing with other broadcasters. Its primary goal appears to be to differentiate itself from other networks, but its promotional efforts have been modest.

Cable networks come in such a huge variety that lumping them all together becomes meaningless. Their goals and means differ considerably. For example, the strategic goal of ESPN and its cohort networks is to continue as *the* preeminent sports service. This differs in brand positioning from most other networks. Cable networks can be clustered by content type (all news, all movies, all sports) or target audience (all children, all military buffs, all women interested in fitness or home decorating or fashion). Competition for brand superiority occurs largely within a group, although the largest cable networks also compete against the broadcast services.

Tactical Approaches

Once there is a strategic goal and a target audience, then the **tactical approach** can be chosen. The main promotional approach, the *internal media tactic*, is when the company uses its own air to schedule promos either on the same channel or co-owned channels and trades space/time on co-owned properties. Instead, or at the same time, the promotional approach can seek wholly new audiences by means of paid advertising in other company's channels and publications. This is called the *external media tactic*. Finally, a media company can seek to foster "events" that generate entertainment news — free but immensely valuable publicity — in other media.

At another level, tactics also refer to the *tools of promotion*. They include, but are not limited to, on-air promos and bumpers, logo-bugs and pop-up titling, print advertising, websites, games and contests, and outdoor and other signage (see Chapter 5). Indeed, thinking up new ways to reach potential audiences with promotional messages is a major part of the job of promotion. For example, the networks need to promote many programs without using up the time for paid commercials. This has led to shorter promos (many are just 5 seconds or less) and new forms of promotion ("Next" corner pop-ups discussed in Chapters 5 and 6). *Increasing competition to build widely recognized logos in America and around the world (**brand positioning**) and retain every possible television viewer has led to the constant on-screen network bug and frequent automated reminders about upcoming programs (**tactical approach**).*

MODEL OF PROMOTIONAL EFFECTIVENESS

Promotion needs to be effective to do its job, but determining all influences that might make spots, ads, or websites more or less effective is next to impossible. Moreover, promotional messages are never totally ineffective (or they wouldn't get made), so the issue is wholly one of degree. The goal seems simple: Maximize a message's influence on its target group. But how to measure that influence is debatable. Some messages are clearly intended to raise ratings, so having ratings go up (or down) is an easy-to-agree-on test. But sometimes, just staying flat in the ratings is a remarkable achievement when one's competitors have gone all out in that time period (such as airing an Olympics or the Super Bowl, which leaves only a few viewers for anything else). So, using ratings as a yardstick of effectiveness doesn't work all of the time.

Moreover, instead of enlarging audience size, some messages have more subtle goals, such as raising awareness (of a new show) or building trust (in a newscast or individual newscaster). Achieving those goals takes a long time, and measuring their degree of success becomes more difficult (or at least, more expensive) than the results may be worth.

Furthermore, many things get in the way of ideal promotional performance: It may be difficult to isolate (or agree on) one target group for a promotional campaign, or social conditions may change without time to alter video or printed promotional messages (natural disasters, scandals). Although consensus exists on many factors that influence television promotional effectiveness in the prime network hours, the list is incomplete and doesn't necessarily apply to other time periods and different media. Moreover, occasionally, breaking a so-called rule can be more effective than following it (called **breakout** in the industry).

Despite all these caveats, the many rules of thumb that practitioners describe in the subsequent chapters result from decades of profitable industry practice. *These rules are generally the best guidelines for maximizing promotion's effectiveness in a given situation.* Some of these rules have to do with structural conditions such as when and where to place promos or ads for programs. Others have to do with elements of content that should or should not appear in a promo under certain circumstances. Because the technical quality of video and audio promos of competitors in any local or national market is likely to be similar, engineering considerations are not much of a concern in this book, but maximizing the effectiveness of promoting specific genres of programs in different time periods and multiple situations does get attention.

To pinpoint the elements that probably affect network promotion of prime-time programs, researchers have repeatedly measured the impact of promotional spots (**promos**) for series programs on ratings, and identified various structural factors that influence television audience size.[3] Some of their findings appear in 1.10 as a diagram illustrating what practitioners might employ to maximize (or minimize) the effectiveness of their on-air promos. The first element in the model is lead-in program ratings, which has long been the biggest influence on a subsequent program's ratings. In prime time, at least, about half the people who watch one show stuck with the channel after watching the preceding show in a sequence, but that estimate comes from averaging many different genres of programs over a long time. It may be quite untrue in any particular case.

The second element (carriage program rating) refers to the size of the audience for the promotion. It seems obvious that promoting a program in shows

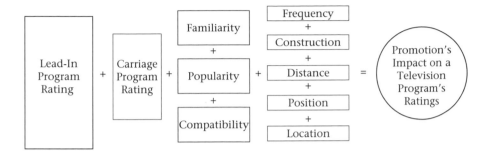

1.10 *Model of promotional effectiveness.*

with small audiences will have little influence on ratings compared to promoting the same show in highly popular programs. But what if the promoted show attracts only a narrowly defined group of viewers? Then promoting in the "right" programs becomes more important than promoting in "big-audience" programs. Furthermore, only a few episodes of any one program appear in a season (some original, some repeats), and drawing conclusions from just a few cases is unreliable. It is clear there are enormous measurement problems.

In general, researchers and practitioners think that how familiar the program is matters (years on the schedule) and how popular it is matters (the bandwagon effect) as well as how closely it matches the programs carrying the promotion (compatibility). After those variables, some other things probably come into play, such as how often the show is promoted (high or low frequency), the way the promo is made (single or multiple construction), how far away in time the promotion occurs from the program's airdate (far or close distance), how the promo is placed in a break (first, last, or middle position), and where the promo appears (inside or between program location). Whether and how much these factors influence specific types of programs is debatable, and the influence certainly differs by the time of day, what the competition is doing, and whether the program is carried locally or nationally.

In addition, factors related to music, voices, and sound effects probably have far more influence on radio program ratings than on television ratings. Different aspects of placement and design affect the effectiveness of printed promotional announcements, and still other factors affect websites — if one were able to define the goal of a promotional site clearly enough to begin to measure it. Nonetheless, the model in 1.8 suggests some avenues for consideration outside a message's quality and content. Subsequent chapters in this book discuss a mix of quality, content, and structural influences on promotional effectiveness, along with legal, technical, and marketing concerns.

ORGANIZATION OF THIS BOOK

In the remaining chapters of this book, the authors discuss many of the strategies and tactics already mentioned as well as additional ones, showing how they have been adapted for particular situations and particular media, some of which were successful and some not so successful. The focus is on current not past practice, although a touch of history sometimes enlivens the story!

The first five chapters provide a broad background in terminology and marketing concepts and the basics of the field. Chapter 1 has outlined the scope of the field of promotion, which includes the issues in the industry affecting promotion and the general targets and goals for the different media. Chapter 2 applies these ideas and others to strategies and practices in the particular situation of commercial radio promotion. Chapter 3 covers the most common practices in promoting local television news and syndicated programs. Chapter 4 deals with the problems of people, facilities, and budgeting in managing stations or systems, and Chapter 5 provides ways to evaluate the designs of different kinds of promotional materials.

The next five chapters deal with promotional strategies and practices in five situations. Chapter 6 looks at the most visible arena of promotion — network television. Chapter 7 shifts to the promotion of basic and premium cable programs, both individually and as groups of channels. Chapter 8 focuses on the Internet and its use as a promotional tool as well as its function as a programming source that needs its own promotion. Chapter 9 outlines the current principles and practices in promoting public television and radio programming. Chapter 10 extends the book's perspective to the global marketing situation bylooking at patterns in world branding of program delivery companies and systems.

At the end of each chapter, a short list of suggested readings appears, including related website URLs and videos. Following the chapters is a Glossary containing definitions for the **boldfaced** words in the text. Next is a Selected Bibliography that contains recent books, articles, and reports (published after 2000) that relate directly to promotion and marketing of media. Finally, there is an index that can help readers find particular topics, concepts, and named individuals or companies in the book.

NOTES

1. Exceptions occur in radio and occasionally in television when stations or channels are co-owned, such as when an AM and an FM in one market are jointly programmed, or very rarely for special programs aired on co-owned channels, such as NBC and MSNBC, CNBC, Bravo, USA, and SciFi Channel.

2. Investigations into the pervasive practice of "pay for play" cost Sony BMG Music Entertainment $10 million in 2005, along with a public agreement to stop bribing radio stations to play its songs. Other major record companies and station groups were also expected to suffer penalties for either instigating payoffs or taking them. In consequence, the role of independent promoters as middlemen between song producers and station playlists is likely to be much diminished, undercutting the big companies' chokehold on radio airwaves.

3. Eastman, S. T., Schwartz, N. C., and Cai, X. (2005). "Promoting Movies on Television," *Journal of Applied Communication Research*, 33(2), 139–158.

CHAPTER 2

Marketing Radio

Gregory D. Newton

Radio, like television, is a nearly unique business because it is marketed to two distinctly separate groups of customers — audiences and advertisers. In radio, successful marketing to the customer who directly provides the revenue stream (the advertiser) requires successful marketing to the other customer (the audience). Thus, radio station marketing has three primary goals:

1. To generate publicity
2. To generate ratings
3. To generate revenue

THE SPECIAL CASE OF RADIO

Unlike managers in virtually all non-media businesses, however, radio station managers have almost no influence over four of the five basic elements of marketing. Most business managers can control the way their products or services are distributed, the prices charged, the characteristics of the products themselves, and the postpurchase services offered. But radio managers have very little, if any, control over any of these.

For example, radio station managers cannot control the price charged for their programming in one of their markets because radio station listening is virtually free to the consumer. Moreover, for most formats, station management has only limited control of the programming itself. Music-oriented stations rely on material that is available only as a result of the decisions made by music companies or satellite-distributed syndication services. News and talk station programming is driven by events beyond the direct control of station management. In other businesses, postpurchase service includes items such as warranties, service contracts, and so on. Although there is an element of service after an advertising buy, postpurchase service for the audience is mostly limited to responding to listener complaints.

Clearly, radio station managers also can't control the place where their station's programming is consumed because listening occurs anywhere — in homes, offices, cars; at beaches and playgrounds; along the street; and anywhere on earth over the Internet. Indeed, it is important to recognize that radio listening frequently occurs while people are engaged in other activities and is secondary to those activities. Except at night, most radio listening takes place away from the home. One-quarter of all listening takes place at work, and more than one-third happens in cars (Arbitron, 2005). Different audience segments tend to listen at different times of the day because radio fits into and around the things people do every day. For adult men and women, listening peaks during the weekday morning and afternoon drive periods; for teenagers, listening is heaviest during weekday afternoons and on weekends (Arbitron, 2005).

Of the five elements of marketing, only one — **promotion** — is fully within the discretion of the station management. Therefore, when it comes to attracting an audience, *marketing means promotion*. Radio has two great promotional advantages over many other businesses, however. First, because radio is present almost everywhere and is consumed by almost everybody, a multitude of opportunities exists for promoting the programming. Second, radio has the invaluable ability to promote itself on air.

A QUICK RADIO MARKETING HISTORY

The role of the radio station promotion manager has changed tremendously over the past half century. Before 1950, very few local stations engaged in much promotional activity. Competition was limited, and most programming came from the networks, so they did the promoting, such as it was. By the mid-1950s, radio stations had created specialized formats to regain audiences that television had stolen. To make the public aware of such momentous programming changes, jobs in promotion were created at many stations. But early promotion managers did little more than process contest entry forms and produce a few on-air promos. These promotion managers often worked only part-time, had other secretarial or production duties, and made negligible impact on managerial decision-making.

Through the 1960s, as competition among radio stations intensified, station **images** became important. Managers built specific identities for their stations using combinations of call letters/dial position, programming elements (touting popular music and their high profile disc jockeys), and nearly continuous listener contests. Attention became focused on creating a consistent image both on air and in external advertising (**congruence**).

In the 1970s, listening to FM increased so much that the number of commercially viable stations in a market doubled and sometimes tripled. More stations led to new formats emerging and more head-to-head competition (at least in larger markets). To keep up and because many had virtually identical formats, promotion managers had to develop **competitive positions** for their stations. The 1980s saw another doubling of the number of stations on the air. Tougher competition necessitated refining strategies for positioning, placing greater reliance on ratings information and other customized **audience and image research** to target more fragmented listeners.

In the 1990s, radio went through tidal waves of consolidation. The elimination of duopoly rules and increases in the number of stations one company could own significantly increased the power and authority of radio promotion managers — now called *marketing managers* or *promotion directors*. The situation of multiple stations with similar formats in a market and aggressive competition among clusters of stations resulted in vital tactical roles for **cross-promotion** and strategic **positioning** of each station's image. Pressure from ownership (compelled by investors to deliver the anticipated economic gains from consolidation) also meant that promotion managers were increasingly called on to create and manage event-driven marketing that included the development of substantial **nontraditional revenue** (NTR), also referred to as *non-spot revenue* (Potter, Williams, & Newton, 2003).

Promotion managers today continue to serve dual goals, operating in the space between programming and sales, with responsibilities that overlap each area. Although large group owners may share ideas among markets and sometimes engage in multi-market contests, most responsibility for radio promotion remains at the local level (unlike in television).

Ideally, management wants to fill the top promotion positions with highly motivated and organized individuals who have skills in a whole buffet of areas:

- Marketing
- Ratings analysis
- Media buying
- Research design
- Positioning
- Creative copy writing
- Technology innovation
- Sales promotion

Beyond such kinds of experience, because promotion directors must serve the needs of multiple departments, creative thinking ability and negotiation skills have become critical. Where once promotion was low on the flow charts, today filling promotion positions with the best possible talent is seen as essential to the success of all stations outside the very smallest markets (and totally automated setups).

RADIO PROMOTION GOALS

Listeners' perceptions of what a radio station represents can be much more significant than the reality of the station's programming (in the short term, at least). In the longer term, the programming needs to deliver on the promise of the promoted perception or there's a negative mismatch. If the listener perceives the station as sounding better, then, for that listener, the reality is that the station does indeed sound better. For example, a station that heavily promotes long music sweeps between commercial blocks may be perceived as less commercial, even when (counting all dayparts) it actually carries more commercials than its competitors. Successful promotion managers undertake activities that will generate talk about the station (**buzz**) and design multimedia positioning campaigns to create perceived advantages.

Generating Buzz

Word of mouth can be the most powerful marketing channel available. Strategies that get audiences so interested in a station that they'll talk about it with their friends can be powerful tools for promotion directors in critical format change periods or other major audience acquisition efforts. Stations have used a number of stunts over the years to announce programming changes, from playing a single song over and over, to running for days or weeks without commercials or DJs. In each case, the idea was to do something so bizarre, so unexpected, that people would have "did you hear . . ." conversations with friends and family members. Buzz also comes when other media pick up on a stunt, although it is harder to generate that coverage if the stunt can obviously be tracked to a station. Nevertheless, "anonymous" giveaways of large amounts of cash in public places and similar strategies have been employed, resulting in newspaper and TV news stories about strange goings-on . . . before the station springs the surprise and reveals its identity.

An Oklahoma City station created perhaps a little more buzz than they wanted when the automated and mechanical "voice" counting down to a format change caused concerned listeners to call local police — who were not too happy when they arrived at the station and discovered that the public's fear of a terrorist takeover of the station was merely a computer-generated station stunt.

2.1 *WHJY "Two Big Boobs." Used with permission.*

Sometimes even "normal" audience acquisition strategies can create substantial buzz. A billboard, like the one shown in 2.1, or other outside media that is shocking or otherwise highly unusual enough to result in surprise can create significant interest within a community.

This billboard, posted in various locations in New England for two months in 2003, led to multiple stories on local television stations and in newspapers in the market. Although some were offended by it ("I don't want my kids seeing that"), it had the desired effect of creating fresh buzz about a long-time market leading station and maintaining the position of the morning show among its target audience.

Positioning

To be successful, a station needs to fit comfortably into the target audience's lifestyle. The promotion director will work closely with the program director and the production staff on **positioning** the station. The goal is to *create a station image that, in the audience's minds, matches their self-image.* In other words, the station should fit into listeners' desired lifestyle, from the music to the logo and slogan to the DJ patter between songs. To help with this process, many stations will develop a single listener that the staff always keeps in mind when working on programming or promotion. For example, consider a rhythmic contemporary hit radio (CHR) station. The sales staff might describe the target audience as 18 to 34 females. But the programming and promotion staff would describe their audience as "Jessica," a 24-year-old public relations associate at a Fortune 500 company. She's single (but would like to be married with kids some day), enjoys music and dancing, is interested in fashion but comfortable in jeans and a T-shirt, lives in an apartment in the city, and works out at the gym after work 3 or 4 days a week. "What would Jessica think?" is the first question asked when a new promotion or programming idea comes up for discussion.

In marketing, perception is reality. Successful marketing managers of all kinds focus on the image or perception of their product or service in the minds of their consumers. Indeed, Randy Michaels, a former Jacor and Clear Channel programming executive, explains that positioning a radio station isn't radically different from what Proctor & Gamble does with various consumer goods (but not identical; look back at 1.1). His point is that, *in radio, positioning is about understanding the competitive strengths and weaknesses in the market and using those to your advantage* (Michaels, 2005). What about a station will be important, different, and believable for listeners? The answer to that question is the **unique selling point** (**USP**, see Chapter 5) and the starting point for positioning a station.

Once you understand your station's USP, the next step is to identify the aspects of your target audience's day when radio can play a significant part and exploit that competitive advantage not only in relation to other radio stations but also in relation to other media consumption. For example, many adult contemporary stations find a competitive advantage in promoting their compatibility with work activities by building contests and other specific promotions around listen-at-work themes. All-news and news-talk stations can build substantial morning and afternoon drive-time cumes by promoting their frequent and regularly scheduled weather and traffic as well as the other news and information that listeners need as they start their day or make plans for the evening.

Another point is that promotion has to be matched to the audience's needs. Tom Peters and Bob Waterman (in their series of books including *In Search of Excellence*) identify this characteristic of successful companies as "Staying close to the customer." Rick Sklar in a spin-off book titled *Radio in Search of Excellence* refers to "Keep[ing] a listener's ear view of radio." He continues, "We radio people, promoting a medium that you can't see, touch or feel, must keep a listener's perspective to win listeners." Successful promotion managers stay close to their listeners by relying on focus groups and call-out and survey research to identify listeners' perceptions of both their station and their competitors. For example, the "Jack" and "Bob" formats are a response to the listener perception that consolidation has created music stations that are overly-restrictive and predictable. These stations promote their broader playlists with slogans that have an anti-corporate radio feel such as "playing what we want," "80s, 90s, and whatever," "we play everything," and "your music . . . your Bob."

RADIO RESEARCH EFFECTS

Research is critical to shaping promotion strategies in several ways. Diaries, Arbitron's frequently criticized method of radio ratings, are the primary source of listening information for the industry (and advertisers). Conventional industry practices regarding audience size, flow, recycling, and maintenance presume that diary keepers can accurately record or remember all their radio listening. This is a significant and highly problematic assumption. Many diaries are filled out some long time after listening has occurred by diary-keepers who attempt to remember the call letters and times of day that they listened for all the stations they heard for the past week. Actual station listening that is unreported because of inaccurate diary keeping, forgetfulness, or uncertainty regarding the station heard is called **lost cume**.

Because of the usual delay between listening and reporting, many promotion managers and marketing consultants believe that a station's position relative to the positions occupied by its competitors is vastly more important for ratings success than actual station listening. Because they are unlikely to recall all their listening accurately, Arbitron diary-keepers are likely to record the station that presents the image with which they most closely identify. In other words, the station that they perceive as closest to their desired lifestyle is likely to be the one that they report listening to, whether or not they actually listened during a particular quarter-hour. Similarly, diary-keepers may not report listening to stations that they heard during the week (perhaps while at work or shopping) if that station doesn't fit their lifestyle. *Therefore, occupying the position most compatible with the lifestyle of your target audience is more important for ratings success than influencing actual listening behavior.*

In selected markets in the United Kingdom and the United States, Arbitron has been testing a method of collecting listening data that is radically different from the much-despised diaries: the **Portable People Meter** (PPM). (For the latest information on the meter's rollout, see *www.arbitron.com*.) The meter — at four cubic inches and less than three ounces, about the size of a pager or small flip-style cell phone — is a passive device designed to be worn by a survey participant. The meter tracks all of the subject's electronic media exposure (radio and television) by identifying codes embedded in the audio portion of a transmission. Thus, it would eliminate the errors of unreported (or over-reported) listening inherent in the diary methodology. (Whether this would be good or bad for a particular station is a hot question.) At any rate, widespread adoption of the new methodology would certainly alter the process of radio promotion, probably by requiring a closer focus on influencing actual listening behavior. In addition, adoption would surely force stations to compete more aggressively for access to out-of-home spaces where listening occurs, such as stores, salons, exercise clubs, and other businesses.

Nevertheless, diaries will continue to be Arbitron's primary methodology, at least for the near future. Armed with an understanding of how radio is perceived and used, promotion managers can assess the best ways to design promotions to achieve specific audience aims.

LISTENER ACQUISITION, MAINTENANCE, AND RECYCLING

When promoting to audiences, directors of promotion have three distinguishable aims. First, they need to institute activities that bring in new listeners (**acquisition**). Second, promotion must encourage long periods of continued listening (**maintenance**). Third, listeners must be enticed to return at different times of the day (**recycling**). The promotion department's main tools are contests, direct mail, and on-air promotion.

Contests and Giveaways

Creating contests and on-air games can solve lots of problems (called **contesting** in the industry). They may be designed to achieve any of the three aims — audience acquisition, maintenance, or recycling — and analysis of ratings generally suggests the best ways to design them. For example, if the ratings show that the station enjoys high **time-spent-listening** (high **TSLs**) but has a small total audience size (*low cume*), an audience acquisition contest like that shown in 2.2 should be used. Notice how the requirements to "Set all your radios to LA's Magic 106" and "Listen each morning," and "Display this sticker on your vehicle" are designed to get new listeners. Winning the contest requires listening to the station for only short time periods. Magic 106 is obviously a station that enjoys high TSLs. The promotion manager has determined that the best strategy for ratings success is to increase sampling of the station by nonlisteners; TSLs will come automatically.

On the other hand, a station that enjoys high cumes but low TSLs might design an audience maintenance-based contest similar to that shown in 2.3. Winning requires listening to KMOO for several hours at a time, thus increasing the TSLs and AQH ratings of the station.

Instead, ratings analysis might show the need for an audience recycling strategy. A station's afternoon drive daypart might be performing well, for example,

Front   **Back**

2.2   *LA's Magic 106 FM Contest. KPWR-FM. Used with permission.*

★★★★★★★★★★★★★★★★★★★★★★★★★★

WIN · CASH
KMOO AM 158
COUNTRY
MUZ■K

JERRY REED	KENNY PRICE	MERLE HAGGARD	TOMPALL & GLAZER BROTHERS	JIM REEVES
TAMMY WYNETTE	SUSAN RAYE	FREDDY WELLER	JODY MILLER	DICKEY LEE
JIM ED BROWN	WEBB PIERCE	TANYA TUCKER	JERRY LEE LEWIS	SAMMI SMITH
DON GIBSON	BOBBY BARE	BILLY WALKER	FARON YOUNG	BRIAN COLLINS
FERLIN HUSKY	ELVIS PRESLEY	ROGER MILLER	DAVID ROGERS	LYNN ANDERSON

© 1972 Wm. D. TAYLOR

WXYZ "COUNTRY MUZIC" RULES

1. This is your free "COUNTRY MUZIC" card. Each week there is a different color card and you must have the correct color card to win. To avoid confusion, destroy your old card at the end of the week.
2. Turn your radio on, listen to WXYZ at 1230 on the AM dial.
3. Playing "COUNTRY MUZIC" is almost like playing Bingo. But instead of calling out numbers, WXYZ will play records.
4. When a record by an artist on this card is played, keep track by using buttons or other small objects to cover the squares. DO NOT write on, mark or tamper with the front of this card.
5. Just like Bingo, you must complete a line across, down or diagonally to win. A new game is started each hour, just after the news. Records played during one hour cannot be counted toward a win in another hour. Clear your card at the end of each hour.
6. Upon achieving a winning card you must call WXYZ at 321-1230 immediately. The game is over when there is a winner. No records past the winning record will count towards additional wins. NO PURCHASE NECESSARY!
7. The amount of the cash jackpot will vary from hour to hour. WXYZ will announce the amount of the jackpot at the start of each game. In case of multiple winners, the money will be divided equally. No checks will be issued until all cards are verified.
8. Winning cards must be brought to WXYZ studios at 1230 Radio Ave. within seven days of winning. You may mail your card, however, WXYZ cannot be responsible for lost cards.
9. Only one card per person. You must be at least 18 years of age. Employees of WXYZ or the participating sponsors and their families are ineligible.
WXYZ's music is selected for its entertainment value. At no time will WXYZ intentionally present it's music in manner that will make winning impossible. However, there are programming factors, both natural and planned which will effect the odds, and your chances of winning will vary from game to game.

Name _____ Phone _____

Address _____ City _____ Game No. ____

2.3 *KMOO's Country Muzik maintenance contest. Courtesy Bill Taylor.*

while mornings are bleak. In this case, the appropriate contest would be one that is heavily promoted in afternoon drive time but requires listeners to listen during morning drive time to win. However, this strategy assumes that nothing inherently is wrong with the station's morning drive-time programming. *One of the worst mistakes a station (or an advertiser) can make is to heavily promote a bad product.* When the morning daypart is dismal because of bad talent or poor programming, promoting morning drive time may hurt afternoon drive-time ratings rather than help morning ratings. Listeners who are turned off by a station's morning drive-time show may decide not to tune into the station at all.

The next time you hear a radio station contest, ask yourself whether the contest has audience acquisition, maintenance, or recycling goals.

Unlike contests, **giveaways** (of money, tickets, CDs, and the like) are typically designed to appeal either to very light listeners of the station ("I've got two free tickets for the first person to call in") or very heavy listeners ("You could win $1,000 if you hear the following three songs played back-to-back anytime this month"). It's important to provide balance between these games and giveaways. Too many complex contests that necessitate long TSLs to participate (or even understand) may leave light listeners feeling completely left out (and give them a reason to tune out).

Both contests and giveaways can be designed to increase **vertical recycling** (listening later in the day), as in "We'll give away this digital cell phone sometime this afternoon," or **horizontal recycling** (listening the next day), as in "Your next chance to win will be at this same time tomorrow." Of the two, horizontal recycling needs are more difficult to determine from ratings data. Specific day-of-week listening estimates supplied by such specialized reports as Arbitron's Fingerprint can be helpful. If midday listening is lowest on Tuesdays, for example, contests and games can be heavily promoted on other weekdays, with the winners announced on Tuesdays.

Very few of a station's listeners actually participate in the station's contests or giveaways. Even fewer win. Therefore, *all contests and giveaways should be designed to be entertaining for nonparticipating listeners.* Contests and giveaway announcements should not become a tune-out factor for most of the station's audience. As a rule of thumb, maintenance and recycling contests and games generally appear only on the air (and the station's website) and rarely involve any paid advertising unless there is also an acquisition goal and sufficiently interesting prize to attract new listeners. Ad budgets are typically reserved for acquisition strategies because they always require some promotional efforts outside the station's air.

Big Prizes

For the vast majority of stations, budgets for contest and giveaway prizes are very limited. To increase the value or number of prizes, stations have two options. The first is creating a sales promotion, described in the section Generating Revenue below.

The second option, available to group-owned stations, is **pooling** contest resources across multiple stations (usually in multiple markets, which effectively creates a regional or national contest) so that the cost assigned to any individual station is minimal. For example, Infinity ran a "$50,000 payday" contest where a lucky caller (to a national toll-free number) won $10,000 five times each weekday. Depending on local needs and the execution details, such a contest could serve acquisition needs (if supported by outside advertising), or recycling (by announcing the hours the contest call would air each day during morning drive, or through a station website or e-mail list) as well as maintenance ("coming up next hour, your chance to win part of today's $50 K Payday"). Although this contest would be prohibitively expensive for a single station in even the largest markets, when it is spread across dozens of markets, the cost becomes manageable for the group (at least for a couple of weeks during a key ratings period).

There are a couple of things to keep in mind when pursuing this approach, however. The terms of the contest — that the contest is running multiple markets — must be made clear to listeners or a station might face legal sanctions. The odds of the winner coming from a particular market are often very small, so the post-contest promotional value may be quite limited. If listeners perceive the contest as impossible to win, its positive impact will certainly be small, perhaps to the vanishing point.

Little Prizes

Contests don't need valuable prizes to generate effective promotional value. During a debate over legalizing gambling in Tennessee, for example, WSIX-AM in Nashville offered listeners a free trip to neighboring Kentucky (where gambling on horse racing is legal) to "Watch for signs of organized crime, pin-striped suits, violin cases, . . . and other gambling related dangers." KNOW in Austin offered the listener with the ugliest car a free paint job, body work, a new sound system, tune-up, new tires, and an oil change. The total value of the prize was around $3,000. All of the items were traded with local retailers in return for free mentions in the contest (**tradeouts**).

To target office listeners, it is common to give away "lunch for the bunch" or "pizza for a month" or "flowers for favorite ——" (secretaries, etc.). A recent approach focuses on working and non-working mothers with young children by offering "daycare dollars" as a drawing prize.

Sometimes the station need not offer any prize at all to have an effective contest. WSEN in Syracuse thrilled listeners with an April Fool's extravaganza in a classic takeoff on an old holiday prank. Winners were to receive a free tour of the Salt Museum (closed for the season), a tram tour of Onondaga Lake Park (closed until June), a tour of the French Fort (opens Memorial Day), a guided walk around the Burnett Park Zoo (closed for renovations), and a ride on the famed roller coaster at Suburban Park (famed mostly because it burned to the ground in 1969). The contest generated numerous entries, received free press coverage in other local media, and helped to reinforce the station's not-too-serious, good-natured image. Obviously, this contest wouldn't suit a station concerned with creating an image of high credibility.

Things Not to Do

Any contest (or any other advertisement) that involves the combination of a prize, chance, and consideration is considered a **lottery** and may be illegal on a particular radio station. Any combination of two elements is safe (giving a prize for a drawing is okay everywhere), but when all three elements are present, the contest comes under the rules governing lotteries (referred to in Chapter 1). Broadcasting information regarding a lottery (other than certain specific exceptions such as state-run lotteries) may subject a station to a fine or loss of license in some states (and maybe the loss of a job for somebody).

Also, contests and other promotional stunts that might hurt people are no-nos. The courts have found contests that could cause harm to the community or risk injury to the participants are "inconsistent with the public interest obligations of broadcasters" and usually have to be avoided, even if they sound like fun. Todd Storz is credited with developing the prototype of questionable "public interest" contests in the 1950s on his innovative Top 40 stations. The most common was a "Treasure Hunt." Typically, a check for $100,000 was hidden somewhere in the community, and obscure clues were given out on the air (obscure because the station hoped the check would not have to be paid). After a certain date the value of the check decreased to a more modest sum, such as $500. Treasure hunters would arrive from hundreds of miles away to listen to the station for clues and hunt for the check.

While treasure hunts certainly achieved audience acquisition and maintenance goals, the results sometimes backfired. First of all, the increases in cumes, AQH ratings, and TSLs from this type of promotion usually are temporary and seldom generate results for station advertisers. Also, ill will can be created because of the unclear clues, and when the check is not found in time, many treasure hunters feel cheated.

Edgier shows are frequently tempted to engage in publicity stunts designed to attract attention. Mancow Muller first achieved "fame" for a stunt mocking then-President Clinton's haircut onboard Air Force One on an LAX runway. He sent out a show sidekick and some friends to shut down traffic on the San Francisco Bay Bridge (so that Mancow could get a haircut . . . although in reality he never left the studio). The mess lasted several hours during morning drive, affecting tens of thousands of commuters, but it brought Mancow and the station nationwide attention. It also sparked a nationwide debate about shock jocks and responsibility. Although the jocks were suspended, Muller moved on to a higher profile job in Chicago (and eventually syndication of his show) and was named *Billboard*'s Radio Personality of the Year the next year (as well as the following two years).

Even stunts conducted in the "privacy" of the station facilities can backfire if participants are seriously injured or the conduct is outrageous enough. Former Tampa shock-jock Bubba the Love Sponge, his producer, and two listeners faced legal charges for the castration and slaughter of a wild boar in the station parking lot as part of a "Roadkill Barbecue" promotion. Although they were eventually acquitted, Bubba was suspended by the station owners. And making the police and fire chiefs and a bunch of listeners mad is probably not good for the station. Although the outlaw image has a certain appeal, it can damage a station's standing in the broader community and create more problems than a spike in listenership would be worth. Besides, the suits (corporate types) tend to like clean images.

Cross-Promotion and Tradeouts

One certain method for reaching light or nonlisteners is to advertise on other radio stations. Many co-owned stations **cross-promote** each other's programming, especially in markets with five or more commonly-owned stations. This happens most frequently when some elements of one station's programming may be appropriate in some way for use on another station in the cluster. For example, the reporters or anchors on the cluster's news/talk AM station can provide news reports during drive time on the music-formatted FM stations.

Groups without a full-time news presence may reach deals with TV stations in the market to use their news/weather/sports personnel in similar fashion, cross-promoting the appearances with the TV station. This has the advantage for both parties of extending the content across additional **platforms** (reaching additional audiences).

Less frequently, radio stations in the same market might buy or trade time with their competitors. When it does occur, the trade usually involves a format change or a new station signing on the air. For example, a station that drops its hard rock format to go to all-talk may allow its former rock competitors to buy time promoting their rock formats (for example, "For all the Rock you used to get here on KXXX, tune to KYYY").

Sometimes two stations with complementary formats may choose to cross-promote each other's programming. For instance, an all-news station and a beautiful music station may trade time promoting each other's formats (using on-air lines like "When you want the news it's here, but when you're ready to relax, tune to WZZZ").

On-Air Promotion

On-air promotion includes not only **promos** for station events (and the inevitable contests and giveaways), but also various short imaging elements intended to complement the programming and further define the station for the listener (called **signatures** when they include the station's identifier; see Chapter 5). The three usual elements of radio on-air are sweepers, liners, and jingles, forms unique to radio. **Sweepers** are short, highly produced imaging spots that include the call letters or an identifying slogan or air talent. They move (*sweep*) the audience from one song to the next while reminding them of the station they're listening to (for diary purposes) and reinforcing the station's image, often by making aural connections between other elements of popular culture and the station. **Liners** serve a similar imaging and transitional purpose, but are simple scripted voice tracks or live reads without music or effects. They can be used to promote upcoming station events or contests, or for general station imaging. To be effective, however, liners must be kept fresh — constantly rewritten and replaced — and the jock has to really sell the information — it can't *sound* written. **Jingles** consist of a few bars of music with the station call letters and identifying slogan sung over them. Producers create several versions for use between songs of different tempos and in different dayparts. Although available for nearly any format, they are seldom used today except on oldies, Adult Contemporary (AC), and country stations (as well as some news and talk outlets). Audiences for most rock, pop, and urban formats would perceive them as "old fashioned."

Most stations will have a production director responsible for producing these identifying elements along with commercials and other recorded materials. Larger operations may divide the responsibilities for advertising from those for promotion, with separate people responsible for commercials and on-air imaging. Individual promos can be entirely created by the local station, but most stations rely on outside sources for at least some music and sound effects.

A number of distributors offer audio production elements through an annual license or library buy-out basis. Stations can purchase libraries of sound effects on CDs, such as the one from the BBC pictured in 2.4.

Similarly, there are companies who specialize in creating and recording custom jingles for radio stations (along with the individual elements of the finished jingles that can later be remixed by the local production director to create additional pieces).

Because consistent and appropriate imaging is as important as programming in a station's success, most stations use only one or two voice-over talents for all sweepers and promos. If the budget permits, this can be an outside talent;

2.4   *BBC sfx CD library. Used with permission.*

otherwise the promotion director, program director, or one of the air staff may be the "voice" of the station. *The voice should fit the format and target audience —* a mature, whisky-soaked set of pipes for a classic rocker, a bright and friendly thirty-something female for an AC, an authoritative baritone for a news-talk station, and so on. **Congruence** between voice, station sound, and desired image are fundamental to effective radio promotion.

EXTERNAL MEDIA

Budgets for external media vary greatly from station to station, and certainly depend on market size. Decisions about buying external space and time are part of the routine responsibilities of promotion directors. Salespeople from competing media in the market (usually claiming a complementary not competing nature) regularly call on radio station promotion managers, and try to secure a fair share of the station's external advertising budget. (Indeed, some stations insulate themselves from these sales pitches by hiring an outside agency to do their media buying.)

Nonetheless, promotion managers have to be familiar with the advantages and disadvantages of each competing medium in their markets and know how they can serve the station, given its format, target audience, image, positioning, and marketing goals. For example, for rock stations targeting younger listeners, having an elaborate Internet site that carries the station's music and includes other content to connect the station to listeners' desired lifestyles and create a sense of community makes good sense. On the other hand, it makes more sense for a talk, all-news, or Adult Standards station to advertise in local newspapers than for a Modern Rock or Heavy Metal station because of the increasingly older demographics of typical newspaper readers.

Effective media buying also requires the ability to show the salesperson why a proposal is too costly and why a counterproposal should be accepted. This necessitates understanding each medium's cost structures. For audience acquisition, the most efficient media buy will be the one with the lowest cost per thousand (CPM) for nonlisteners in the station's target demographic. Typically, *paid external media is primarily for acquiring new listeners, so efficiency is what is wanted.*

TV Spots

Television stations that use customized ratings reports such as Tapscan and Strata may be able to calculate appropriate demographic-based CPMs for nonlisteners of a radio station. Making that information available to a radio station helps sell TV spots. Of course, the overall effectiveness of any promotional campaign will depend not just on efficient media buying but also on the creativity, execution, and overall appeal of the advertising. For radio stations, the competing media to evaluate make a long list:

- Broadcast television
- Cable television
- Newspaper
- Telephone directories
- Internet
- Outdoor
- Transit
- Sometimes, even other radio stations

If the budget is big enough, all-news and news/talk stations can reach their target audiences by advertising on cable news channels or broadcast TV newscasts (although those are among the more expensive spots on highly-rated stations). Country stations might go after their target audiences by advertising on a television station's country music special or on the cable network CMT. For alternative stations, local spots on edgier cable offerings like Comedy Central, or niche cable channels like Fuel, or X Games on ESPN may be attractive.

The saving grace for most radio station budgets is that local newspapers, cable systems, and television stations often trade advertising time (on a dollar-for-dollar basis) with radio stations. The promotion manager, in conjunction with the sales manager, is responsible for developing such advertising trades (tradeouts) and then making effective use of them. Irrespective of whose idea it was, *giving away the radio station's airtime has to bring solid benefits to the station.*

Print and Internet

Print media, such as newspapers and magazines, are other advertising options for radio. Promotional inserts in newspapers, which can go in selected copies of the paper, are especially useful for targeting specific geographic areas within the larger market. Cable system **interconnects** may also be able to deliver zoned advertising. Some larger markets also have local or regional magazines in which radio stations can advertise.

Telephone-directory advertising can be especially useful for stations desiring to reach newcomers to a market. Directories of various types are particularly important in rapidly growing markets, and most markets now have at least two competing telephone-directory companies. Small ads or listings in the yellow pages may have some limited value for reaching potential listeners or clients, but the inside and back covers are the real prizes. They make a really attractive option for stations trying to target new listeners.

2.5 *CD101 "The Lounge" web screen. Used with permission.*

Web pages on the Internet are certainly another popular way to promote radio stations, because a well-conceived and maintained website can connect listeners to the station in many ways and generate non-spot revenue for the station. The screen shot of a CD101 page in 2.5 showcases both of these advantages. The lack of hype is appropriate for an alternative station (and especially one that also promotes its local, non-corporate ownership), and the highlighted affinity credit card allows listeners to earn points toward goodies in the station's prize closet, returns a portion of purchases to the station (as well as creating a marketing database), and connects listeners with advertisers by awarding bonus points for use of the card at those locations.

On the web, a station can supply opportunities for the most loyal and active listeners (the ones who go often to the website) to give feedback on music and other programming. Contests and merchandise offers are easy to display on websites. Depending on the user's connection, sound files with sample music can also be downloaded or the station's music can be "streamed" live, a popular option for many "at work" listeners.

Outdoor and Transit

Outdoor advertising is oh-so expensive, and the bad news is that it is seldom offered on a trade basis. Outdoor will generally only be cost-effective for stations in large markets with high-volume traffic routes (and thus, substantial numbers of commuters to be targeted). *The long-established cardinal rule for billboards is to keep the message short; three to five words make the most effective message (and eight words are the maximum).* A second, but less repeated, rule *is to make the message provocative,* as was the case in the "boobs" example in 2.1. Just putting up pretty call letters and frequencies are not enough to provoke changes in behavior (**acquisition**).

By using information such as Arbitron's Fingerprint, stations can determine the most effective geographic areas for their outdoor advertising because the software supplies ratings information by zip code. Stations then can target their outdoor placement to areas with good signal coverage but low listenership among the station's target demos.

There are two basic types of outdoor bulletins: poster panel and painted. The standard *poster-panel billboard* runs 12 feet, 3 inches high by 24 feet, 6 inches wide; to create a 24' image, 10 to 15 sheets of printed poster paper are glued to it. *Painted bulletins* are usually 14 feet high by 48 feet long, and each is custom designed and painted by hand. Because of different **aspect ratios** between painted and poster bulletins, the same graphic design can't be used for both. Painted boards sometimes allow for special effects; cutouts, for example, can be attached to the board to extend either its height or width. Because of the cost of repainting, painted bulletins are less flexible than poster boards and usually are sold for a period of one year. Poster bulletins are altered by repapering over the existing poster and may be purchased for a few weeks or months (although 3-month buys are usual).

Transit advertising on subways, buses, taxis, and trains is another option in some, mostly larger, markets. Audience demographics vary depending on the geographic area and who rides or sees the vehicles. For example, the demographics of riders of buses and subways usually differ markedly from those of taxi or suburban commuter train riders, but the outside of all these vehicles may be viewed by the same inner-city population as they travel across town. In the largest markets, several types of transit advertising are available: busboards (side, rear, and front), bus stop or station posters (including airports, subways, and train terminals), and taxi boards or cabtops. Similarly, mobile video screens, perhaps including audio, may be available in some markets to target potential audiences on the street. *All these are traveling billboards and take only limited messages.* Many transit vehicles also sell space inside the bus, cab, or subway for signs (cards), which is especially useful for advertising long-term contests and promoting news. Finally, the promotion manager probably has responsibility for the custom painting of station-owned remote vans, boom boxes, sales cars, and so on. The principles of emphasizing the message and stating a USP or benefit apply to all these media as well.

GENERATING REVENUE

Beyond traditional advertising sales, two key tactics for gaining revenue for the station are **sales promotion** and **event marketing**. Both of these can motivate clients to invest more money in a promotional activity, but then they expect more in exchange.

Sales Promotions

Not every client of a station should be involved in a sales promotion. High-profile events should be reserved primarily for big spenders. After all, their businesses' images are being directly attached to the station's precious image, an invaluable commodity and a risky strategy for the station. At the same time, to protect advertisers' interests, only a limited number of businesses at one time should be involved (**exclusivity**), and few remotes and other sales promotion activities should be scheduled in the same time period.

Quite frequently, sales promotions are tied to the generation of new business accounts for the station. For example, the promotion manager at an El Paso station wanted to design a $10,000 giveaway but lacked the money in the budget. Working with the sales manager, the promotion manager designed a month-long spot schedule at $1,000 each for 12 clients. The spots were scheduled to run during the first quarter, when inventory pressures were low. Out of the total $12,000, $2,000 was to cover sales commissions and expenses, leaving $10,000 for the contest prize. (All clients had to be new businesses for the station; no retailer that recently had advertised on the station could participate in this special package.) As part of the promotion, each client received a free remote on one of 12 consecutive Saturday afternoons. To participate in the contest, listeners had to register during the broadcast from the client's location. The result was a $10,000 cash contest prize, motivated listeners, a dozen new clients who saw the station's drawing power demonstrated live at their locations, a happy general manager, a contest that cost nothing, a pay raise for the promotion manager, and at least one very satisfied listener.

The rule for any sales promotion is that it must serve both the audience's interests as well as the advertisers' to effectively serve the station — because ultimately the two are intertwined. If the audience doesn't care about the promotion, they won't show up. If the audience doesn't show up, the client says, "radio doesn't work," and that advertiser is lost. The goal is to create something listeners haven't heard or seen before, a unique hook. Another make or break variable is whether sufficient time remains to promote the event (at least one week, often much more). *Last-minute efforts rarely succeed.*

Event Marketing

Event marketing is another critical revenue stream for many stations, but it is far from a simple process. Large events require major long-range planning efforts, substantial investment (which is at risk if the event fails), and a long-term perspective. Although promotion directors are generally expected to develop and sustain a number of annual events, *the scary reality is that most such projects will not see a significant profit (and may even lose money) in their first year or two.*

Because of the tremendous resources required to manage a large event, stations typically do no more than one per quarter. Smaller operations or stations without a history of successful event marketing may be limited to one or two each year. Organizational ability and negotiation skills are critical in this area. Working on a large event, a promotion director will have to not only develop the basic idea for the event but manage all the following:

- Oversee arrangements for facilities to hold the event (including bad weather plans if the event will be outdoors)
- Coordinate both the entertainment and revenue aspects of the events with staff in programming and sales (developing the marketing plan for the event)
- Develop the budget for the event
- Select and contract with talent, vendors, and sponsors
- Arrange insurance and security to address various risk issues
- Manage the execution of the event

How about a Fourth of July music and fireworks celebration sponsored by a country station. The event has the appropriate flag-and-family appeal for the target audience, and it would undoubtedly be attractive to a number of large advertisers. But what would be required?

The Venue

This would obviously be an outdoor event, so the number of possible sites in most markets will be few. Site selection would probably be required a year (or more) in advance. The promotion director would need to do a site survey of any location that wasn't already extremely familiar, looking at such issues as:

- Traffic flow and parking facilities and conditions in case it rains either the day of the event or the day before, in the parking area as well as the venue itself
- Space for side activities (a "family fun" picnic area and game zone, perhaps)
- Options for sponsor or souvenir booths or food trailers

- Opportunities for signage or other promotional outlets on stage, around the venue, and in the parking lot (video displays, public address announcements, inflatables)
- Existing venue contracts with food and beverage providers (which may effectively limit some of the station's sponsor options)

Although the basic rental charge for the location may not seem very costly, during the site survey the promotion manager will also need to address such issues as:

- Access to the venue for the bands and fireworks technicians to load in
- Union labor requirements
- Clean-up costs
- Charges for utilities hook-up (electricity)
- Other potential charges, including access to secure money-handling and storage facilities

Several of these items may greatly increase the total cost.

The Entertainment

Projected ticket revenue will define the budget for entertainment. Most stations will expect to cover the operational cost — the performers, the facility rental and related charges, on-site security and other event day operating needs — with the gate receipts (ticket sales). All other revenue becomes profit. Let's say the station could sell 8,000 tickets at $10 apiece. That $80,000 would probably allow a budget of $25,000 to $35,000 for music, sufficient for one established star supported by one or two new, upcoming acts and a half-dozen regional and local bands. In the largest markets, a second stage providing a location for continuous music might be possible, if the budget is adequate and the site large enough. The established and upcoming bands should be booked months in advance, although hungry local acts can be arranged closer to event time.

The fireworks will be expensive, equal to or perhaps more costly than the music budget for a professional display. And of course, the promotion director will have to address a number of issues relating to the fireworks and work with the local fire prevention and law enforcement authorities to make sure the display complies with local laws. Good fireworks companies will be busy around the Fourth, so booking far in advance will be essential.

Sponsorship of the Event

Advance planning is also critical here. Many companies set their summer promotional budgets and calendars during the previous fall, so the promotion director needs to be ready to pitch the event to them at that time. In other words, *anything less than a 12-month time frame probably isn't going to work.*

To best serve the needs of both the program director and the sales manager, it's generally a good idea to design the event with multiple levels of sponsor participation. This can help keep the on-air mentions from getting too cluttered with long lists of sponsors (not every client will need to be in every spot, although a few might be), and will help create a variety of attractive options for the sales staff to present to prospective participating clients — who will also appreciate a less cluttered environment.

For example, there might be just one presenting sponsor ("Budweiser presents the Country 99.9 Red, White, and Boom Fourth of July Celebration") who will receive mentions in every spot and in all other marketing of the event from direct mail to the tickets. The sponsor of the family picnic area will be mentioned only in the on-air promos that highlight that part of the event ("between bands on the main stage, grab a bucket of chicken and join us in the KFC Family Picnic Area with games for the kids and music by the Foggy River Boys"). Similarly, individual sponsors of the main music stage, the fireworks show, and other activities will receive on-air mentions only in the subset of promos highlighting their part of the event. *Sales staffs don't always keep the "be entertaining" imperative in mind (and thus keep advertiser lists short), so the promotion director regularly needs to remind everyone.*

Promos

To determine how many spots the station can run, on-air promotion has to be negotiated with the program director in advance. Once the parameters of the event and its marketing are defined, the sales department can solicit sponsors and package the various levels of sponsorship, and the production director can create the spots. The sales staff should have a deadline of at least 48 to 72 hours prior to the start of the on-air run for delivering final sponsor contracts. It is important for the promotion director and sales manager to agree that once the promos begin to run, any additional sponsors will only receive mentions in the remaining promos — the station won't be in the awkward position of adding additional spots (and potentially wrecking the entertainment value of the event as radio programming).

Day of the Event

Once the big day arrives, the promotion manager has several responsibilities:

- Coordinating station staff on-site
- Making sure the money is collected and the performers are paid
- Keeping the event on schedule . . . union overtime can quickly destroy the budget!

After that, it comes down to praying for good weather, smooth traffic flow, and loud amps. Meanwhile, the event promoter bounces between problem solving and traffic control.

MERCHANDISING

Merchandising involves the distribution and sale of customized station products, from key chains to coffee mugs to apparel — virtually anything that can be emblazoned with the station call letters, logo, or other identifying characteristics. Some stations have found that clothing, in particular, can also be a revenue generator. KATT in Oklahoma City, a heritage rocker that has long been one of the top stations in that market, met with great success selling KATT/Rock 100.5 T-shirts and ball caps through a chain of truck stops across the state. Many other stations make their shirts available via the station website.

Most stations maintain a closet full of small branded items — key chains, refrigerator magnets, bumper stickers, buttons, pens, note pads — to use as easy giveaways for listeners at station remotes. These little reminders can help with audience maintenance goals, as well as keep the station at the top of the listener's mind when it's time to fill out an Arbitron diary.

Like billboards, bumper stickers can only handle a very few words, such as in the main WOWO bumper sticker shown in 2.6. (Note that there is a mini-sticker at the end of the main one, intended to be taken off and put on such teen paraphernalia as binders, books, T-shirts, car windows, mirrors, and so on.) Also, the logos show that Pepsi and Marathon gas paid for these bumper stickers (thousands of them), but they only got tiny spaces on the sticker. Too many novice promotion people give away the value of bumper stickers to advertisers instead of reserving it for the station. Despite having advertiser logos, this sticker primarily promotes WOWO and its oldies format.

2.6 *WOWO bumper sticker. Used with permission.*

COMMUNITY AND MEDIA RELATIONS

The goal of a community-relations strategy is to develop one-on-one relationships with current or potential listeners. Word of mouth is widely cited as the most effective form of advertising, and public relations efforts (PR) can be highly effective in generating word-of-mouth advertising. PR strategies include live on-location broadcasts, station personality appearances, and station tours, as well as publicity and press releases.

Remotes, Appearances, and Tours

Remotes, broadcasts from locations other than the station's studio, often occur in conjunction with sales promotion activities, but they also may be used to generate higher visibility for the station's personalities. Broadcasting from the top of a flagpole, interstate billboard, underwater cabin, or other outrageous locations may generate both free publicity for the station and greater listening among former light or nonlisteners. Some remote broadcasts may even originate from outside the station's coverage area. For example, some stations have sent their most popular personality on an around-the-world tour (usually part of a travel agency sales promotion) that included broadcasts from "30 countries in 30 days." Another gimmick for edgier stations is to send a controversial personality to the site of a hot scandal to stir up participants with live interviews, pseudo-investigative reporting, and so on.

More run-of-the-mill **personality appearances** may involve speeches to local civic groups, a station softball or basketball team, interviews on local broadcast or cable television shows, and public participation in community events. As everyone learns the hard way, the station personality needs complete instructions regarding the exact time and location of the appearance and an ample quantity of station giveaway items (bumper stickers, photos, and so on). If the appearance is before a civic organization, the personality may want to show a brief videotape about the station, which needs to be provided, along with suitable projection equipment. The promotion manager should provide the organization's chairperson with the personality's biography, arrange for media coverage by the local newspaper and television stations if appropriate, and provide photographs and another copy of the personality's biography to the editor of the organization's newsletter. Better to have overkill than a wasted opportunity and annoyance all the way around.

Station tours commonly are conducted by the promotion manager. Various high school, civic, and even listener groups often want to see the studio facilities. Some stations have even sponsored vocational radio programs (for groups such as the Boy Scout Explorers or the local high school radio club). The promotion manager typically becomes the organization's advisor and in return gathers a nearly inexhaustible supply of energetic station interns.

Special remotes and personality appearances can be powerful maintenance tactics. They give loyal listeners the opportunity to identify closely with the station. At station-sponsored community events, loyal listeners should receive special consideration (such as priority seating, free tickets, or station giveaways). Such perks may be earned by random on-air invitations, direct mail, or telemarketing efforts.

Publicity and Public Relations

Promotion budgets can frequently be stretched through the careful application of **OPM** — Other People's Media and Other People's Money. This may be as simple as keeping the newspaper media critic informed of the week's sports broadcast schedule or as complex as creating a mystery character who randomly gives away $100 bills around town and later is revealed to be the station's new morning personality — but only after the newspapers, television stations, and even other radio stations have covered the story. For major events, many sponsors should be willing to promote the event in their other marketing efforts, including print, broadcast, and outdoor advertising along with website and point-of-purchase materials. For example, the Budweiser distributor who was the presenting sponsor on a big Country 99.9 Red, White, and Boom event could also create and maintain display signs promoting the event (perhaps with entry slips for a giveaway of backstage passes or something similar) at liquor stores, grocery stores, and convenience stores in the market.

Press releases are written notices of newsworthy events. They generally are handled by the promotion manager and should be sent out for all station events, including internal job promotions for station personnel; the hiring of new personalities, sales, and managerial staff; and winning broadcast industry or local civic awards. Press releases should be sent to the local newspapers, television stations, broadcast trade magazines, and the employee's hometown newspaper. Press releases about publicity stunts should be sent to all the competing media in the station's coverage area along with the trade press. New station programming, call-letter changes, studio location shifts, and technical improvements also should be announced in press releases. Promotion managers should routinely maintain biographical data on all station management and air talent, because it can be needed in the next hour when a call comes from a newspaper editor seeking filler before deadline.

MORAL DILEMMAS

Are there limits to what is acceptable practice for attracting an audience? For example, what ethical issues are involved when a station gives away breast augmentation or other plastic surgery as a contest prize? Many stations have done exactly that (a St. Louis station reported nearly 100,000 entries in one such contest).

Sometimes the issue is clearly fraudulent behavior, such as rigging a station contest so that current or potential clients (or client's friends or relatives) will win. Contest prizes may seem innocuous, and sometimes there are so many winners of something every week that who wins hardly seems to matter. What would you do if your general manager asked you to fix a circus promotion so the disabled 6-year-old child of the station's largest client could be "Circus Queen for a Day"?

Note that FCC rules require licensees to fully and accurately disclose the "material terms" of all contests and to run the contest as announced or advertised. Material terms include all factors that define the operation of the contest and affect participation in the contest. Beyond the legal technicalities, however, each station and promotion director needs to clearly define expectations for what is acceptable and what isn't. Edgier formats (alternative, active rock, some urban stations) and shows like Mancow Muller's need to meet audience expectations for rebellious behavior that may at times border on antisocial (an approach that admittedly carries a cost in broader public and advertiser perception). Even they need to have some limits, however, that are understood within the station. Station management and air talent who have failed to understand the limits of "acceptable" behavior have often paid the price in the long run, contributing to the industry's troubles before the FCC and Congress. Some actions, while they might provoke some reaction and appeal to the station's core audience, can cost too much to simply be written off as "the cost of doing business" and promotion directors (and the entire station management team) need to balance the "brilliant" impulses of jocks with the overall needs of the station and community.

SELECTED READINGS AND WEBSITES

All Access, *www.allaccess.com.*
Arbitron (2005). *Radio today 2005.* Available at *www.arbitron.com.*
Association of Radio Marketing Executives, *www.a-r-m-e.com.*
Michaels, R. (2005). *Positioning Your Radio Station.* E-book available from *www.danoday.com.*
National Association of Broadcasters (Eds.) (1984). *Radio in Search of Excellence.* Washington, D.C.: NAB Books.

Peters, T. J., and Waters, Jr., R. H. (1982). *In Search of Excellence: Lessons from America's Best-Run Companies*. New York: Warner Books.

Potter, R. F., Williams, G. C., and Newton, G. D. (2003). Juggling brands: The pressures and perks of radio promotion directors in the age of acquisition. *Journal of the Northwest Communication Association, 32* (Summer), 78–95.

Radio Promotion Directors Academy. Audio CD's available from *www. creativeanimal. com*.

www.abc.com
www.billboard.com
www.clearchannel.com
www.rronlin.com
www.radioandrecords.com
www.sirius.com
www.xmradio.com

CHAPTER 3

Local Television Promotion: News, Syndication, and Sales

Douglas A. Ferguson and William J. Adams

Stations differentiate themselves from the rest of the multichannel universe by focusing on *local* programming, which for most stations means local newscasts. The other major sources of image income are their sports and syndicated programs. The approach to promotion advocated by industry experts is **integrated marketing** (IM), which unifies a station's efforts to reach and maintain audiences and advertisers under a single strategic and tactical umbrella. *Such an umbrella approach treats all promotional media as a unit; it utilizes a common design for all audience and advertiser materials, whether those materials appear on the air, on the web, or in print or outdoor media. It emphasizes creating crossties between promotional efforts.* Viewers see IM when on-screen and website graphics for affiliates match those of the network. The most effective station promotion is **congruent** across all the media.

As group owners buy more and more television stations, they demand more sophisticated marketing of expensive programs and imaginative ways of approaching local and regional advertisers. Although some of this promotion is handled at the group level or comes from networks or syndicators, the exigencies of tight deadlines, last-minute changes, and local conditions make it necessary for stations to do their own production of daily news promotion, if the station carries newscasts.

About 630+ stations are affiliated with the traditional full-service broadcast networks (ABC, CBS, and NBC) and thus retransmit at least 16 hours of daily network programming. This leaves them time to produce (and promote) local newscasts but not much else. Most of these stations offer early and late news and may produce early morning and noon newscasts as well, but their promotional efforts focus on the evening news and associated websites. FOX affiliates get fewer hours inside and outside prime time, but they are required by the network to produce a mid-evening newscast, scheduled at 9:00 or 10:00. The 200 or so affiliates of Univision and Telemundo get full day and evening schedules from the Spanish-language networks and may add local news to the mix.

Other commercial stations, carrying mostly older syndicated series and regional college sports, operate under somewhat different conditions than affiliates of the bigger networks. They get far fewer hours from their networks and thus have less assistance with promotion and more programs to promote. Most of these 350+ stations are affiliates of UPN, the WB, PAX, or perhaps a religious network such as CBN, and must themselves promote all their many hours of non-network programming to the extent they can.[1]

BIG FOUR NETWORK AFFILIATES

A powerful two-way relationship exists between the Big Four broadcast television networks (ABC, CBS, FOX, and NBC) and their affiliated stations, which greatly affects the amount and kind of promotion viewers see on the air and how they think about their stations (their **images**). At the same time, changes in network affiliation, such as occurred in great numbers during the 1990s, drastically altered some stations' identities. *Promotion became the main tool for explaining such identity changes* (involving new call letters and channel numbers, new news anchors, new prime-time shows, and sometimes a shift in language) *to audience and advertisers and building the stations' new images*. Moreover, altered television standards and delivery systems, like the advent of HDTV, have affected the underlying audience perception of local television service. Indeed, the switchover from analog to digital channels is creating huge promotional challenges for local stations. Promotion has to explain the new digital video landscape to viewers as the various new services unfold.

The affiliate–network relationship is built on the principle that the network supplies programming and the affiliate is its outlet. The networks promote their programs within other programs they carry and spend some money on print advertising, all of which benefits local affiliates because this programming comes already promoted in the best time periods. The networks, however, have rules pertaining to the promotional ads they air. The most important of these rules is that *local affiliates cannot preempt any of the network's time to promote their own local and syndicated shows*. It is up to the station to find effective ways of promoting its non-network programs.[2]

Promotional Priorities

How does local program promotion fit with network programming? Does the local affiliate seek audience flow into or out of network shows, or should it concentrate on its own dayparts without considering the impact of local lead-ins on network programs? What role does the website play? What promotional options does the affiliate have when it preempts a network program? How promotion managers treat the affiliate–network programming mix promotionally establishes their relationship with the network, and these relationships differ markedly among the more than 830 affiliates of the Big Four. Most stations develop a formalized strategy regarding the programming and promotion mix.

One of the first principles is that *a promotion department cannot promote everything*. There just isn't enough time to produce and schedule on-air promotional material for all of a station's programming, even though the network hours come pre-promoted. Affiliates therefore focus their promotional efforts on those dayparts that bring in the most revenue: local news, early fringe, prime access, late news, and sports. But even those dayparts have to be prioritized. Because most affiliates' local images are tied to their evening news performance, about 75 percent of a station's promotional effort goes to promoting its local news, mostly on the radio but sometimes in newspapers and *TV Guide*. The typical affiliate allocates most of its syndicated program budget to early fringe and access, acquiring such expensive off-network and first-run shows as *Wheel of Fortune* or *Oprah* to anchor these important time periods. Because of the high cost of such shows, about 20 percent of a station's promotional effort goes to attracting an audience for the programs that fill these two key time periods. Only about 5 percent of an affiliate's promotional effort is left for promoting other non-network or network programs. The general principles are to *promote the programs that bring in the most revenue*, and *promote the programs that cost the station the most money* — usually but not always the same programs.

On-air promos are key to any station's promotional effort, and on-air often has more dollar value than all external media. Surveys indicate that 90 percent of viewers learn what to watch from on-air promotion. On-air promos also provide a unique opportunity to target viewers who may be tempted to switch to another channel.

Network Support Materials

Summer is the time when affiliates get ready for the premiere of the new fall network season. During summers, stations have to collect material on new and changed network prime-time and daytime shows. The networks provide their affiliates with downloadable prime-time promos, advertising and promotion kits, **tie-in packages** (of shared theme graphics and music), web page graphics, and information about **co-op** promotion to support network shows.[3] Stations can purchase banners, decals, and posters to download from their networks. To integrate their marketing with their networks' (following an IM approach), stations are then able to dovetail local promotional efforts with network styles in web and on-air graphics, video designs, and music. In addition, most syndicated shows turn over in the fall, too, so summers are busy times for affiliate marketing managers.

During midsummer the networks send the stations completed episodes of new fall programs via closed circuit. Promotion managers record them for later use in on-air promos and for sales aids for the sales department. The networks also send tapes of the new fall promotion campaigns first shown to managers earlier in the year at the annual network affiliates' meetings and usually screened at the annual meeting of **PROMAX** (Promotion and Marketing Executives in the Electronic Media), which is held during June in the United States. This key trade association is described in 3.1.

The networks also send the affiliates completed promos for new and returning shows with new campaign animation and music. Some networks produce **combination promos** with an open space at the beginning for insertion of material about local access shows. These "combo promos" are designed to stimulate audience flow, not only from local to network programs, but also in reverse because a strong network lead-off at 8 p.m. aids local prime-access shows, usually the biggest moneymaker for stations after local evening news. Advance tune-in occurs when the audience recognizes that adjacent programs are a combination, especially if they are similar in appeal.

Network promos, unedited footage from new programs, and other video materials are scheduled at predetermined times throughout each week and then sent to stations via satellite as part of a daily **electronic press kit** (EPK). Color photos and radio promos are delivered over a private Internet, such as *www.affiliatepromo.com* for NBC affiliates. These materials can be edited for use in paid advertising, to create on-air promos, and to fill out station websites. The networks also send much of their advance promotional material directly to local newspapers. Included with press information are black-and-white pictures, outlines of specific episodes, and names of guest stars.

Networks periodically offer **satellite talent interviews**, in which stars of network series and specials are available for local interviews. These events are also known as **satellite media tours** and allow stations to bring well-known personalities to local programs, such as extended newscasts and interview programs. The affiliates and the network gain a big promotional benefit by running these interviews, especially before the premiere of a new program, and they have further life on websites for a month (but beware of sudden cancellations of struggling shows).

During the last few years, networks have even made deals with major sponsors to cross-promote events built around the September premieres, such as ABC and McDonalds and CBS and K-Mart (see Chapter 6). Such deals provide large amounts of local promotion, which is basically free to the local station.

3.1 Promax

PROMAX is the global, non-profit association that designers and executives at nearly all American stations, networks, studios, and design producers join, as well as thousands of marketers and designers of media promotion around the world. The association sponsors six international conferences around the world (United States annually in June, plus Arabia, Asia, Australia, Europe, and Latin America in other months), and it gives the annual Medallion Awards for top promotional design. According to PROMAX's website (*www.promax.org*), this trade association is "dedicated to advancing the role and effectiveness of promotion, marketing, and broadcast design professionals in the electronic media." Its 2005 membership brochure cleverly depicts the four types of members on the cover: *executives*, who are probably most interested in increasing audiences; *associates/freelancers*, who are the designers most concerned with actual creative products; *academics*, who need current information; and *students*, who'd like an iPod (and might get a job).

Cover of 2005 PROMAX Membership Brochure. Used with permission.

Co-ops are deals for joint network/affiliate advertising offered only during periods prescribed by the networks. Co-op funding is restricted to the amounts set by the network for each station and offered only for such times as the fall premiere weeks and the ratings periods in November, May, and February. Occasionally, such as when a network changes anchors, co-ops may be offered for news. Some networks also require that the advertising be limited to specific network programs on designated days. A variation on this practice occurs when a network buys ad space in the 100+ versions of *TV Guide* and then customizes each ad with the local affiliate's channel number.

A typical co-op print ad, such as in 3.2, contains an evening's lineup of programming and is called a **stack ad**. Space is occasionally provided in the ad for the station's news or prime-access programs, or stations can simply add column inches to the top or bottom of the supplied ad slick. In the example, *Joey* is shown airing at 8:00, *Will & Grace* at 8:30, and *The Apprentice* at 9:00 (or 9, 9:30, and 10, depending on local daylight savings time). The network reimburses the station for the cost of only half the ad (called the network program portion). Affiliated stations must also pay for the space they use to advertise local programs (usually local news). Co-op is a great vehicle for associating late local newscasts with popular network hits.

Networks also swap local on-air time in prime time for designated promotional spots earlier in the day. For example, NBC has a "Nine For Prime" plan in which stations get a 30-second **availability** (industry jargon for an open commercial slot) in prime time in exchange for running nine network promos on weekdays (and four on the weekend days) in local time periods. NBC specifies that the nine promos run once in the hour before *The Today Show*, once afterwards, once in daytime, twice between 3 and 5 p.m. (ET), twice during the 5 to 7 p.m. news block, and twice during **access** (the hour before prime time). Weekend swap promos run twice between 6 a.m. and 4 p.m. and twice between 4 p.m. and prime time. Computers keep such scheduling from becoming a nightmare!

An affiliate's degree of participation in co-op plans depends on the value the station places on outside media promotion for network programs. Some stations tie their success closely to the fortunes of the network. For participating stations, co-op is offered 20 weeks a year (out of the 52 weeks that have to be promoted), and a stream of day-to-day promotional aids arrives, often far more than any promotion director can actually use. In the case of an affiliate with a struggling network, however, joining in the network promotional efforts may be less than rewarding. With the advent of digital television and more options in video delivery from the Internet, DVDs, DVRs, and direct broadcast satellite, even the traditional affiliates rely less and less on their networks. To a greater extent than in the past, the local station must place its own priorities ahead of its network's priorities, especially as the financial relationship between them changes.

3.2   *Joey/Will & Grace/The Apprentice co-op stack ad. Used with permission.*

SMALL-FIVE HYBRID AFFILIATES

At former independent stations, the promotion manager functions with less out-side support in advertising, press relations, on air, and general promotion. Unlike affiliates of the Big Four networks, the hybrid stations get fewer promotional spots, graphics, press releases, or built-ins coming down the pipeline. At one time, true independents were on their own until the emergence of FOX Broadcasting in 1986 (now a major network), followed by UPN and the WB in 1994, and PAX in 1999. During this time Univision and Telemundo expanded their program schedules and also acquired sizeable numbers of affiliates. Stations now affiliated with these networks are **hybrid** stations, partly affiliated, partly independent.[4]

Promotional Practices

Although the promotional needs of hybrid and network-owned and -affiliated stations are similar, their promotional practices are different. Hybrids face the perplexing problem of promoting 18 to 24 hours of daily programming (that is because UPN and the WB, for example, provide only two hours of prime-time programming on most days). Early on, hybrid stations competed with traditional network affiliates by promoting themselves as movie or sports stations, but the coming of all-movie and all-sports channels on cable and satellite providers forced most of them to change that tactic.

A better alternative for hybrids and true "indies" is to promote off-network series. Because the four major network affiliates usually hold the top four ratings positions in a market, competing independent stations vie for fifth place. Hybrids purchase most of their programming from program distributors that strive to compete with the marketing prowess of the big networks. Nowadays, station promotion directors can expect promos for the high-priced syndicated shows to resemble in quality those received by their network-affiliated brethren.

Then there are the older not-quite hits. Much of the promotion hybrids get for them fails to reach network-quality standards, and many come with minimal promotional support. When distributors make electronic kits of on-air promotion materials available, they usually include episodic promos in various lengths, generic promos featuring the series stars, open-ended interviews with the stars, and **wild lines** (out of context clips) for stations to utilize in multipromos covering blocks of programs.

Indeed, because weekly shows get so little promotional attention from stations (they can't showcase everything), promoters of some syndicated once-a-week programs bypass the local station altogether by using websites to market directly to viewers. In the case of low-rated or small-niche programs, such as the *U. S. Farm Report*, advertiser and audience tie-ins are possible as never before.

Most syndicators, however, seldom speak directly to audiences in the consumer media, largely because their programs are scheduled at different times in different cities (and because they don't see audience promotion as an effective way to spend their money). Although syndicators purchase enormous quantities of advertising space to promote their programs, it is almost exclusively in the trade press and directed toward selling their programs to stations (as discussed later in this chapter), not directed toward audiences.

Themes and Slogans

Competing successfully in a television universe of hundreds of channels forces stations to give branding a high priority. Promotion managers traditionally promoted their channel numbers, but repositioning by cable systems and reassignment for HDTV ended that strategy. After all, more than 75 percent of viewers receive their local signals via cable or satellite, with the percentage nearing 90 percent in markets where satellite providers carry local stations.

Regardless of a station's degree of dependence on a network affiliation, **themes** that characterize a station's programming play a big part in on-air identification, and they serve to label a service by creating an image for it. Television stations usually commit to a good overall theme for the long haul, and some of the best-known stations have had a single theme (or variants thereof) for decades. Classic examples include "We're 4" in Boston and later New York, "Here's 2" in Pittsburgh, "Go 4 It" in Detroit, "3 for All" in Philadelphia, "Straight from the Heart" in Knoxville, "Going Places" in Green Bay, "The Land of the 3" in Hartford, "LA's Own" in Los Angeles, and the widely used "The One and Only TV 4 (or TV 9 or TV 2)." More examples can be found by clicking on individual states at *www.tv-ark.org.uk/international/us_index.html*, which shows many of the great on-air campaigns for American and international stations.

THE IMPORTANCE OF ON-AIR SCHEDULING

For *all* local stations, *scheduling on-air promotion is certainly as important as creating it.* A well-produced promo needs to be seen — and it needs to be seen by the right audience. The competitive station schedules promos in the same way it handles commercial spots for its best client — by targeting a key demographic or psychographic group in advance of a promoted program's airtime. Leftover avails (unsold airtime) generally are not good enough to sell programs effectively, and when the station and the economy are strong, there are few leftovers.

Because most stations recognize the importance of promoting their shows, they work out systems for clearing promotion spots during all time periods, regardless of the sales climate. This system commonly is called **fixed-position promotion**, because the promotion department actually contracts with the sales department for fixed times throughout the day. These times can't be sold to commercial clients except on rare occasions. The times may be specific (30 seconds at the 3:00 p.m. break) or for specific dayparts (90 seconds between noon and 3:00 p.m.). A billing system usually is established for these spots for internal accounting purposes. Therefore, the promotion and the sales departments must reach an agreement that strikes a balance between the need for creating commercial inventory to sell and the need for building an audience to sell.

Maximizing Availability

It is important to know what availabilities exist before producing on-air promotion materials. Commercial breaks usually are divided into 30-second multiples: 30, 60, or 90 seconds. Five-, 10-, and 15-second spots also have become increasingly common, especially when 15-second **bookend promos** are used to lead into and out of commercial segments (called **pods**). When the sales department sells a heavy schedule of 10-second spots to clients, 20-second available spots are created. Few advertisers, however, produce 20-second commercials. The marketing manager who knows in advance can make 20-second promos especially to fill these spots. Marketing managers should read sales availability reports so that promo production plans can be tailored to a possible overabundance of abnormal commercial lengths, such as 10- or 20-second spots.

In addition to warehousing odd-length promos, combo spots, shared IDs, and audio tags are the other main tactics for maximizing leftover positions at stations that have only a limited number of fixed positions (or none). **Combo spots** mention more than one program. They maximize the effectiveness of whatever positions are available. Combo spots also can be useful for promoting a programming block to help create audience flow between programs.

When local stations show their station identification and simultaneously give part of the screen over to promoting a program (in a corner box, as background, or in split screen), they are using **shared IDs**. Sharing is a valuable tool that greatly increases the total amount of program promotion possible in a single day. A 4-second identification that splits the screen between program promotion and station ID combines the station's logo with information about an upcoming program. The typical affiliate might have only about twenty 30-second spots (or fewer) available for promotion in one broadcast day, and worse, many of those fall outside the best times for promotion. Often, too few people or the wrong demographic group is watching, so promoting key programs (local news, early fringe, and access-hour shows) is largely wasted. Using shared IDs on the hour, and sometimes the half hour, can effectively double the number of programs that can be promoted by the station. Shared IDs are especially useful for promoting familiar shows, especially stripped off-network series that have been carried on the station for many months.

Because the FCC requires a *legal* ID only to identify a station's call letters and city of license with either audio or video, there are many ways to construct a *shared* ID. For example, topical video of a special guest can be pulled from a talk show and combined with a topical audio announcement. The networks also have adopted shared IDs. Not only do they add opportunities for promoting network programs during network dayparts, shared IDs also encourage promotion of network programs during local programming. Affiliates are more willing to share IDs with their network (as opposed to reserving them for promoting local shows) than give up 30-second available spots in local programming for network promos.

Another effective method is the over-credits **tag** (a vocal promotional announcement). Audio copy usually is mixed with the last few seconds of the program's theme music while the credits are rolling but squeezed smaller to present a video clip. In a technique borrowed from the networks, many prime network programs now provide a vertical split-screen for the local news anchor to tease the upcoming late local newscast because audience size is crucial to the ratings for the news. Sometimes the station chooses to promote the last network show even earlier in the evening to bolster its ratings and its value as a lead-in to late local news.

Scheduling Guidelines

For any local station, despite all the talk of "appointment TV" from some of the networks, the promotion of programs is closely tied to what is being shown today or tonight, not "this Wednesday" or "next Saturday." This is especially true for stations whose focus is on local news, but less so for stations whose central theme is a local sports franchise or high-demand syndicated programs. For any station, promoting today's local news story or tonight's network lineup creates a greater sense of immediacy and makes the promotion more appealing and thus potentially more effective.

To ensure the effectiveness of well-produced promos, seven guidelines should be followed in scheduling on-air promos at television stations:

1. *Establish promotional priorities.* Promotional priorities are the product of three-way communication between the programming (or news), sales, and promotion departments. Clear priorities are especially crucial during ratings periods. Because the station can't promote all its programs, it should establish which ones are important for sales. Nearly all marketing managers use a gross ratings point (GRP) system with weekly goals. Gross ratings points are sums of all the ratings points in a week's available spots. Here, the quarter-hour ratings for programs on either side of a break containing a promo are averaged to get a "break rating," and all the break ratings for the week are totaled. Presumably, a 300 GRP target will reach all viewers 3 times (100 percent ratings $\times$ 3).

2. *Use topicals before generics.* Unless a show is a newcomer and needs thematic promotion, topical (specific) promotion of daily episode content is always preferred. Topical promos should also be run more often than

generic promos. Frequent exposure of topical promos is needed because the content changes every day.

3. *Target on-air promotion.* Schedule promotional material in programs that reach the audience desired for the program. A promo for the late movie may be wasted in the late local newscast if the audiences are not compatible.

4. *Give news promotion top priority.* Local newscasts often dominate a local station's image. A highly-rated, early local newscast builds network news audiences, which in turn swell viewership of the station's access-time programs. Because of the importance of news, a base should be established for the early and late newscasts with good generic image promotion. The anchors' personalities are usually vital, promotable elements of local newscasts. Generic spots for top personalities should be produced and scheduled in addition to image promos for the entire newscast. This base should then be reinforced with daily topical promotion.

5. *Keep a good rotation.* Separate promos for the same program by at least half an hour. This separation allows for sufficiently frequent exposure without excessive repetition.

6. *Keep informed of network on-air promotion.* Keeping an eye on network promo schedules helps in evaluating the network's promotional efforts for individual programs. Spot matching (keeping the episode and temporal sequences correct) is essential when the affiliate is supporting network programs. The station also must try to avoid promo duplication (both airing the same spot) when switching between network and local feeds during breaks.

7. *Focus on the chronology of the program schedule.* Audiences are less likely to memorize the time of shows than they are to learn what program comes after what program. Promos that teach the temporal sequencing of the program schedule often are effective in promoting audience loyalty.

Nowadays, promotion managers can purchase computer software to maximize promotional goals. Effective Media Services sells a program called GRiP it! — software that converts GRP priority targets into an efficient promo schedule. GRiP it! captures all promotional inventory directly from station logs, allows promotion plans and priority levels to be set based on GRP and reach goals, and then allocates promotional inventory automatically using proprietary optimization data. For example, most *Oprah* viewers are the same viewers that watch early morning television. (As a result, King World requires its Oprah stations to run at least three promos for Oprah between 6 and 9 a.m. in order to qualify for co-op dollars.) GRiP it! allows users to specify available commercial lengths, the ratio of commercial lengths to each other, the days of the week promotions will run, cut-off times, and fixed promotions (boilerplate) to be run every week.

NEWS PROMOTION

News is the arena in which most network affiliates choose to compete for ratings supremacy in a marketplace. At virtually all the 800+ affiliated television stations in the United States, including FOX affiliates, promotion of news has the highest priority. At many of the 300+ hybrid television stations, promoting an "early" late newscast in prime time is a typical strategy. WGN in Chicago, for example, carries an early-late newscast named "WGN News at Nine" (or "Ten," depending on daylight savings time), meaning the show appears an hour before most affiliate late news at 11:00 p.m. Another strategy is to counterprogram affiliate news by scheduling and promoting prime-time movies, sports, and off-network sitcoms. However, the station that is number one in news ratings usually is number one in overall ratings and in total dollar revenue in the market.

News promotion messages fit into two broad categories: *long-term campaigns* (using **generic** spots) and *short-term topical promotion* (using **specific** spots). Long-term campaigns are useful for competitively positioning anchors and reporters or upcoming programs, such as a revamped noon, early evening, or late evening newscast. They also can be used to mount assaults on the ratings leader in the marketplace or to demonstrate bragging rights by the station leading in the ratings.

The second type of news promotion is the daily topical that requires no more than one or two days of lead time. The subjects of these promotions are local story exclusives, special features on current issues, or timely reactions to such public events as celebrity scandals or court decisions relating to local issues. For example, 3.3 shows a young child smoking and captures some of the ugliness of cigarette detritus, pairing all that with the happy news anchors who are going to help society solve this problem, maybe. Whatever the feature or medium, *every piece of promotion should have a goal that is both achievable and measurable.*

Early fringe programming provides a good opportunity for some stations to steal viewers from competitors' newscasts. Custom research can tell a station running an afternoon talk show how many viewers in a particular demographic group watch, say, at 4:00 p.m. but then switch to a competing station for the 5:00 p.m. news. A well-placed promo can encourage these viewers not to switch. For example, a station that learns its 4:00 p.m. *Ellen* program attracts older women (who watch another station's news) can give heavy on-air promotion to an upcoming news story on the needs of the elderly at 5:00 p.m.

Defining News Goals

The three common objectives of news promotion are to gain ratings supremacy, person- ality acceptance, and newsgathering credibility. Everyday promotional tactics are as direct as simple announcements of news features or new program times or the

3.3 *Action News 13 topical. (WTVG) "Local Teens Choose to be Quitters." Used with permission.*

acquisition of major newsgathering equipment such as weather radar, news helicopters, or satellite newsgathering gear. More precise acquisitional goals include altering the demographic mix of the audience by capturing the 18- to 49-year-old women currently viewing the competition or attracting viewers from an ethnic group that makes up a significant portion of the demographics in a market. In large cities with diverse ethnic populations, such as Houston, Los Angeles, or Detroit, targeting local audience subgroups is an important strategy. Not all stations can compete effectively for the dominant audience group, so seeking other ethnic subgroups or nightshift workers may be appropriate news targets. In practice, news promotion mixes acquisitive and retentive goals, but the most effective campaigns usually give primacy to a single goal.

Ratings reports show the times when a market's **HUT** (homes using television) level goes up. The typical causes are bad weather, a major news happening, or some other factor that causes more viewers to watch television news. Ratings analysis will spot which station gets most of the viewers during these increases. The station perceived as the most credible generally gathers the largest news audience during major news happenings where visual content is secondary. Stations with exploitative news reporting do better with coverage of weather disasters, family tragedies, and dangerous accidents, where the lurid pictures grab attention.

Successful promotion can also cause the HUT level to rise. Analysis of a series of rating books will tell how much audience increase came from new "turn-ons" as opposed to "switches from competitors." When poor weather or some other outside factor causes the HUT level to increase for all stations in a market, *the amount of increase at one station by comparison to competitors suggests the part promotion played.*

In highly competitive situations, stealing a rating point from competitors really amounts to a difference of two points: one the station gained and one the competitor lost. And two rating points, as any research director will say, is a substantial success story.

News and Promotion Consultants

Virtually all news directors at network affiliates in the top hundred markets subscribe to outside research companies for periodic analysis of their newscast content, their news delivery, and the professional and personal appeal of their news personalities. This information is available to the promotion manager, who should participate in meetings between the station's news staff and the consultants.

Two important agenda items in discussions with news consultants are how to make the news product more profitable and how to use the station's news personalities for promotion. Research indicates that some anchor personalities are perceived by audiences as especially credible and consequently they appear to deliver headlines in news promotion better than others. Some anchor personalities appeal to younger audiences; others are more popular with women. Whatever the strengths and weaknesses, the best features should be exploited by promotion.

Equally as important as data gathered from outside research firms is information compiled internally from ratings books. Careful study of program audience demographics often suggests more efficient scheduling of on-air news promos. For example, if the current goal is to attract more male viewers to the newscast, clearly promos for news should then be scheduled in programs that attract a larger audience of men. The tough part is to get the sales department to give up some commercial time in local sporting events.

The latest influence on research is the rise of *promotion consultants*. Stations can hire promotion consultants to conduct on-site training seminars that show creative service directors how other stations have gained success using specific tactics. Information is available at *www.602communications.com* regarding the foremost promotion consultant, Graeme Newell. Another way to learn about promotion is to join an online discussion group dedicated to television promotion (for example, *www.vault.com/go/to.jsp?place=25156*).

Consultants can advise on the typography in news promo signatures (usually an animated logo with a soundbed, as described in Chapter 5) and the titles for news features, which should be closely coordinated with the station's overall look. These are significant elements in establishing station identity and important strategic tools. News graphics should be selected with long-term use in mind because news program logos often are retained for years (and then modernized rather than discarded). Capturing the desired station image in high-quality logo art and good animation is worth the extra cost and can be justified by amortization over the life span of their use.

News Campaign Themes

Like every commercial product ad, ideally, every promotional advertisement should "ask for the sale" and give a **benefit** the viewer will get from watching. Viewer benefits can be stated explicitly (as in "your most reliable news source") or implied (as in "a professional news team, on your side," and so on).

However creative a campaign, the promotional *theme* comes first, and it should be embodied in a simple statement. A campaign concept that uses wordy messages can be broken into stages and taken one step at a time in separate pieces of promotion. The most successful advertising campaigns in television news have evolved from simple statements or concepts and continued to build in scope and reach. News teams seldom attain leadership position overnight; they take months or years to build momentum.

Beneath the gimmickry and flash of most news promotion, a dozen basic themes used alone or in combination appear in most promotional campaigns. When deciding which theme to use, it is crucial to determine whether the campaign should strive to retain current viewers (**retentive**) or acquire new viewers (**acquisitive**). Some campaigns focus on the attributes of news personnel, others on the attributes of the newscast or station:

1. *The leading newscast.* If a station can lay claim to the highest ratings in its market, it can use this achievement as a promotional tool. This "News Leader" campaign usually serves a retentive function for the station by reassuring its viewers that they have chosen the best channel for news coverage. The top station in the San Diego market, KFMB-TV in 3.4, has a dramatic news set that embodies its leadership position in the market (and won an Emmy award for creator Devlin Design).

3.4 *KFMB-TV news set. Used with permission.*

2. *The professional newscast.* This type of campaign tries to communicate the high standard of professionalism practiced by a news anchor or team. This positive message focuses on the expertise or dedication of the newscaster. A professional campaign serves a retentive function. When a station has suffered from a ratings drop or has introduced a new anchor-person, however, such a campaign becomes acquisitive.

3. *The folksy anchor.* News anchors are highly visible and serve an important role in their communities. It sometimes becomes useful to portray them as ordinary citizens with everyday concerns in a "people like you" campaign. This campaign works especially well if the audience can be convinced to identify with the anchor. Primarily in small markets, ready identification with news anchors breeds long-term loyalty.

4. *The hardware newscast.* When a station acquires a new piece of newsgathering equipment, it can use the equipment as the basis for a short-term promotional campaign. Many stations have produced promos touting their fancy helicopters, "live" news vehicles, sophisticated weather graphics, or local weather radar. This promotional strategy primarily serves an acquisitive function by impressing potential viewers with the newsgathering capabilities of the station.

5. *The live-on-the-scene newscast.* This type of promotion concentrates on promoting the station's live, on-the-spot coverage. The increased availability of remote equipment and satellite delivery gives stations the opportunity to dominate competitors by providing a constant stream of live coverage from distant places, including the hot news spots in other countries. Research usually shows that live on-the-spot coverage is a significant determinant in newscast preference, demonstrating its acquisitive role in middle and larger markets.

**YOU'RE LOOKING AT
THE SUBJECT OF OUR MOST
DISGUSTING NEWS EXTRA...EVER!**

 It can live up to three weeks without food or water. It eats virtually anything from food to glue to hair to paint chips. It's a notorious spreader of food poisoning and carries 100 different types of bacteria. If a nuclear holocaust were to occur, it is likely to be the sole survivor. It may be in *your* modest apartment or palatial estate. How do you know? And how do you defend against it? Tom Hooper reports.

**COCKROACH · STARTS TUESDAY
ONLY ON NEWS AT TEN,**
(WHEN YOU'RE NOT EATING)

3.5 *WITI mini-doc (about cockroaches). Used with permission.*

6. *The feature newscast.* Some stations find it profitable to air lots of news specials and mini-documentaries (short news series included within evening newscasts) to bolster audience interest. For example, WITI-TV produced a multi-night feature about cockroaches that was both fascinating and disgusting (see 3.5).

In-depth news comes from a

3.6 *KSL-TV news team billboard. Used with permission.*

This strategy works acquisitively but only with about 5 percent of the audience. It also can be a maintenance device in that multipart mini-docs encourage the newscast's regular audience to watch more often.

7. *The deep newscast.* This refers to the newscast with the most in-depth coverage among stations in the market. The long billboard for KSL-TV in Salt Lake City shows off the faces of its news staff and makes a little pun out of "long line" to illustrate its in-depth coverage (see 3.6). The more competitors step up their pace and story count, the greater the opportunity to stress depth of coverage and attract more mature, upscale viewers. Such campaigns usually are most effective as long-term retentive campaigns, but function acquisitively for the target demographic group.

8. *The new newscast.* When a station adds news programs, expands into hourly headlines, or revamps its newscast by changing anchors or remodeling its news set, the change can be made the basis for a promotional campaign. Generally, news expansion themes, such as "Your 24-Hour News," have positive audience appeal. An effective "new newscast" campaign will serve to acquire new viewers curious to see the changes announced by the station, but then the station needs other means to hold them.

9. *The best newscast.* The claim of being the "best" newscast (as in "the one and only") can be made in conjunction with the claim of being number one, or it may be made separately and accomplished either through promoting station or system awards or viewer testimonials. The image of a newscast can be strengthened by testimonials. Community leaders, celebrities, and news anchors from an affiliate station's parent network can effectively laud a station's newscast in promos. The station's own news talent also can be used to sell the newscast to viewers. Some network affiliates utilize network anchors for this purpose, such as having the top ABC anchor participate in a promo endorsing a local ABC affiliate's newscast.

10. *The community newscast.* Promos and ads that stress the ways the newscast represents the needs and interests of viewers can create a "community minded" image for a station or cable system. The value of promoting community involvement is a powerful long-term acquisitive strategy.

11. *The constant newscast.* Another news strategy emphasizes the ongoing and continuous nature of coverage and wakefulness of the news team. The theme usually reminds viewers that "our news team is always here, working for you." Such a strategy is largely retentive.

12. *The convenient newscast.* This strategy plays on the availability of syndicated news programs to local stations. To compete with 24-hour cable news, some stations use the claim "We're there when you are," meaning "on-demand," which definitely is acquisitive.

Daily News Promotion

Everyday news promotion, whether on air or in print, is more direct than campaign promotion. In most cases, the goal is to gain a viewer within 24 to 48 hours. The information a promo sells may be that day's headlines, a special feature, or a one-time-only live appearance of a nationally known personality. Billboard copy has only six to eight words to cover the topic, and print ads are much the same because fewer than half the people who see ads read beyond the headlines. One 30-second promo, however, can combine promotion for three news features and hold attention because the ad unfolds out of the viewer's control. It is important to sell everything salable about news features in the spot or ad while keeping the words to a minimum. Daily promotion is quick selling; a promotion manager has only a limited number of print, television, and radio spots to do the job.

News Teases

News headlines and teases may be much shorter in length than regular 15- or 30-second promos. Many stations take advantage of their 3- or 4-second station identifications to promote their news with a quick headline. Other teases may be packaged with a brief commercial so that the whole pod lasts 10 or 15 seconds. The size of the audience for these brief messages within prime time is much larger than it is for longer promos scheduled outside of prime time, so the potential impact is far greater.

Writing the headline itself goes one step beyond writing billboard copy. There is a big difference between saying "The Sox win the big game" and "See the final highlights of the Sox game at 11." News headlines on television and radio should not be miniature newscasts but should whet the viewers' appetite for watching the news. As often as possible, headlines and teases should refer to an exclusive feature in the next newscast.

With local news, the reporter's job is to *tell* the story. The promo writer's job is to *sell* the story in the tease. *The golden rule of tease writing is "Sell, don't tell. Don't inform, compel."*[5] In every topical news promo, the promo writer wants to achieve the following objectives:

1. Get the viewer's attention.
2. Interest the viewer in the story (hint at the content without giving away the story).
3. Give the viewer reasons to care (by communicating the *viewer benefit*).

According to promotion consultant Graeme Newell, the viewer benefit should do at least one of the following:[6]

1. Offer information that viewers can act on or use to improve their lives.
2. Offer information that viewers will share with family, friends, and coworkers (such as Gee Whiz Video).
3. Offer the viewer a memorable or emotional experience.

The day after a news story has run, ideally, a **proof of benefit** (POB) promo reminds viewers of the particular benefit provided by the station's newscast. Some stations set a goal of 300 GRPs for their POB promos.

Frank N. Magid Associates released a sobering study in 2003 that reminded promotion managers to "keep it real." A survey of 2,200 viewers found that 30 percent were so turned off by exaggerated news promos that they tuned away from over-hyped newscasts. The study also reported that only 53 percent were motivated to watch a newscast after seeing an on-air promo, which was still better than alternate media promos (cable, 40 percent; radio, 40 percent; billboards, 16 percent). Only 32 percent could even remember a specific promotion for a local newscast. Print advertising was particularly ineffective at creating an impression.[7]

Cross Promotion

Cross-plugging news features is almost like getting a free promo. **Cross-plugs** aren't charged to commercial time and don't show on the programming log. Their only costs come from the time for a newswriter or program producer to insert the plug somewhere in the program. Within the news itself, many newscasts tease the features coming up right after each commercial break with copy that reads, "Stay tuned for . . . right after these messages." This type of tease also is called a **bumper.**

Stations that have two early evening newscasts — 5 and 6 p.m., for example — can take advantage of the earlier newscast by having the 6 p.m. anchor appear about 45 to 50 minutes into the first hour with a tease for the 6 p.m. feature stories. Early in the day, the networks' morning shows all have local minutes blocked out in which stations can insert a mini-newscast. Such miniature headlines also may contain a plug for exclusive news features in the early, noon, or late evening newscasts.

Weather breaks always should contain the name of the program, the channel number or call letters, the station's URL (on screen), and perhaps the name of the weather personality — as in, "Channel Seven's Herb Brooks says we can expect rain later today." When people talk about the weather, they have a tendency to repeat the entire statement they heard and create their own word-of-mouth promos for a station's name or weather personality.

Every station runs a large number of public service announcements daily, and it often becomes possible to have news personalities prepare some of these charity or community-oriented spots. Every free mention on the air is a personal promo for the station as well as for the news personality, generating goodwill and a sense of community involvement.

Press Relations for the News

Facts about a station's news personalities and daily news features belong in everyday press bundles. Most newspaper columnists shy away from reviewing mini-documentaries and news features, primarily because newspapers compete against local broadcasters for news coverage, but at times special features can be telephoned to the newspapers. Uncommon timeliness or an outrageous fact uncovered may stimulate interest. When columnists have a slow day, they may be eager for that extra information. Fifty-two efforts in a year are worthwhile if just one gets a splash in the papers that ultimately raises ratings.

A promotion staff member should make daily runs through the newsroom to inquire if the news anchors intend to make appearances on their own (not arranged by the promotion department). If so, the promotion department should furnish biographical materials, a photographer, or other useful assistance. In the larger markets, news personalities are celebrities of such magnitude that they frequently have agents or business managers to handle their public appearances. When this is the case, coordination is required to bring about the maximum amount of goodwill.

Promotion departments occasionally set up a speakers' bureau to assist station personalities (and often management and production staff as well) in public appearances. Before initiating such a project, the station's news personalities should be polled to assure their interest in participating. A speakers' bureau requires brochures to mail to community service and industrial organizations that regularly use speakers, parade personalities, contest judges, and grand marshals.

The brochures need periodic updating and at least two mailings a year. Obviously some of a station's news personalities will welcome a speakers' bureau more than others, but the more a station's talent meets the public in functions, the easier it is for the promotion department to expand its viewing audience and create station goodwill.

Mini-Docs, Features, and Projects

Promotionally-oriented news operations schedule news mini-documentaries, magazine features, and special news series to take advantage of their on-air and online promotional potential. When broadcast, promos are placed well in advance of air dates in major rating periods. In some markets the major rating periods are so competitive that choosing and promoting non-headline news features has been polished into an art form. Because most of the headline news is common to all stations, rating battles are won and lost on the quality of promotion of these extra features. Most stations promote their mini-documentaries as an item within multiple-show promos. If the mini-doc has segments lasting through an entire week of newscasts, however, it warrants its own promotional effort.

Depending on the length of newscasts and the size of feature reporter staffs, news directors may schedule anywhere from one feature per rating period to two or three per week. If the news contains a sizable number of promotable features, the news promotion budget should take into consideration the cost and facilities needed to inform the viewers about when and where the features will appear. It is not uncommon for local news stations to be running different promotable features at the same time and offering supplementary information on their websites. *The promotional advantage usually goes to the station that ties together all media with a consistent, unified, creative design.*

Media Advertising to Support TV News

A station's own airtime is the most flexible kind of advertising because commercial availabilities can be used (over the sales manager's loud objections) when unexpected news stories occur. External media can be exploited, too.

Radio

Radio time is especially useful in emergencies because it is relatively inexpensive and requires little lead time for production, and most of the larger radio and television stations in a market have similar coverage areas. Even for routine daily promotion, talk radio and all-news radio have the ideal demographics for teaching potential viewers of evening television newscasts. Advertising on these stations has exceptional promotional value because of information radio's timeliness.

In-car listening is the largest type of out-of-home radio listening. In cities with little or no mass transit (think of Boston, Los Angeles . . .), the car radio is a distinct medium in its own right. Promotion in drive-home traffic has strong carryover effects for evening television news audience size. Evening drive is usually the television station's last chance to promote its latest headline story or remind the "arriving-home/turn on-the-news" crowd of special features planned for that day's early newscast. In many markets, the competing television stations regularly use special telephone lines from their news facilities to deliver last-minute radio promos directly to several radio stations. Produced and executed well, this last-minute news promotion via radio stations can achieve extra rating points, drive down the competition's ratings, and actually steal audiences from other media and outside activities.

Advertising on radio allows more detailed promotional content than either transit or billboard messages. For both campaigns and daily announcements, radio adds depth to the promotion effort. And because spot radio advertising has some flexibility in length (30 or 60 seconds), more than one message can be stacked on another. **Stacking** is of special value for news because stations that have 60-, 90-, and 120-minute newscasts accommodate larger numbers of magazine and non-headline news features than stations doing half-hour newscasts. Because news directors choose these features not just for their informational and credibility value but to attract larger audiences, the station's on-air promotion producers can **billboard** several news topics within each 30-second spot and can run them back-to-back within a 60-second spot for individual newscasts, features, or a combination of early fringe, news, and access programming.

Print Space

Because major news features and mini-documentaries generally are scheduled for major rating periods, the number and size of print ads to support them usually can be estimated accurately in the annual budget. Most daily newspapers have a weekly television supplement, similar to *TV Guide*, which lists seven days of television fare. These supplements generally have greater staying power near home television sets and, in many cases, higher readership than the newspaper's daily television section. Because of the supplement's longer ad deadline, it usually carries generic station ads, as well as specific promotion for preplanned news features. Mini-docs intended for the February and November ratings periods often require a lengthy period of preparatory research and writing, and they should be easy to plan for in print promotion budgets.

Other Media Options

In large, spread-out cities with little or no mass transit, billboards along highways and main streets have greater value for news promotion than in other cities where train, bus, and subway advertising reaches millions of people daily. Because of the lead time for printing billboard and signs, and the very limited number of words that will be effective, billboard and transit advertising usually are restricted to *generic* reminders to watch a newscast or sport series, as in 3.7. This generic ad for the Cubs on WGN-TV refers to the whole season of games,

Just One Of The Highlights
From Last Season's Number One Show.

The Cubs On

See all-new exciting episodes this season.

3.7 *Generic ad for the Cubs on WGN-TV. Used with permission.*

not any particular game, and might easily have appeared on bus sides and transit posters, as well as in magazines.

Billboards and transit are sometimes used to introduce new anchor personalities or changes in program times. If a news promotion budget can afford reminders to "Watch the news when you get home," train, bus, and subway posters are a good buy.

Whatever the medium, the length of the advertising message must be measured against the cost per thousand people reached (cost per hundred for smaller market radio) and the speed of delivery. Other elements in media advertising strategy are the timing and size of buys. For certain times in the year, it is wise to overbuy in anticipation of major news events. In particular, planning up to a year in advance (as discussed in Chapter 4) and calculating for at least two last-minute buys of space to promote unpredicted news features during rating sweeps is sophisticated strategy and money smartly spent.

SYNDICATED SERIES MARKETING

Despite the supremacy of news promotion, local stations must also attract viewers to their syndicated programs. Materials are readily available for first-run shows, or promotion managers can create their own. As mentioned earlier, topical promos are always better than generic spots.

Syndicators (distributors of shows) often offer co-op plans to stations for some hit shows. For example, King World offers stations up to 50 percent cost-sharing for promotion of the program *Dr. Phil*. The plan targets women aged 25 to 54. For stations that offer the program for the first time, the plan recommends a media mix in September that spends 50 percent on cable advertising (specifically on Style, Oxygen, Soap Net, WE, Lifetime, HGTV, Disney Channel, Food Net, ABC Family, TLC), 30 percent on outdoor advertising, and 20 percent in radio (specifically on Soft AC, AC, Religious, Jazz, Oldies, Country, and Gospel formats). For continuing syndicated shows, the mix is 60 percent cable and 40 percent radio advertising, but only during the November and February **sweeps** (when Nielsen conducts measurements of all 211 television markets).

Promotion of off-network series is less difficult. After all, the shows are already well known, so syndicators offer little help. Stations don't have to explain the **backstory** or overall plots of such shows to their viewers; they can concentrate on that night's episode ("Watch Grace trip Will tonight!"). Nonetheless, the ongoing grind of keeping up with handfuls of promos and other advertising for series episodes, daily news teases, and news features takes energy and enthusiasm.

PUBLIC SERVICE PROMOTION

Public service promotion allows a network, station, or cable operator to position itself as the friend and ally of its audience and, at the same time, draw new audiences to its programs. While other media in a market use their advertising, promotion, and public relations resources to tell their audiences how important they are, stations (and cable systems) using public service promotion actually can perform invaluable services on behalf on their audiences or subscribers. These services can enhance a station's image and improve its ratings and build audience loyalty for cable operators. Most of all, public service is an opportunity to give more exposure to its local on-air personalities.

The two major elements of on-air public service are public service announcements and public affairs programming. **Public service announcements** (PSAs) are announcements for which no charge is made to promote activities of federal, state, or local governments, the activities of nonprofit organizations (such as the United Way or Red Cross), or any other announcement serving community interests (such as messages urging listeners or viewers to vote). PSAs can be highly produced spots using actors or station personalities at remote locations. Most radio and television stations and many cable systems also air a simple audio-over-slide "community calendar" listing upcoming local activities.

Most stations are inundated with local and national PSAs, often to the point where demand exceeds the supply of airtime. Stations or local broadcast associations usually organize rotation plans that manage the flow of spots. These rotation plans generally work against the impact of any individual spot, delivering the reach but seldom the frequency required for impact. Because public service announcements are a large part of a station's community outreach, they need to reflect current public issues and needs.

Three Approaches for Stations

The strategies of public service efforts can be divided into three broad categories: passive, active, and interventionist. Stations and, increasingly, cable systems commonly are classified by community groups and business organizations according to their public service policies and practices. The *passive* stations and systems present no more than the required share of public service announcements and rotate them in accordance with their license commitments. *Active* stations and systems involve their staffs and airtime in advancing local causes. They typically associate themselves with established community projects and charities, furnishing enormous amounts of support to ongoing local institutions such as hospitals, rape crisis centers, and mental health facilities. They may take on local fund drives and turn them into annual crusades. They use local personalities, tie in local sponsors, coordinate with dozens of community organizations, and powerfully persuade their audiences to participate. By allying efforts with other media, stations can get printed flyers and radio announcements provided "in kind." As depicted in the poster in 3.8, WCBD, Channel 2 in South Carolina,, got behind the town of Mt. Pleasant's effort to encourage children to discover the arts.

Interventionist public service promotion requires that the broadcaster or cable operator identify specific social problems and, in alliance with such partners as business, government, and organized volunteers, intervene in those problems on behalf of the audience, while meeting a number of the station's or system's public service, ascertainment, and promotional needs. The basic idea is to use the airwaves to allow *others* to find solutions to problems, not for the station to tell the community what to do.

Campaign Resources

The judicious selection of a problem is crucial to whether or not a campaign will work. Obviously, a local television station or cable system is not going to solve the issues of world peace and nuclear disarmament. It might help mediate a school board problem, however, or encourage a dramatic increase in volunteers to alleviate specific local problems.

The major difference between large-market and small-market participation in interventionist public service is a matter of scale. Social problems are as easy to find in small cities as in large ones. The key challenge faced in conceiving and mounting the public service or promotional approach in small markets is securing staffing and dollars. One is advised to select only projects that realistically can be implemented and to take advantage of the close community ties usually found in smaller cities by leaning heavily on local resources. A community group or business that wishes to sponsor costs, provide staffing, or supply services (such as distribution) usually can receive on-air credit — a form of institutional advertising that may well bring them business. Moreover, spots crediting local service groups and businesses with support often can be counted by the station as part of its PSA commitment. Because each case is different, it is prudent to check station (and group) policy. If these obstacles are surmounted, a campaign has a powerful way to fuel itself with money and personnel.

Another approach is to sell a campaign to one or more clients, thereby increasing the station's revenue during slow sales periods. In this case, the on-air material must be logged in as commercial matter. A third approach — split logging — allows the station to log a campaign spot as "other" except for the sponsor's tag, generally logged as "commercial matter."

The best way to maximize the value of community involvement is by ensuring that the public service activities are fully integrated into the station's overall

3.8 *Artfest poster. Used with permission.*

identity umbrella. Management can gain credit in the public's mind through consistent promotion of its activities on behalf of the community. But remember the old saw: "If you keep it to yourself, don't expect the public to know about it." When the station's overall promotional strategy, including theme and IDs, reflects public service commitment, the message will get to the public.

SALES PROMOTION

Television is a dual-product medium. Its customers are audiences and advertisers. Although the most visible forms of promotion are those targeted toward the audience, most of the local media's money still comes from advertisers. As a result, much of any station's promotional budget must be used to convince potential sponsors to buy time. Moreover, as movies and sports migrated to cable channels, local stations had to turn to syndication in order to develop some kind of personality to set them apart from everyone else in the market. These shows rely heavily on national advertising that needs a large audience to sell national time. As a result, most of a syndicator's promotion budget is aimed at getting the stations to buy the programs, not the public to watch them. In selling time to advertisers or selling shows to stations, promotion plays an enormous role.

Marketing Syndicated Programs to Buyers

Today, most local television stations choose from dozens of potential programs to fill their non-network hours with syndicated materials. Because most of these programs look very much alike, which programs the stations choose to buy and how much they are willing to pay has a lot to do with how the program alternatives are promoted.

Older Network Series

Syndicated materials fall into three payment types, each of which is promoted slightly differently. The three types are straight cash, cash plus barter, and straight barter. Older off-network series, most of which ran a decade earlier — such as *Home Improvement* or *Seinfeld* — are offered to local stations for a straight cash payment. The syndicator's job is to get each station to pay more per episode. This is accomplished by emphasizing three things in sales promotion conversations and materials: how well the show did during its network run, how loyal the show's audience is, and how well the show has performed with key demographic groups in other (similar) markets. Such information often will be reflected in brochures, handouts, and episode guides, which focus on former popularity, the stars involved, or the numbers in markets where the show is now running. The text of print ads for older syndicated series typically states how each series is doing in comparison to other similar programs, how much it has improved its slot's ratings compared to whatever it replaced, and how strong the program was the first time around.

For scheduling reasons, local stations tend to want half-hour rather than one-hour shows and typically series not old enough for cable or new enough to cost big bucks. Syndicators therefore concentrate money on a few perennial hits, such as *Gilligan's Island*, or on the other two types of syndication where potential profits are higher. Very little support is offered to stations to help promote these "evergreen" series, but most stations are content to lift scenes for their own promos. This may change, although not to the local stations' advantage, as the owners of these "limited use" shows discover the potential of DVD sales. A shift away from direct cash sales to stations may occur in favor of direct sales to the public, but at this writing, the direct DVD market receives very little promotion as yet. The industry seems to think just releasing a set is sufficient.

New Network Series and First-Run Hits

Newer off-network series such as *Friends, Will and Grace*, and *That '70s Show* or hit original syndicated programs such as *Oprah* are sold to stations for *cash plus barter*. The syndicators want cash for each episode but also want advertising time to sell on the national market, and stations will both pay and give up time to get these exceptional programs. These shows have proven track records and are in big demand, so the majority of syndicators' promotional dollars are spent on these shows.

Promotion for hot syndicated shows is designed to get local management excited and in the mood to bid large sums of money for the exclusive rights to the program. When *Home Improvement* was in this category, the syndicator's reps arrived in costume, presented station personnel with tool belts filled with chocolate tools, and did an entire entertainment routine before showing a videotape highlighting the funniest moments from the series. The video presentation also contained a personal appeal from the stars. Because several stations already were bidding on the program, such promotion might seem like a waste of resources, but these promotional efforts were not designed to "sell" the show. Rather, they were meant to create excitement, heat up the bidding war, and increase what each station is willing to offer. For a program like *Everybody Loves Raymond*, a great deal of the promotion was what the industry calls **schmoozing** — meeting the stars, going out to fancy dinners, getting expensive promotional items. Today, such major hit programs as *Smallville* draw bids from several stations in each market, as do original series such as *Jeopardy, Wheel of Fortune*, and *Dr. Phil*.

Trade publication advertisements for such hit programs often skip numbers, as in the ad for four familiar series in 3.9. The distributor, Carsey-Warner-Mandabach,

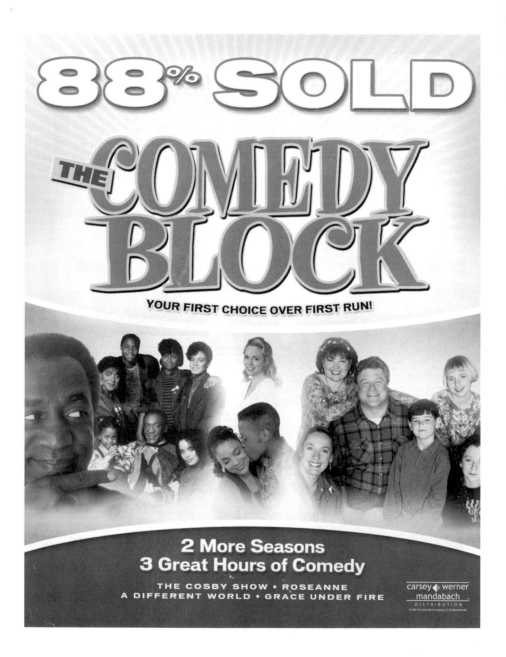

3.9   *88% Sold: The Comedy Block. Used with permission.*

offers all the shows as a comedy block to stations with a headline saying the block has already been sold in 88% of the U.S. market.

Everyone already knows such shows are great, so in their huge trade-magazine ads, the syndicators can choose to emphasize the stars as Carsey-Warner-Mandabach did for its comedy block, or they can list the markets that have already gotten on board or point out that some desirable series finally has become available.

Syndicators will make big promotional efforts for original shows that have proved to be sustainable. They will try to create excitement about them by using teaser advertisements spread over several full or part pages or even through several magazine issues. Such ads slowly build, revealing the show's title only on the final advertisement page. Syndicators may also spend hundreds of thousands of dollars creating huge displays for national conventions, elaborate press kits, and even special promotional items. For example, the syndicators of *Regis and Kelly* made dolls of the stars that they gave to station personnel. Many syndicators also set up **photo ops** (opportunities) with the stars, shooting quick Polaroid shots for the low-level station staff and guests, while providing professional, autographed, and framed 8x10 inch prints for potential buyers.

Other First-Run Series

More routine, or lower-rated original series like *Divorce Court* and first-run original series with no track record (such as the *Tyra Banks Show* or *Robin Quivers* in 2005) make a third type of syndication. These programs are licensed for **straight barter** (for time instead of cash). The stations and syndicators split the advertising time during the program by dividing the number of commercial minutes between them, and each sells its time separately, keeping all the revenue. First-run shows have no track record when they are newly offered, so they require promotional campaigns emphasizing that they are shows the audience can't get from the networks. At other times, the promotional message for barter shows emphasizes how much the program is like something already successful. This was the case when *Dr. Phil* got started, because his format had been incubated within the hit program *Oprah*.

Print advertising for barter series tends to emphasize market penetration and word of mouth in the form of testimonials or media hype. The ad for *Access* in 3.10 illustrates the program's growth in ratings in one market over the previous year, making a pun of the series' name and its intended time period.

Sometimes the advertisements themselves are designed to look like movie posters rather than television promotions. There is also a great deal of personal contact in marketing such shows, accompanied by many promises of promotional help to the station to get the series off to a strong start with viewers. The

3.10   *Print ad for a new weekly barter show,* Access. *Used with permission.*

trick is to generate enough interest for stations to take the chance on an untried show and commit time. Syndicators strive to get in on the ground floor with deals that lock in stations for several years. With the enormous success of such original syndicated series as *Wheel of Fortune, Judge Judy, Hercules, Xena,* and *Andromeda,* not committing early has become a potent risk factor for stations. On the other hand, only one in 10 or 12 such shows succeed, and far fewer become real hits.

Follow-Up to a Buy

Once a barter show is sold in a new market, the syndicators follow up with promotional packages designed to help the station promote the series to the audience. Video cuts, often mentioning the station by name and the time the show will run, occasional guest appearances by the stars (in the biggest markets), and print ads are usually included with the sale. In many cases, stations will be given a promotional allowance, taken out of any cash payment, to allow them to create their own promotional messages. A few barter shows are huge moneymakers for the syndicators, and these, therefore, generate the most promotional effort from them.

To aid in sales commitments, the syndicator's promotional materials provide information on how much money and effort will be committed to promoting the specific programs to the public, the reputation of producers, the reasoning behind recommendations for scheduling, appropriate ratings goals, possible tie-ins with successful series, and other information that may affect ratings or the show's chance for financial success. In more practical terms, the syndicator will provide (usually on a weekly basis) promotional clips that can be run whenever the station wants. These clips can be edited to mention the station directly and the time the show is being run.

Marketing to Advertisers

In addition to attracting audiences, stations are in the business of convincing potential advertisers to buy time. Depending on the size of the local station, or more often nowadays, the size of the group owner, separate departments may be established for sales promotion and audience promotion. If there are two, they should work closely together to embody the same theme, graphics style, and approach to getting the message across. After all, advertisers and regional spot market buyers also watch some commercial television. No station wants potential buyers getting conflicting messages just because two separate departments are at work. The actual materials sales needs vary from simple flyers to elaborate four-color brochures, to merchandise, and perhaps to full multimedia campaigns — depending on the size of the market. The amount of money that has been invested in obtaining a program and, of course, the revenues generated by the station or group of stations determine the amount of effort that will be made to market the show to advertisers.

The task of the sales promotion staff is to facilitate communication between advertising staff and advertising clients. Most local stations concentrate their efforts into three areas: the regional spot market, local advertising agencies, and direct contacts (the owner of the retail or service business).

Many *large advertisers* set aside a portion of their budgets to buy time on local stations, dividing the country into geographic regions with similar characteristics. For example, a car tire company might want to emphasize one set of tires in a southern region with a lot of rain and other tires in a northern area with a lot of snow. The regional spot market allows a company to reach different audiences. Naturally, local stations want part of that money, and staff puts together proposed groups of programs and buying schedules to meet the sponsors' goals. This gives the advertisers several options they may want to consider, usually on a GRP basis (how many spots will they have to buy to reach, for example, 80 percent of the audience at least three times).

One of the keys to successful sales is personal contact, and sales, promotion, and management should work together, sharing the local promotional load in dealing with local *advertising agencies*. For example, it is important for salespeople to remember birthdays, graduations, anniversaries, and other events in the lives of clients. Station managers also often keep close social ties to their regular advertisers. Gifts for the holidays are also common, as is taking clients out to lunch to discuss potential buys and so on. In fact, almost anything that will help develop a friendly, personal relationship with clients is considered acceptable.

Although local business people know something about ratings, demographics, and so on, many have no idea of how to read a ratings book and don't know a great deal about the audience or coverage area. This means the promotional effort has to be much more personal and less technical than at the regional level. *Ratings data communicates best when it is reduced to graphs or charts that local clients can easily understand.*

It is assumed that *local sponsors* want to know and like the people with whom they do business. They want to think of the station staff as friends, and they often develop loyalties that have very little to do with audience size or even past successes. In many communities, the management, sales, and promotion people go to the same church, belong to the same clubs, and have kids on the same teams as the potential sponsors.

Basic and Specialized Materials

Besides promoting programs to viewers, the promotion department usually prepares the actual materials needed for the personal sales contacts. The types of materials fall into two categories: basic and specialized. *Basic* (or tangible) *materials* are provided to nearly all clients and agencies and can be revised as needed. These materials include rate cards, information sheets on special opportunities (such as package deals offering quantity discounts), coverage maps showing the station's signal coverage area, program schedules (usefully separating network series from the locally produced or purchased ones), and audience ratings and demographics data. Such materials also often include comparisons with the competition.

Specialized (or intangible) *materials* are selected by the sales staff to meet the needs or desires of specific clients. Such materials include information on specific shows, biographical data on personalities or stars, success stories and testimonials, and clippings from newspapers and trade publications. Sometimes client lists are included to show which other clients are buying time. In addition, specialized demographic or sales data may be included.

To keep a consistent image, even with this specialized material, stations usually utilize **shells** — preprinted sheets that can be filled in with whatever information is needed. An example of a shell from a FOX affiliate appears in 3.11, telling advertisers how well the syndicated *O.C.* has been doing since its move to Thursdays at 8 p.m. and emphasizing key demographic groups.

Such sheets always have the station's logo and identifier, perhaps a slogan or brief selling point, and contact information. (Note the "borrowing" of an NBC branding slogan by a FOX affiliate in 3.11.) The completed materials are placed in elaborate preproduced four-color covers or in professionally designed folders as **leave-behinds** for the client. The actual information provided in the promotion materials often comes from Nielsen ratings books, or may come from the affiliate's network or the syndicator of the program as part of its promotional effort to keep the station happy.

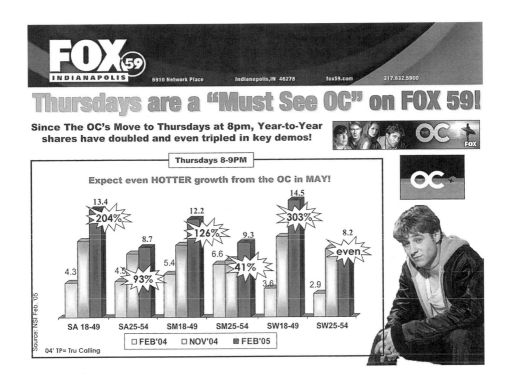

3.11 *FOX 59 shell for O.C. for advertisers with "borrowed theme." Used with permission.*

Events and Contests

Often, local advertisers lack the resources to understand how well an advertising campaign is working. As a result, stations can design sponsor-related public promotional events to visibly prove the effectiveness of a station's advertising, such as contests that generate foot traffic coming into advertisers' stores. Contests are big pluses in convincing advertisers to keep buying time.

Going still further than in-store contests, KSL in Salt Lake has run a Christmas event called "Quarters for Christmas" for many years. The idea is to collect money to buy shoes for needy children at holiday time. During the afternoon news and during special weekend events, people are allowed to come on TV and give the money they have collected. Businesses also set up collection sites and then deliver the money on the air. Other businesses come on to offer such things as new clothes, food, or special deals in which shoe recipients can come in and select gifts for other family members. In short, a promotional event has been turned into an annual community tradition.

Taking another approach, a Kansas FOX affiliate tied its own promotion to the success of *American Idol* by capitalizing on its potential for audience interaction. At random points in the show, a number would flash on the screen. Audience members then called in, and a specific number caller was asked a question about the station's prime-time programming. A correct answer won a jackpot while an incorrect answer passed the money over and let the jackpot continue to grow. To support such contests, large schedules of on-air and newspaper promotion for the show and contest were run.

Another valuable tactic is to turn the audience into living billboards. Public television has done this for years with T-shirts, mugs, tote bags, and anything else they can think of — putting local station call letters (or PBS) on items given out at pledge drives. Giving such labeled things as prizes has the added advantage of appealing to viewers' egos, because most want to show off what they have bought or won.

GUIDELINES FOR SALES PROMOTION

Jim Janicek, a respected director and producer of promotion and interstitial programs, as well as long-ago creator of ABC's T.G.I.F. campaign, created a list of ten guidelines for successful sales promotional efforts at the local level:[8]

1. *Always make emotional contact with clients.* Stations and advertisers are seldom sold by lists of benefits or numbers alone. They are motivated by a desire to be part of the experience.
2. *Find an angle that sets your station apart from the competition but not too far apart.* Originality is not a great selling point with either stations or advertisers.
3. *Get to know the clients.* Personal contact is essential, and records indexing the names of children, past buying behavior, and other background are useful.
4. *Create a strong, easily recognized and coordinated image to guide an entire campaign.*
5. *Test new ideas on small groups before going big.* Ask yourself, "Would I enjoy this event or game if it were presented to me?" Remember to make the product emotionally more appealing than the competition's product. If you don't buy the pitch, neither will anyone else.
6. *Challenge the ways things have been done in the past.* Make your promotions stand out, but be careful not to go too far. You don't sell by offending your audience or sponsors.
7. *When the competition gets tough, shift the battlefield in your favor.* What can you offer that is unique about your station's product?

8. *Build an army of supporters.* If you can get the receptionist, secretaries, sales, production, and promotion people behind you, it is a lot easier to sell management.

9. *Deliver the same message over and over, every chance you get.* Resist the urge to change focus or add something new unless you have absolute proof that the original strategy isn't working. Too many messages just confuse your audience.

10. *Take the word* fear *out of your dictionary, and don't rely on "experts."* Many great ideas have been lost because promotion people were afraid to try something new or because the experts already knew it wouldn't work. Promotion is a creative endeavor, and promotional staff cannot be creative by copying other people's work.

SELECTED READINGS AND WEBSITES

Albiniak, P. "Coming Up at 11! Viewers Don't Care," *Broadcasting & Cable*, June 9, 2003. Retrieved online at *www.broadcastingcable.com/article/CA303768*.

www.602communications.com
www.broadcastingcable.com
www.katz-media.com
www.kleinand.com
www.nielsenmedia.com
www.promax.tv
www.tv-ark.org.uk/international/us_index.html
www.tvspy.com/Marketing/Marketing_archive.cfm?t_MarketingMatters_id=84
www.vault.com/go/to.jsp?place=25156

NOTES

1. UPN and the WB supply between 2 and 3 hours of prime time daily to their affiliates; PAX supplies 5 hours from 6 to 11 p.m., and Univision and Telemundo both supply full service equaling ABC, CBS, and NBC.

2. When stations preempt network shows for any reason, any network promos for that show should be covered with network promos for some other show that the station is carrying.

3. FOX, for example, provides a *members-only website* where affiliates can download pictures, numbers, and brochures, and so on for any program on the FOX network. This information then can be tailored to specific local or regional clients. The FOX website features a section where local affiliates can file examples of successful sales or other promotional campaigns they developed, and other affiliated stations can adapt these ideas. The website also provides non-public access to the network's top promotional people, who will help with local campaigns.

Along with such private websites, networks provide a wide array of computer-based CD-ROM and video materials that affiliates can run on a laptop computer to impress a potential sponsor. These materials usually are produced by the network's sales promotion department and are free to affiliates, with few restrictions on how they can be used.

4. Other semi-independents remain, such as those affiliated with religious or ethnic groups, and some true independents, but the proportion (about 5 percent) no longer warrants separate consideration. For all practical purposes, commercial broadcast stations are comprised of two groups: those channels attached to Big Four networks (affiliates) and those channels aligned with the five smaller networks (hybrids). They are all affiliates, but the hybrids retain some semblance to the old-time true independents.

5. Source: Graeme Newell, "Teasing Tip of the Week: Sell Your Coverage," *Marketing Matters Archive. www.tvspy.com/Marketing/Marketing_archive.cfm?t_MarketingMatters_id=840.*

6. Source: *www.602communications.com/602pdfs/whitepaper01.pdf.*

7. Paige Albiniak, "Coming Up at 11! Viewers Don't Care," *Broadcasting & Cable*, June 9, 2003, retrieved online at *www.broadcastingcable.com/article/CA303768.*

8. Enumerated at the 1994 PROMAX Image Conference and here paraphrased for promotion by syndicators to networks, networks to affiliates, and stations to advertisers.

CHAPTER 4

Management, Research, and Budgeting in Promotion

Michael O. Wirth and Ronald J. Rizzuto

Organizational structures in broadcasting and cable are quite inconsistent from company to company. Responsibilities in stations, networks, and systems depend on such factors as corporate policy, tradition, size, income, mission, and management style. Over time, there has been an increasing shift toward a marketing perspective for four main reasons:

1. *Greatly increased competition for audience attention, as the number of channels proliferate and audiences fragment*
2. *More and more costly investments in programming*
3. *Rising importance for Internet strategies*
4. *Increased concern by government regulators (e.g., the FCC) with indecency, lotteries, payola, hypoing, and community relations.*

The virtually constant pressure from competing multichannel programmers — cable, DBS, wireless cable, and conventional broadcasting — has led to a much greater emphasis on marketing as companies battle it out to acquire and retain viewers and subscribers. The increasing importance of marketing and promotion positions can be seen in changing job titles, staff sizes, salaries, budgets, and associated responsibilities.

ORGANIZATIONAL HIERARCHIES

Where once they were really low-status jobs, marketing and promotion have achieved places of prominence nowadays in the organizational structures of broadcast and cable networks, stations, and broadcast and cable groups. The fields are now dominated by vice presidents of this and that at the network and group levels. What is new is that stations, systems, and certainly networks now have at least one person, fully or partially assigned, to program and sell their website. Larger companies have somewhat larger Internet staffs. This reflects climbing revenues from web advertising as well as the integration of websites into the marketing, promotional, and content strategies of these larger operations.

Network Configurations

Each broadcast network now has a half-dozen or more vice presidents or directors involved in some way with marketing and promotion. At ABC the titles include vice presidents of on-air promotion, creative services, on-air graphics, and marketing of special projects, as well as art directors. At CBS and NBC, more links between advertising and promotion have been created at the vice presidential levels (with VPs of marketing operations, advertising and promotion, advertising and creative services, and advertising and promotion, as well as graphics) under an executive vice president of marketing at CBS and a senior vice president of on-air advertising currently at NBC, although these configurations are fluid. FOX uses more traditional naming in its network broadcast division, such as vice president of on-air promotion and senior vice president of marketing. Generally, the activities at each network can be grouped into four broad functions:

- *on-air promotion,*
- *print advertising and promotion,*
- *affiliate advertising and promotion, and*
- *Internet advertising and promotion.*

Different individuals deal with promotion for such program content as daytime, comedy, variety, specials, children's, news, and sports. Usually, within each network hierarchy is a press information unit concerned with program kits, press releases, interviews, and star tours. Altogether, several hundred people, situated on the East and West Coasts, are assigned these tasks. While on-air spots are handled by the department designated to produce promotion, trade materials are usually supplied to systems by a separate affiliate marketing department.

Cable's Variations

The widely distributed cable services, such as HBO, TNT, and USA, also have large staffs to handle the various subdivisions within promotion, marketing, design, and graphics, and they purchase a great deal of consumer and trade advertising. Revealing its marketing orientation, HBO has a vice president of Brand Image and a creative director of Brand Image. Many cable networks employ outside agencies to handle the production of their trade advertising messages and their media buys.

The smallest cable networks try to get by with a handful of promotion and marketing employees, and as a consequence, they can supply less advertising support to their system affiliates in the form of on-air promos and camera-ready art or paid national advertising in program guides and other consumer publications.

Most new cable networks understandably concentrate their efforts on purchasing trade advertising aimed at gaining more system affiliates. The ad in 4.1 provides an example of a comparative promotional message designed to reach potential systems (and their group owners) by touting the channel as a vehicle for advertising. Formerly, the International Channel and now AZN Television, the cable trade ad emphasizes AZN's narrow targeting and points to the channel's high potential for reaching Asian Americans and, by implication, its rapid growth as a place to advertise.

Station Staff Sizes

Who does the day-to-day work? At broadcast stations, promotion tasks fall to just a handful of people compared to the major networks. Staffs range in size from only one to a dozen or so people. In small radio stations (49 employees and under, as defined by the FCC) and in television stations in markets beyond the top 100 (usually having fewer than 99 employees), the tasks associated with promotion are generally handled by just two or three overworked people.

Major market stations, of course, have larger staffs because having more media outlets in big cities increases the promotional challenge, due to the fact that more money is spent on advertising in these markets by agencies, and because larger stations produce more discretionary income. *More money being spent in the market means bigger financial rewards to be gained from higher ratings from better marketing. More profitable stations have a greater opportunity, if management desires, to emphasize promotion.*

4.1 *AZN trade ad targeting cable systems. Used with permission.*

GROUP OWNERSHIP'S INFLUENCES

One important indicator of promotion's influence is its relative position in management's personnel hierarchy — the oh-so-important job title, as already illustrated for networks. While the 1,000 largest radio stations have evolved hierarchies similar to those at television stations, 10,000 or so remain relatively simple organizations. *Market size, economics, power, automation, and commitment by top management determine the role of promotion.* Many radio promotion managers continue to play dual roles in programming, advertising and sales, or station management, a switch of hats that isn't always as successful in practice as it looks on flow charts.

However, with the rise of multi-station clusters made possible by the change in the FCC's Duopoly Rules and with increased local competition, many radio stations became more sophisticated virtually overnight in the 1990s. Large group owners established full-time promotion departments or positions, increased promotional budgets, and increased the staff time devoted to promotion. Expansion of group sizes between 1990 and 2006 also led to standardization of promotional and marketing efforts among commonly-owned stations and systems. On the plus side, this development enhanced corporate identity, allowed for greater use of research expertise, and spread marketing costs. On the negative side, it has led to more look-alike promotion across the country and far fewer of the imaginative oddball efforts that used to come from inexperienced part-time promotional staffers, probably to media managers' and lawyers' great relief.

In recent years, at both radio and television station groups, the demands on headquarters' promotion and marketing staffs have ballooned, leading to designation of a unit or person (such as a group vice president of marketing and promotion) at the corporate level to coordinate promotional efforts. Such a person consults on local promotion problems, and conducts joint meetings among station department heads, frequently in tandem with top management.

Cable multiple system owners (MSOs) tend to be even more rigorously centralized than broadcasters, supplying most promotion and marketing materials in identical form to hundreds of cable systems scattered across the country. Historically, cable MSOs have spent little on local customization of materials, preferring to save on costs by using the same bill stuffers and promotional offers in all markets (see Chapter 7). Many local systems thus merely redistribute the generic materials supplied by their MSO and the pay cable networks they carry. *As multichannel competition from telephone companies and DBS increases, however, MSOs will soon have to give their divisions the autonomy to promote and brand themselves through the use of locally unique campaigns.* They will have to get in the game to stay in the game.

SALARIES

Besides job titles, another status indicator is how much the job is worth in $s, and, as might be expected, the salaries paid to broadcast and cable promotion personnel have wide variance. Cable promotion personnel are the most highly paid, followed by television, with radio promotion personnel, not surprisingly, receiving the lowest compensation on average. But there are always exceptions.

According to the National Association of Broadcasters (NAB) and the Broadcast Cable Financial Management Association, the median annual compensation (salary + bonus) received by television promotion/publicity directors is almost $54,000. Median annual compensation for television promotion publicity directors ranges from $30,500 in markets 151+ up to $128,000 in the largest television markets (1 to 10). By market size, these figures are reported in 4.2.

As shown in 4.3, the median annual compensation paid to radio promotion directors was almost $40,000, according to the NAB. The median annual compensation paid to radio promotion assistants was about $26,000. However, the range in salaries is large and dependent on market size and market rank. For directors of radio promotion, median annual compensation varied from $30,000 in the smallest markets (151+) to $60,000 in the largest markets (1 to 10).

As illustrated in 4.4, salaries for cable marketing directors vary by size of operation. Annual salaries range from $90,000 in markets with 125,000

4.2   *Television promotion/publicity director median annual compensation.*

Market Size	Median Salary + Bonus
All Markets	$53,669
Markets 1–10	127,950
Markets 11–25	96,393
Markets 26–50	82,175
Markets 51–75	58,500
Markets 76–100	53,500
Markets 101–125	40,955
Markets 126–150	36,649
Markets 151+	30,500

Source: National Association of Broadcasters/Broadcast Cable Financial Management Association. (2003). *Television Employee Compensation and Fringe Benefits Report.* NAB: Washington, DC.

4.3   *Radio promotion personnel median annual compensation.*

Market Size	Promotion Director	Promotion Assistant
All Stations, Nationwide	$39,922	$25,750
Markets 1–10	60,000	32,448
Markets 11–25	46,000	25,000
Markets 26–50	36,269	25,090
Markets 51–100	35,000	21,500
Markets 101–150	36,000	29,000
Markets 151+	30,000	20,000

Source: National Association of Broadcasters. (2004). *Radio Station Salaries: 2004.* NAB: Washington, DC.

4.4   *Cable marketing director typical annual compensation.*

Cable System Size – Subscribers	Typical Compensation*
125,000	$90,000
200,000	$110,000
300,000	$125,000
500,000+	$150,000

* Cable marketing directors also typically receive an annual bonus of 15–20% of their annual compensation.

Source: Carlsen Resources provided compensation data from a proprietary data base.

subscribers to $150,000 in markets with 500,000+ subscribers. In addition, cable marketing directors typically receive bonuses of between 15–20% of their annual compensation.

Unlike cable systems, the salary for publicity directors for cable networks does not tend to vary with network size. Regardless of network size, the typical base salary ranges between $110,000 and $150,000.

BUDGETS

Still another big status indicator is how much money the promotion and marketing director has to spend. On average, the most profitable television stations (meaning the O&Os and those affiliated with ABC, CBS, FOX, and NBC) devote 2 to 3.5 percent of their net revenue to advertising and promotion. The promotion manager with a $3 million budget is usually farther up the managerial ladder than the competitor with just a million or two. Less profitable stations, such as WB and UPN affiliates and the few remaining independents, spend 4 to 5 percent of their net revenue on advertising and promotion. Radio stations typically spend between 2 and 4 percent of their net revenue on advertising and promotion. Finally, the typical cable system also spends between 2 and 4 percent of its net revenue on advertising and promotion. One can expect that the top station almost always spends more on promotion than the lower ranked ones.

RESPONSIBILITIES

Another status indicator is the list of responsibilities associated with the job. In the last decade, many television stations have broadened the promotion manager's responsibilities to include such duties as research, art, and even programming. More and more stations refer to the station department head as the Director of Marketing and Promotion, and directors always have underlings, which is an important status criterion.

Whether a person is situated at a network, group, system, or station, the diverse responsibilities associated with promotion require broad knowledge. In small operations, most of this expertise will be used daily, whereas specialization will be the case in larger organizations. At any rate, promotion personnel generally are charged with four distinct functions to enhance the station's, system's, or network's economic position, programs, and image:

- *audience promotion* (including acquisition and retention),
- *sales promotion* (meaning materials for selling advertising),
- *community relations, and*
- *research.*

In addition to these four functions, the duties of promotional personnel may involve other station or system responsibilities:

- *brand image,*
- *press relations,*
- *daily news promotion, and*
- *general administrative responsibilities.*

Audience promotion by broadcast stations can be acquisitive or retentive and focused on branding or tune-in, and it is divided unequally between internal and external promotion. For broadcasters, on-air remains far more important than external advertising. About half of television stations place their on-air promos in unsold available spots while the other half work with assigned schedules (as discussed in Chapter 3). Most radio stations, on the other hand, use fixed-spot schedules for promos, partly because radio is so highly automated these days. Not surprisingly, television stations report that topical news and sports promotion have the highest priority among acquisitive efforts, whereas point-of-purchase promotions (games and contests in retail stores paid for by advertisers) rank highest for radio promotion managers.

In the case of cable, as the traditional business matured in the 1990s, the emphasis shifted from acquisition to retention. However, the situation reversed again as cable systems began offering bundled packages of telecommunication services, such as digital tiers with video-on-demand (VOD) and near-video-on-demand (NVOD). Emphasis on acquisition was boosted once again as a result of regular offerings of high-speed Internet access, IP telephony (VoIP), and other interactive services. Thus for cable, acquisitive marketing strategies and techniques are back at the forefront, as the plethora of on-air spots now show.

At the same time, tune-in promotion, so basic to TV and radio, has simultaneously become necessary to cable — not only for building program ratings but also as a continuous reminder to subscribers of the value received (the maintenance or satisfaction-building function). In the multichannel world, branding of both cable systems and cable program networks should be an essential part of any promotional strategy, as illustrated in Chapter 7.

Television stations continue to focus on station image and news campaigns, but, borrowing from radio, on-air contests have become another crucial element in efforts to build bigger local audiences. Contests remain essential to audience maintenance in radio, while station image campaigns have become more important to gaining new radio audiences. Community involvement now is an element in three-quarters of acquisitive and retentive promotions for radio stations and over half of all television promotion. These efforts are illustrated in upcoming chapters.

PROMOTION AND MARKETING RESEARCH

Research is a complex aspect of media that all management has to understand in great detail. The risk of failure has become too great for uninformed decisions, and research provides most of the decision-making information for managers. Not only are the images of networks, systems, and stations to their audiences and advertisers crucial to their success, their profitability usually rides on program ratings and satisfied viewers/listeners/subscribers. In addition to research focused on programming and personalities, networks, systems, and stations use research to guarantee the success of their promotion and marketing campaigns — insofar as possible. The potential costs of unsuccessful campaigns in wasted time, effort, and dollars are too great to be allowed if they can be avoided.

Research affecting promotion and marketing can occur at four points in relation to any specific project. Research can:

- *provide a benchmark to measure the marketplace at a project's outset,*
- *be used to isolate an achievable goal for promotional or marketing efforts,*
- *pretest the effectiveness of a campaign concept, and*
- *measure campaign performance after the campaign has occurred.*

Stations, systems, and networks use two kinds of research affecting promotion and marketing: *primary* research to aid in developing and evaluating advertising and promotional campaigns and *syndicated* (or secondary) *research* to determine audience composition and viewing patterns. **Primary research** (so named because it involves direct contact with respondents and is not recycled from some other use) usually is conducted by the station, system, or network producing the campaign or by a research firm it hires to collect information on a particular campaign or a local market. The research focuses on concept testing, image, product, and segmentation or audience identification. These all do different things: Concept testing tests an idea on a small sample of people before it is launched to the public at large. Image research measures how effectively an image campaign is working, after the idea passes the concept stage. Product research examines public attitudes and behavior regarding purchases (or viewing in the case of promotion). Segmentation or audience identification research refines the general public into target audiences more desirable to advertisers.

Syndicated research, on the other hand, is conducted by the two main national ratings and research companies, Arbitron and Nielsen. Stations, systems, and networks purchase relevant portions of their national or marketwide databases. Beyond the ratings, which measure the size of the audience, these big research companies supply special reports on request, but the information still is secondary because it is based on data collected for some other purpose.

Image versus Product Research

Image research examines how the audience thinks about a network, station, cable company, newscast, or program. It can focus on an institution's image or on a specific product's image. *Image research is concerned with the audience's perceptions and how to tap into audience attitudes.* Research into images investigates an audience's interests and needs and then addresses questions about the degree to

4.5 *KUSA's 9News image promotion with theme. Used with permission.*

which a network, station, or cable system appeals to those interests and meets those needs. The illustration in 4.5 is an image ad for of the Denver NBC affiliate's evening newscast, *9News*. It shows the faces of KUSA's four news personalities, along with the theme "Colorado's News Leader."

Benchmark research tells what the audience *already* thinks; the next step is to understand how to change attitudes and, hence, behavior. This requires research into the product. For networks, stations, and systems, the product usually is a particular entertainment program or mix of programs, a newscast, or service activity. A marketing campaign that carries a message that the product does not deliver cannot succeed. Management's job is to decide whether to proceed with a promotional campaign primarily on the basis of the research, although experience and instinct also can play a role.

The flip side is that a particular product's **identity** (the true nature of a product) may have more to offer than its **image** (the manufactured and marketed perception of a product) among its audience or subscribers suggests. Basing marketing strategy solely on a current perceived image could miss an opportunity to build on unknown (to the audience or subscribers), but highly desirable, elements of a product's identity. *Congruence between identity and image is usually the ultimate goal.* (A revamped radio station sometimes tries to establish a commercial-free image for a few months, and then slowly changes its identity by adding commercials while hoping to hang onto its "more music" image.)

Concept Testing

Concept testing explores the appropriateness of specific campaign ideas for current viewers, listeners, or subscribers. Ideally, acquisitive promotional concepts should be tested with members of the target demographic group who do not now view, listen, or subscribe to the client network, station, or system, although that's pretty hard to do for a reasonable cost. Retentive concepts, on the other hand, can be tested with the potential audience as well as with those easy to reach current viewers, listeners, or subscribers. **Concept research** includes the testing of formats, slogans, campaign ideas, music, and graphic styles. It may include matching an existing image to new promotional messages and finding out how audiences respond to new image elements.

Because the results so often are misjudged or misused, concept testing is controversial among both creative staff members and management. For example, a common misuse of concept testing is to assume that the results of a qualitative test will predict how well a subsequent promotional campaign will perform in a quantitative sense. Concept testing does not necessarily produce a "winner." It is most helpful in doing two things: first, locating strengths or running up red flags about any given creative approach, and second, establishing a first-read from the audience on what the content of different campaigns *means to them* (as opposed to what the researchers think it means).

Qualitative concept testing of audience acceptance of particular images as they are associated with a given promotion can be important in shaping a campaign. However, the degree of acceptance in some brief study should not be used as the final, deciding factor in accepting or rejecting further development of a campaign. Tiny modifications can lead to subtle changes in audience response. How spots actually depict an idea makes a huge difference.

Segmenting Audiences

Research comparing the effectiveness of various external media in targeting particular audience segments is conducted more often by advertising agencies and national ratings companies than by individual broadcasters. Ad agencies and ratings firms care the most about having hard numbers that show the relative effectiveness of newspapers, magazines, direct mail, or outdoor media for use in selling their clients' products, so they foot the research bill. Television networks and affiliates, on the other hand, rely heavily on their own air because of its great reach and message frequency and relatively low cost. Most radio stations and cable networks and systems emphasize external media when they want to attract *new audience groups* because they reach only their *existing audience* with their on-air messages. *It takes external media to reach new people.*

The large cable programmers such as Time Warner and Viacom are able to blanket multiple cable networks with **cross-channel promotion,** a highly desirable strategy. Promoting a notable program across their varied owned-cable channels allows them to utilize on-air promotion more effectively — and more cheaply — than smaller cable programmers who have only a single channel for reaching the public and who have to pay for external media to reach larger potential audiences.

Stations and cable systems have somewhat different concerns from advertisers and from each other because "selling news" and "selling subscriberships" are certainly not the same as selling clothing or cars, and selling viewing of individual programs is not exactly the same as selling monthly packages of programs. Media that work well for consumer products and services may not be cost-effective for marketing station images or gaining program tune-ins or subscriptions.

Local market ratings books carry some information about the audience segments reached by various media in the market, but the detail usually is insufficient to serve individual station or system needs. Occasionally, therefore, research on the audience reached by various media has to be commissioned by a network, station, or cable system. For example, individual television stations can order local market studies that will show which media their particular viewers use to learn about upcoming television programs.

Public radio and television have special media research needs because they want to learn which media most effectively generate memberships. Cable systems require media evaluation to determine which media perform best in reaching nonsubscribers and potential **upgraders** (current subscribers who can be persuaded to add various additional services).

PRIMARY RESEARCH METHODS

This and the following section cover the basics of primary and secondary research only as they apply to program promotion and other station and system marketing needs. *The first principle is that research designs and data collection and analysis methods need to fit the research objectives.* Qualitative research uses open-ended questions and is analyzed informally. This method is employed with small groups of people because it is time-consuming. Quantitative research uses fixed responses on a written or oral questionnaire. It lends itself to statistical analysis if the random sample of survey respondents is large enough. Networks, stations, and systems use both quantitative and qualitative research, although certain topics and types of questions lend themselves to different research designs and methods.

The second principle is that questions about image and concepts tend to be answered most effectively by qualitative research while questions about media usage tend to be best answered by using quantitative analysis. For example, if a television or radio station wants information about its image or about the image of its on-air personalities, a series of focus groups may be held with viewers or listeners to obtain in-depth qualitative information on viewer perceptions.

On the other hand, if a television or radio station wants to know how many people are watching or listening to a particular program or during a particular daypart, some type of fixed-choice questionnaire will be used to gather the desired quantitative information. Answers to questions about news and program product often come from a combination of research methods.

Television and radio survey audiences differently. Broadcast and cable networks and television stations usually focus their quantitative research efforts on surveys that reach very large random samples of television viewers. Radio stations focus their quantitative research efforts on surveys that reach only listeners to a particular format or a particular age group. For example, a radio station whose target audience is women 25–34 may conduct ongoing telephone surveys of women 25–34 within the station's market area to help identify which songs in its format are most preferred by the target audience. The station could hardly care less about the opinions of older or far younger women.

All types of networks, stations, and systems also use small focus groups to obtain qualitative information about such questions as which news anchor seems most trustworthy, most professional, or most friendly. Cable systems use quantitative mail or telephone surveys when they are seeking to increase subscriptions or to measure customer satisfaction.

Surveys

Surveys can be conducted by telephone, by mail, over the Internet, or in person. Telephone surveys are probably the most common method of primary research by broadcast and cable television. Because most U.S. homes have telephones, and tens of millions of individuals have cell phones, researchers have access to nearly any universe or audience. Telephone surveys are the most cost-effective, time-efficient way of reaching a large, representative sample of television viewers, radio listeners, or cable subscribers. Unfortunately, a lot of people are besieged by intrusive sales solicitations and simply hang up on innocent researchers. Mail surveys take longer to conduct and achieve much lower return rates than telephone surveys. Mail is used relatively infrequently in local station research because of its high cost, but it is especially convenient and cost-effective for cable companies who can conduct mail surveys of their subscribers inside the monthly bills. Also, mail surveys may be the only way to elicit responses on complex issues or answers to lengthy lifestyle questionnaires. Asking viewers to document their viewing patterns across a week (in a diary) also necessitates a written and mailed questionnaire.

Generally, telephone surveys are somewhat cheaper and yield more generalizable results for broadcasters and cable systems or networks than mail surveys if the questions are appropriate for telephone and if the desired population can be reached. For example, a cable television system that wants to measure subscriber satisfaction could include a questionnaire in its monthly billing statement or make telephone calls to a sample of subscribers and ask the questions.

The mail questionnaire approach likely will achieve a very low response rate (about 20–30 percent) and the results could be very misleading, because the type of person who completes the survey probably does not represent the vast majority of people who did not fill one out. A properly conducted telephone survey will achieve a much higher response rate (up to 75 percent), and the results can be more representative of the entire population of subscribers. Sometimes, the problem of people simply hanging up when they are called is remedied by informing them in advance (by mail) that a survey telephone call will soon be placed, so they don't treat it as a sales call.

Internet surveys are notoriously lopsided in responses because potential respondents can so easily choose not to respond. Thus, all respondents are self-selected, and may fill out questionnaires for reasons of ego or particularly strong feelings on a topic. This means that the average person, especially ones with only modest concern about a topic, are likely to be missing.

In-home surveys are similar to telephone surveys in that they ideally involve large samples of people and utilize a random selection of respondents. For this method, researchers go to private homes and conduct one-on-one interviews with selected participants. The types of questions asked in telephone and in-home surveys are similar, but in-home surveys have the advantage of permitting the use of pictures (aided recall) and actual copies of printed ads and video promos.

However, despite their positives, the high cost of in-home studies and safety concerns have limited their use. Some research firms continue to specialize in this approach because of the advantage of showing pictures and the potential for interviewing people in-depth. Respondents can also make comments about matters the questionnaire might not address but which could be useful.

Focus Groups

Focus groups are a different kind of tool and are widely used in broadcast and cable promotional research. The research is qualitative and typically uses samples of fewer than 100 people, usually in small groups of 8–12 at a time. Participants often are identified in malls or office buildings and asked to come to a public place at a later time. They then are interviewed and tested in a controlled discussion format that may include showing videotapes or administering written questionnaires. Subjects typically are paid a fee of at least $20 for their participation. Thus, focus groups tend to attract people with a lot of time on their hands and that want the money.

In promotion research, focus groups can be used before, after, or instead of surveys. Prior to large-scale telephone or mail surveys, focus groups can help identify issues and pretest the wording of questions. They also can be used as follow-ups to surveys to gather open-ended responses on key items, thus providing a further qualitative explanation of the responses. Focus groups permit testing of visual and auditory materials (such as pictures, videotapes, print layouts, and music selections), and they commonly elicit insightful examples on responses that are difficult to obtain in quantitative surveys.

However, focus groups often are used without support from more systematic quantitative studies. This can lead to problems of bias and lack of generalizability. Focus group samples rarely are selected randomly and thus have a built-in bias toward people with plenty of spare time.

Auditorium and Theater Testing

Theater testing usually involves test groups of 50–100 people or more. A written questionnaire may be administered before and after a videotape screening or between playback of song fragments, or alternatively, measurement can be electronic (with knobs or buttons to pull or push). As with other research, these groups must be selected at random to represent the desired population. The theater approach has the advantage of permitting both image and product testing. Its disadvantage is that the large size of these groups often prevents extended interviewing to obtain related qualitative data. The theater testing method is widely utilized to test the pilots for television shows as well as the popularity of rock and country song selections. This method is used infrequently in promotion and marketing research.

Cable Testing

Cable testing has become popular for program testing and can be applied to evaluating promotional concepts and campaigns. Typically, researchers contact participants in advance of a program's airdate and request them to view a specific program on a designated cable channel. The program readily can incorporate selected promotional (and advertising) spots that others may or may not see. After the program, participants are called on the telephone for an interview.

Unfortunately for researchers, few cable companies authorize such use of their channels.

SYNDICATED RESEARCH

All broadcast stations, broadcast and cable networks, and most cable system operators have access to syndicated ratings. The major ratings companies also provide standardized market research of many other types each year and conduct customized research studies on request. Their fees, however, tend to be much higher than those of small firms specializing in customized studies.

In case you didn't know, Nielsen rates the national broadcast TV and cable networks, and Arbitron's RADAR rates the national radio networks. Nielsen supplies local market television ratings, and Arbitron supplies local market radio ratings. Their methodologies have a big influence on promotional practices, especially at the local level. In consequence, *understanding their methods and terminology has become essential for those who create promotional and marketing materials that apply ratings information.* Consult such books as Webster, Phalen, and Lichty's *Ratings Analysis: Theory and Practice of Audience Research* (2006) and Wimmer and Dominick's *Mass Media Research* (2003) for the fundamentals of ratings and research, which are far more than this chapter can cover, but some aspects related to promotion and marketing can be pointed out.

Television Ratings

National broadcast and cable television network ratings derive from Nielsen's metered households. These homes and apartments usually keep their peoplemeters for up to 5 years, and viewing is measured constantly. Because ratings come daily in larger markets, many TV stations hold daily tactical meetings to maximize both programming and promotional opportunities and priorities. Midsized and smaller markets, however, are rated only during portions of each year (varying from four to eight or more 4-week periods), utilizing the much vilified in-home diaries.

Stations virtually always plan for increased promotion preceding and during ratings **sweeps**. Because local television ratings in a majority of markets still come from diaries filled out by viewers, stations heavily promote their channel numbers as well as individual programs. The resulting ratings are tremendously important to stations because one rating point can bring in many thousands of dollars in additional sales revenue in the following season. Thus, promotional messages directed at advertisers spell out every advantageous rating and use visually catchy sales sheets, such as in 4.6, to engage advertisers' attention.

4.6 *FOX59 shell for ratings information about the syndicated* The Simpsons. *Used with permission.*

Radio Ratings

Arbitron is the only company that provides local radio ratings. It uses pocket-sized 7-day diaries in which listeners are expected to record their daily radio listening both in and out of the home. The listeners then mail their completed diaries back to Arbitron for analysis. Arbitron obtains random samples of listeners in each market, and sample sizes are as large as the stations (and advertising agencies and other purchasers) are willing to pay for.

Arbitron's data collection methods influence most stations' promotional activities. For example, stations often utilize promotional slogans such as "WXXX — write it down!" or engage in heavier promotion on Thursdays (when diaries begin) and on Wednesdays (when laggard diary-keepers are attempting to remember their radio listening for the previous week). Many stations distribute small promotional items by the thousands to listeners, such as the pens in 4.7 imprinted with the station's logo, as well as other office items such as Post-its, large clips for papers, rulers, tablets, and mouse pads. Such items can be ordered

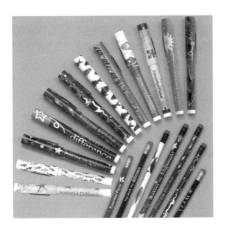

4.7 *Pens as audience promotional items. Courtesy Baudville, Inc.*

in large quantities from promotional merchandise companies such as Baudville, and the stations hope they function as reminders in offices.

Another approach is to distribute phone stickers with emergency numbers in the hope that they will be seen many times a day and remembered when diaries are filled out. In the expectation that most diaries are filled out in home kitchens, refrigerator magnets have become another common promotional item. Because much of radio listening takes place in cars, travel cups and hot/cold mugs as shown in 4.8 may find permanent places in listeners' daily lives (and memories).

4.8 *Cups and mugs as audience promotion. Used with permission.*

In addition to addressing audiences, one way that radio stations commonly use Arbitron ratings information is in trade magazine ads addressing potential advertisers. The hand grabbing an Indiana map in 4.9 was intended to draw advertisers' attention to (some of) WOWO's audience size figures (presumably from Arbitron). The ad depics WOWO's listenership as dramatically larger than that of its competitor WIBC.

Both Nielsen and Arbitron let station representatives have access to the actual station diaries for a market, and stations can hire specialized consultants to review their diaries to look for mistaken attributions and other clues to the causes of low ratings. Promotional success can be judged from the number of diary-keepers who correctly record the station's current identifier or slogan. The

4.9 *WOWO trade ad targeting radio advertisers. Used with permission.*

result of inadequate identifying promotion is often some very odd naming in diaries that does not get attributed to the right station.

PROMOTION BUDGET STRATEGY

Scary myths surrounding the budgeting process can be dispelled by analyzing exactly what a budget is. In simple terms, a **budget** is a management tool, a plan for what a station or system wants to do expressed in numbers. Being able and willing to create and defend budgets is what separates the underlings from the managers. Local marketing and promotion managers must formulate and execute campaigns that will increase audiences and solidify (or improve) station or system images in local markets. To meet this challenge, a plan of action is certainly needed. Departmental budgets become the monetary guidelines within which promotion departments accomplish (or fail to accomplish) their goals.

Budgeting Objectives

Marketing and promotion departments usually are regarded as "support" arms for stations and systems. Therefore, promotion and marketing managers need to know the goals of all other departments before devising their own action plans. Answers to questions such as the following provide essential information:

- *How many sales promotion or client parties are forecast for the coming year?*
- *Will there be a major revision in the programming or channel lineup — and if so, when?*
- *How will the new fall season be advertised?*
- *Is the news department planning a change in format or style?*
- *Is the station or system intending to add new features, services, or on-air personnel?*
- *What kind of community activities are planned for the coming year?*
- *What major changes are expected in the competition's programming?*

Ideally, the promotion or marketing manager should spend time with each department head searching for information about projects that may need promotional support. Of course, records from previous years provide many clues. After gathering facts and figures, the manager combines the other departments' goals with the promotion department's plan for routine advertising and promotional expenses.

Managers of promotion must understand their station's position in its market, know the potential weaknesses in programming that will need substantial promotional support, and anticipate promotional and programming moves by the competition. Detailed discussion with other department managers should provide the critical information for effective promotion budgeting.

A formal system for promotional planning requires information about four areas:

- The *plant* (the promotion department's work area)
- The on-air and print promotional *product* (in-house and out-of-house promotional production needs and sales support needs)
- The department's *personnel* (hiring, training, and personnel evaluation needs)
- The department's measures of *productivity* (research and other information needed to assess achievement of its productivity goals)

These four areas should guide strategic planning sessions and systematize budgetary considerations in the marketing and promotion department. Practically speaking, most station promotion managers have a drawer in which they throw paid bills and scraps of paper noting the next year's events and the financial problems with this year's events (and their bright ideas for dealing with them). Some very organized managers use filing systems or their computers, but a place for scraps of paper is essential for pressure periods when there's little time to think and write.

An important principle of effective promotion is that a department's goals must be measurable. Promotion managers should assign a date for completion of the tasks necessary to achieve the goals and indicate who is responsible for each task. In large departments, a detailed written plan is an effective motivational tool for staff members (related to eventual salary increases) and should be presented to the station or system manager for approval. When the plan is approved, the promotion or marketing manager can move on to the next step. For example, a television station may want to increase favorable publicity about its major evening news anchors. To accomplish this promotional goal, specific tactics must be developed with respect to advertising (in radio, print, outdoor), on-air promotion, and public relations. Measurable goals could include the following:

1. *Increased audience recognition of the station's news anchors*
2. *Increased ratings for the station's evening news*
3. *Increased number of favorable newspaper stories about the station's evening news anchors*
4. *Increased qualitative ratings (measuring likability) of the news anchors*

These are practical and achievable goals because they are concrete.

Applying Dollar Figures to Goals

Once the basic framework for budgeting exists, the next step is to apply dollar figures to each goal. The first step in the mechanics of budgeting is making direct contact with the business office. It will supply a flood of proper forms, a chart of account numbers, and the highly detailed administrative information needed to complete sections of the promotion or marketing department's budget. The forms for budgeting generally are broken down into about nine categories: Personnel Administration, Office Administration, Travel and Entertainment, Technical Supplies, Advertising Expenses, Printing, Sales Promotion, Research and Other Advertising, and Promotion. A typical line-item budget is illustrated in 4.10.

Accounting for Trades

In addition to cash expenses, there are many ways to pursue advertising, promotion, and publicity by using trade (barter) agreements. Each station or system has its own philosophy regarding tradeouts. Some do it, and some do not.

4.10 *Example of line-item budget.*

2006 Proposed Budget

Account Number			
0010	Base Salaries		$85,616
	Salaries for Promotion Manager, Assistant Promotion Manager, & Part-time Secretary		
0020	Overtime		1,800
	Client Reception	600	
	Premiere Party	600	
	Community Project	600	
0130	FICA		6,687
	.0765 on wages up to $90,000 per employee		
0140	Unemployment Taxes		423
	2.35% of first $6,000 in earnings per employee		
0200	Travel and Entertainment		23,750
	Client Reception (January)	1,500	
	Network regional meeting	1,000	
	PROMAX Seminar (L.A.)	2,000	
	Premiere Party	11,000	
	Local Travel	750	
	Community Project	7,500	

If the station does it, trade maneuvering is limited only by imagination and attitude. It is crucial to understand that the station's on-air inventory is being traded away, typically for (1) air time on a radio or TV station or on a cable system, (2) newspaper space, (3) outdoor signage, or (4) concert or sporting event tickets. However, the station or system manager and sales manager have to be consulted before entering into most trade agreements. Trades can't give away too much of the station's potential income.

Contracts for all trades must be drawn up, signed, and kept on file; oral agreements are absolutely inadequate. Although no cash changes hands, the sales and accounting departments must specify the dollar value of traded airtime and whatever was received in return (because of all-important IRS reporting requirements). For example, if a station or system trades for 500 circus tickets to distribute in an over-the-air contest, the sales department must know the total worth of the tickets so that equivalent value in spots for the circus show can be scheduled.

Preparing the Presentation

After diving into that drawer and sorting out all the bills and notes from this last year (technically called "reviewing the various line-item expenses"), the manager of marketing and promotion next writes a detailed explanation of proposed expenditures for the coming year. Making lots of notes during the formulation of costs is very helpful in writing the explanation. Under the heading of Travel and Entertainment, for example, only total figures such as $23,750 appear on the official written forms, but the promotion manager must attach a description of how that $23,750 will be spent over the course of the year.

A narrative description (cribbed from what happened last year and how the process is expected to be different in the coming year) is necessary for each line item. These written explanations will be particularly helpful when the promotion or marketing manager has to make the formal budget presentation.

Monthly Spreads

After the marketing or promotion manager has applied dollar figures to goals, arrived at totals for each line item, and written a short descriptive narrative for each expenditure, the budget must be allocated across the total year to produce the monthly spreads. It is crucial to know not only how much the department wants to spend for the whole year but also when it wants to spend it.

Estimating expenses month by month (the **spreads**) will indicate key periods of heavy expenditure and give an accurate picture of activities to be accomplished on a monthly basis. Although every company's budget form varies, basic accounting principles require:

1. *Inclusion of the current year's budget information*
2. *Estimates of how close to budget a department anticipates being at the end of the current budget year*
3. *The figures the promotion and marketing manager is preparing for the next budget year*

Next, put new batteries in the calculator. Then, when line items have been tallied and cross-checked and the narrative description of each line-item expense has been drawn up, the promotion manager can consider the first draft of the budget complete. Ideally, research, computation, and creativity should come together in a neat package that describes the promotion or marketing manager's plans for the next 12 months.

Formal Presentation

It is highly desirable that department heads approach the budget presentation session in a positive and flexible frame of mind. The presentation is necessary because it allows three things:

1. *A chance for the marketing or promotion manager to identify opportunities, define problems, help coordinate efforts, formulate new programs, and propose new actions*
2. *An illustration to top management of how creative and practical the department's plans are*
3. *An opportunity to push for acceptance of promotion's proposed budget and to defend its programs*

After the presentation, the marketing or promotion manager may have to make structural or dollar changes before receiving final approval. Once approval is given, the business office usually issues the final copy of the budget to each department.

BUDGET EXECUTION

Two elements are the keys to budget execution. One is **forecasting**, the prediction of events and their associated expenses. The other is **accountability**, which shows how things happened and what was responsible for differences from predictions after the fact.

Forecasting is of considerable value in administering budgets effectively. The highly-organized promotion and marketing manager will set aside one day a month (say, the 15th or 20th) to analyze the activities and expenditures planned for the upcoming month. This practice invites advance planning (forecasting) to make sure that projects are completed on time and to ensure that expenses are accounted for in the correct month. A successfully executed budget also requires a built-in system of accountability. This system should provide information that permits monitoring and directing the activities of a large department. Usually, such a system is called a monthly **variance report**. It requires delving into that drawer for notes on why an item, say a series of radio ads, went over or under budget. Variance records tend to be per job and typically are a bunch of slips in a drawer (that same drawer!) that are saved for the monthly report and next year's budget planning. Some companies do it quarterly, some weekly. Constant variance reporting allows the department head and top management to keep tabs on expenses.

To fill out a formal variance report, the department head needs to know the budgeted amounts (projected) for the month versus what was actually expended during the month. The station's business office provides this information after it has closed the books for the month. It is the manager's responsibility to explain any variances between budget forecasts and actual expense, that is, whether the amount is higher or lower than projected. This information lets department heads know exactly where they stand at any given time during the year. Frequently, companies ask for a quarterly report on departmental budgets as well as a report at midyear. Reports of this type should be regarded as "promise versus performance" reports. Those who are behind will be the first to know and can revise their plans accordingly (or their plans will be revised for them!).

As competition within the telecommunications marketplace continues to grow and as the role and importance of the Internet continues to spread, managers of promotion and marketing at television stations, radio stations, and cable systems will need to become increasingly sophisticated in how they manage and implement their marketing and promotion plans. As the competitive landscape becomes more complex, managers will need access to a wide array of primary and secondary research to be successful in the marketplace. Increased competition and complexity will also require managers of promotion and marketing to become better financial managers to maximize the efficiency with which their departments operate.

SELECTED READINGS AND WEBSITES

Stafford, M. R., and Faber, R. J. (Eds.) (2005). *Advertising, Promotion, and New Media*. Armonk, NY: M.E. Sharpe.

Webster, J. G., Phalen, P. E., and Lichty, L. W. (2006). *Ratings Analysis: The Theory and Practice of Audience Research*, 3rd ed. Mahwah, NJ: Erlbaum.

Wimmer, R. D., and Dominick, J. R. (2003). *Mass Media Research: An Introduction,* 7th ed. Belmont, CA: Wadsworth.

Woods, G. B. (1995). *Advertising and Marketing to the New Majority: A Case Study Approach.* Belmont, CA: Wadsworth.

www.nab.com
www.ncta.com
www.tvb.org

CHAPTER 5

Designing On-Air, Print, and Online Promotion

Susan Tyler Eastman

Designers and managers of promotion and marketing need to be able to defend their decisions about promotional materials and say why one design is more likely to be more effective than another. At the network and major station level, such designers and their bosses normally have plenty of experience and a track record to back up their decisions, but local designers and managers of promotion need verbal ammunition to fight frequent skirmishes. And the heads of stations and systems need to be able to communicate effectively with the people who plan and realize promotional designs. This chapter provides some bullets for the art wars.

Battles occur because the inclinations of general managers, the ideals of news directors, and the preferences of art designers frequently clash with smart promotional practices. Corporate vice presidents and station managers tend to favor the broad, familiar, and prudent in promotional design, but what seems safe to them too often targets too many audiences or the wrong audience for maximal effectiveness. News directors tend to want their important news stories presented with heavy-handed seriousness (and talking heads) rather than with a light touch, even though humor and sensational action are known to attract more viewers.

Sometimes in-house and out-of-house art designers present the greatest problems for managers of marketing and promotion. The station has hired these people and paid for this art, so their work must be good, right? The problem is that art directors like to win awards for promotional design. Acknowledged or not, there is peer pressure among commercial designers to come up with award-winning ideas. And awards seem more likely for promotional designs with trendy themes and innovations in multilayered logos than for hackneyed slogans and very simple logos. Moreover, awards seem to come more often for elaborate video campaigns than for routine newspaper ads. Few ads for television programs in program guides and local newspapers are large enough to stand out from the surrounding commercial clutter, so they get little attention from art departments, and indeed, print has largely faded away as a medium of persuasive communication for local and national television and local radio. At any rate, a regular tug-of-war sometimes goes on between the understandable desire of the art director for "good design" by artistic criteria and the manager of promotion's urgent need for promotional effectiveness. What helps is if they both speak the same language and agree on the aims.

This chapter presents some guidelines for judging whether promotional materials are likely to be effective in doing their jobs. To learn how to implement art ideas, courses in computerized graphic design are necessary, but familiarity with these ideas will speed the learning process and will aid those managers who never draw a picture.

EVERYTHING COUNTS

The first rule of the TV screen, radio airtime, and print advertising is that nothing is there by accident. Everyone is aware of the millions of dollars spent in producing major television commercials. Every second of time and every frame of a television ad's design have been scrutinized for maximum impact and maximum appeal. No details of background or foreground or sound are left uncontrolled. Sets are built, costumes are constructed, cameras are aimed, hair is sprayed, and faces painted to create exactly the desired effect. The equivalent occurs in radio: The absence of predetermined sound ("dead air") is anathema, and every second of precious ad airtime is carefully scheduled for maximal effectiveness.

Viewers and listeners know all this, perhaps unconsciously, and they recognize the carefully structured nature of commercial messages. On-air spots touting programs (**promos**) are merely another type of commercial message, usually produced in a shorter time with far smaller budgets than most commercials. The promo's ultimate goal is to make money for the station or network, and viewers and listeners are quite familiar with that intent. Therefore, promotional program spots and on-air identifiers must be constructed as carefully as their competition — the commercial spots — to have a chance of effectiveness. Every detail must contribute to the desired effect or be eliminated. Saying "that's close enough" is rarely good enough to win the battle for viewers. *Visual and auditory control of every element is essential for effective promotion.*

The Goal of Effectiveness

The overwhelming criterion the designer or manager of promotion must hold out before others is "likely effectiveness with the target audience." To deal with art staffs and persuade others to support some design ideas over others, managers of promotion need three vocabularies. They need one set of words to spell out the proposed *function and purposes* of specific pieces of promotion that programmers and corporate managers will understand — the overarching strategic goals that were described in Chapter 1. They'll want to know *what part of the program or service is to be promoted and who is the message for.*

Designers and managers of promotion need a different language to classify the content of promotional pieces — that art staff and promotion coworkers will recognize — including the proper names for the tools that design staffers work with and the basic concepts used in message construction. Third, managers need a *set of criteria* for determining likely effectiveness to objectively arrive at their own evaluations of design ideas — before they are realized in costly video, print, or sound. These are the everyday principles of communication, often labeled "rules" in this chapter and also called "guidelines" in this book. They have to educate their staffs, design colleagues, and other managers so that they understand the importance of these criteria in making effective promotional messages.

Sticking to Simplicity

KISS is one paramount idea in nearly all designs that are effective for promotion. **KISS** stands for "Keep it simple and stupid" (or alternately, "Keep it simple, Stupid"). That means valuing straightforwardness over intricacy. That means seeking easy readability over clever lettering. That usually means prizing adaptations of tried-and-true themes that have been shown to work in similar markets over untried promotional concepts. Adhering to KISS means the manager of promotion must find the strength to send sample artwork back to the designers whenever "art" has undermined simplicity.

Many billboards and signs that can be comprehended by a consumer standing right in front of them become incomprehensible at 40 or 60 miles per hour. Innovative promotional concepts that can be decoded with a little thought will be incomprehensible to most people who merely give them a passing glance. The 94 HJY billboard in 5.1 exemplifies ready understandability without complexity that defeats the message — but only IF you come from New England where the Red Sox (and maybe the weather!) had been "cursed" for 86 years (since Babe Ruth was traded to the Yankees after the Sox's World Series win in 1918).[1]

The point is that no one is obliged to look at promotional advertisements or listen to on-air spots. People won't bother decoding or deciphering some ad they

5.1   *KISS billboard: "CURSE THIS!" Used with permission.*

just happen to see or hear. (If you aren't from New England, the 94 HJY billboard won't even be noticed, whereas if you are a Sox fan, wow, it's really exquisitely clever!) Trade reports estimate that the average person is flooded by some 8,000 commercial messages every day. Why should anyone put any effort into figuring out a piece of promotion? It is the obligation of the promoter to make the message come through to a casual glance or momentarily tuned-in ear, despite the lack of attention given to ads and spots.

Breakthrough and Routine

Certainly original ideas have a place in promotion. Implementing a new idea for a contest or a humorous twist on a plot line for a sitcom spot is vital to keeping promotion exciting for audiences and morale high for the promotion staff. Promotion departments like to win recognition for their efforts, too. Achieving **breakthrough** in some aspect of sound, design, or concept indeed is crucial to exceptional marketing success, and standout promos, unusual sound signatures, and innovative print ads are likely to be highly effective with viewers. As 5.2 shows, PBS likes awards just as much as commercial networks and often tries for a humorous twist.

Most breakthrough ideas appear first in campaigns for big advertisers or promotion for the major television networks, where pretesting and big budgets are the rule (unlike at most local stations). Wherever they come from, good ideas that succeed in breaking out of their environments to capture immediate attention do win awards, and then they get swiftly copied. The top promotional designs often win Medallion Awards from PROMAX and the Broadcast Designers Association (BDA), the dominant trade associations for people in media promotion

5.2 *PBS: "Be More Original." Used with permission.*

and marketing design. These associations make DVDs of award winners available to local managers of promotion so they can "steal" ideas.

There are occasional exceptions to the rule that consumers will not make an effort to decode promotional ads: A radio contest may intrigue a teen listener who will call the station to learn what's needed; a sports fan will find the time and channel of the game no matter how confusing the ad. But the day-to-day battle in local television promotion revolves around getting people to watch ordinary television shows — the evening news and a couple of rerun stripped series that already are familiar to most viewers from previous years on a network, as discussed in Chapter 3. At the broadcast and cable network levels, promotion focuses on prime-time shows competing with similar shows on other channels (the topic of Chapter 6). In radio, the usual goal is to build daily patterns of listening that extend from one time period into the next, as already spelled out in Chapter 2.

In essence, the practice of effective promotion is more a matter of efficiency and productivity than extraordinary innovation. The ability to capture the essence of a routine news story or the twist in a familiar sitcom plot is the skill of value to a promotion manager. And this is a skill that novices can learn.

KEY MESSAGES

Meeting the criterion of KISS need not mean being out of style. Currently hot designs for television use multilayering in complex sequences of fast-paced images. Promotional spots, signs, and ads can also be trendy, but to succeed, the key promotional information needs to stand out. In television, the **key message** is either the day/time/channel of a program ("Tomorrow at 7:00 on Channel 3") or in branding messages, a service's name (such as a broadcast or cable network's logo).

Because the key message appears (or should appear) in all promotional materials, it sometimes gets confused with other messages that managers want to see in their promotion. At the local level, the key message is *not* topical information about a newscast or names of the stars or details of a program's plot (although these elements make one piece of promotion different from another). *The key message to be emphasized is the **where and when** of a program or, for generic non-program promotion, the **where** of a channel.* As long as the art leads the viewer's eye (or ear) to that key information, the design probably meets the KISS criterion.

Keys for Programs on Local Television

The "where and when" of promotion are so vitally important that they are sometimes called the *essential whats* of local television promotion. The **identifier** of the channel carrying a TV program and the time the show begins are nearly always the where and when messages that need to be implanted in a viewer or listener's memory, not a program's name. Because the public is flooded with so many commercial messages, the best a promotion manager can hope to do is to get someone to remember where and when a desirable show comes on television (or radio). If the viewer vaguely remembers "tonight at 7:30 there's a show I want to see on Channel 10," the promotion manager's job has been accomplished. That viewer need not recall the program's name. If the viewer remembers only the program title, then a hunt for the right channel at exactly the right time becomes necessary — secondary steps that viewers can easily be distracted from — when repetition of a good promo would have left a memory of that key information.

Effective topical promotion focuses more on the where and when of programs than on the titles of shows. Indeed, big billboards that scream the name of a syndicated show or its stars and bury the channel location and time of the show largely are wasted advertising. They make money for the billboard company but do little to lure viewers or listeners to stations.

Keys for Formats and Stations

The managers of radio promotion, many Internet services, and creative services directors of some narrowcast cable networks have somewhat different problems from the promotion directors of television stations and the popular cable networks. On many radio stations and some online and cable channels, there are relatively few specific programs to lure listeners or viewers to, so the message to convey is the *format* of the station (all-news, top 40 country hits) or the niche of the cable network or web service (all baseball, all food, all movies, and so on). The format must accompany the *identifier* of the service: in the case of a radio station, it is some permutation of its tuner position; in the case of an Internet service, its URL; and in the case of a cable network, its name. Thus, the two parts to the key message are *channel and format* for radio, *URL and format* for Internet services, and *name and format* for many small cable networks. Formats need not be spelled out, but can be merely implied.

For example, formatted radio stations typically use identifiers like X100 or Magic 101.5 that combine some hint of their music formats along with their dial positions. Even people who have never heard of X100, for example, are quite unlikely to think that the station is all-news, easy listening, or classical music. Unique twists to call letters (K-ROQ, KNUS) also signal certain kinds of formats and identities. Qs, Zs, Xs, and other words are conventions for popular music formats targeting young listeners that most people unconsciously recognize (and KNUS is "news" when said aloud). Rounding, such as to 100, represents an approximation of an FM dial position (somewhere between 99.5 and 100.5).

Keys for Networks

Nationwide promotion is very different from local promotion because, unlike television and radio stations, broadcast and cable networks lack a promotable channel number. A network's affiliated stations have different channel numbers in different markets (a CBS affiliate may be a Channel 4 or 5 or some other number; A&E can appear on any of the double-digit channel numbers). Networks therefore are left with only their network names (ABC, Lifetime, Spike!) and program titles (*CSI*, new or in rerun) or events (such as NFL games) to promote. But for the major services, the network names are already widely known and need not be salient in most ads; it's only the programs that matter. Viewers can find them, especially if the programs on are on one of the Big Four broadcast networks. The ABC Sports ad in 5.3 illustrates national tune-in promotion from a network. The intense faces in combination with the huge words "Indianapolis 500" speak so loudly that little else is needed, although ABC's network logo and the day/start time come through clearly once the reader's interest is caught.

Normally, for specific series or special events, the three elements promoted by networks are the *what, who*, and *when*. *What* refers to the essence of a program, which is usually conveyed by its title, unless poorly named; *who* refers to the stars' names or faces (if any can be recognized); and *when* is the time (or times in different zones). These are the classic elements in a network program promo or magazine advertisement ("Watch the latest winner on *American Idol* tonight at 9:00"). A FOX spotlight logo, for example, conveys the general *where*, and local affiliates may add their own designations, such as on "FOX 59 or FOX 23." Note that FOX 59 probably does not tell viewers where the channel actually is on their local cable system. Saying precisely *where* is only possible on local radio and in regional guides and newspapers. On network programs, *where* often ends up being a string of several channel numbers on print ads. (Look ahead at 6.7, which is about a *Saturday Night Live* special.) Because *TV Guide* and most newspaper ads for prime-time shows are placed on the exact airdate, naming the day of the week (the rest of the *when*) is not necessary for network ads and co-ops.

One other condition that changes the key message somewhat is when a program is on-demand, as discussed in Chapter 7. When offered by a video-on-demand (**VOD**) service, the key message becomes the program title (*what*) and the name of the service (*where*, vaguely); there is neither day nor time if the subscriber can have the program anytime!

SOURCE IDENTIFIERS

Logos, wordmarks, and signatures are the three primary elements of self-identification in promotion — the elements that signal which channel or service

5.3 *ABC Sports ad for Indianapolis 500. Used with permission.*

is being watched, listened to, or promoted. Each broadcast and cable network, television and radio station, and online service has either a copyrighted logo or wordmark for use on all its printed advertising and other materials, as well as a unique signature and a small logo-bug that are used on the air. While television networks and stations have elaborate visual identifiers in colorful graphics usually accompanied by a sound effect, radio stations are recognized by their elaborate sound signatures. Radio also uses brief sound jingles (the equivalent of bugs) on the air, and each station has a logo for use in printed materials, on the sides of remote vans, and in spots for television, often incorporating a theme in a short phrase.

Logos and Bugs

Formally, a **logo** is the *graphic identifier* of a network, station, or company — a two-dimensional design that represents the name of the company in abbreviated form. An ideal logo can be used in large or small size, in various colors or in black and white, and animated or stationary and is thus suited to print, television, and online. Four network television logos — ABC's circle with lower-case letters, the CBS eye, the FOX spotlight, and the NBC peacock — have become deeply embedded in people's consciousness, and other media companies struggle to achieve that same level of recognition. The network logos are priceless brand identifiers with infinitely valuable worldwide recognition, and constant vigilance aggressively protects them from imitation and duplication without permission (reproduction usually requires paying big fees).

Logos are valued and protected at the local level as well. Because nearly a hundred television stations (and hundreds of radio stations) have identical numbers, they try to achieve original logo designs unique to their stations. Figure 5.4 shows the logo for a Jacksonville, Florida, television station appearing on Channel 4. This station logo can be used in colors or black and white and large or small; it can sit still in print or whirl around in video and merge with other video elements (the seeming blurriness comes from the three-dimensionality of the on-air number 4). To be a registered trademark, this logo has to differ from that of every other channel 4 in use in America.

Nowadays, large full-screen logos usually appear only in the 2-second breaks between television programs to identify and brand the network or channel. Instead of using valuable airtime to name a service, tiny "bugs" are superimposed on the screen during network and local shows and serve to identify programming sources. A **bug** is a miniature logo, normally appearing in the lower right-hand corner of the screen (although Speed uses the top right and Disney and CNN the lower left). Everyone immediately recognizes the NBC network bug in 5.5, for example, even without colored feathers in the peacock's tail and no matter how small it appears. Bugs remind viewers of where they are in an increasingly

5.4   *WJXT Channel 4 logo. Used with permission.*

cluttered television environment. About half are transparent (TBS's half-globe, UPN's oval, BET's star, Food's circle, Oxygen's Oh!), and about half consist of solid white letters and shapes (A&E, MTV, TNT circle, Hallmark's crown), although thin letters, such as those for the Sci Fi bug in 5.5, permit some background to show through and seem semi-transparent. A few bugs are colored (Nick's orange blob, MTV2's two-headed dog, The Weather Channel's blue screen), and some revolve (Discovery globe, Travel globe, Fox News cube, and sometimes the VH1 cube). Some can be animated so that they move cleverly in some way (winking CBS eye, waving USA flag) for special presentations. Interestingly, AMC uses only its URL (*amctv.com*) as a bug. Logos and bugs may be identical except for size or may move or add an element such as the network's name, as both NBC and Sci Fi currently do to their bug forms.

In the 500-channel universe, bugs serve an informational function by telling viewers where they are — knowledge especially useful to TV surfers and users of JUMP or BACK buttons. They also help embed the name of the source of a program in the minds of those who must later fill out diaries to record their viewing.

5.5   *NBC and Sci Fi logos and bugs. Used with permission.*

FOX made an innovative use of bugs when it touted its prime-time airing of *Star Wars: Episode 1 — The Phantom Menace* by placing animated R2D2 bugs in several days of other programming. Only special programs can be promoted this way, because the special bug preempts the regular program bugs.

Logo-bugs also appear on printed stationery, all sales handouts, and other printed items coming from a media source. They are also prominent on websites and imprinted on such small giveaways as key chains, pens, cups, and so on. Somewhat larger logos are used on paperweights, caps, totes, T-shirts, and other promotional merchandise.

Wordmarks

A local television station or cable network may have a logo but is equally likely to make use of a stylized **wordmark**, a particular way of writing the station's channel number or company's name. For example, when it means the cable network, the word "spike" is written in cursive-like printing with a capital S, an exclamation mark, and a small "tv" underneath. Wordmarks have the same trademark protection as logos and serve the same communication function (indeed, distinguishing between the two is sometimes rather arbitrary). The smart television station adopts either a logo or an easy-to-read wordmark that works in print and on-the-air, whether blown up large (full-screen) or squeezed very small (in a bug), whether reproduced in black and white or in color, or whether in motion or still. It then uses that wordmark constantly in one standardized form to keep its name in front of potential viewers and advertisers. Figure 5.6 illustrates some wordmarks long used by the Headline News and Nickelodeon cable networks.

New services need to invent logos that both distinguish them from established or competing networks and communicate the nature of the program content. One tactic is to combine a graphic element with the spelled out name of the service or channel, a **combined identifier**, because an unfamiliar logo might not be quickly identified without supplementation. At the time the Tennis Channel came along, the Spanish-language network Telemundo was already using a dramatic stylized T, leaving the Tennis Channel to invent some variation. As 5.7 shows, the two Ts differ in style although both make striking yet simple statements. Because it is the newer service, the logo for the Tennis Channel adopts the practice of combining the graphic T with its spelled out name, although one might imagine the words fading away at some future time. While the use of block lettering makes Tennis Channel's name clear and easily readable, the slant of its T gives dynamism to the high-contrast graphic. Note that the curved slash intersecting Telemundo's T creates its own dynamism while looking very different — more stable and formal.

One failing at some stations occurs because of management's refusal to settle on only one main wordmark or one main logo (or a combined logo/wordmark). Having more than one basic design for the way the company's name is printed

5.6 *Headline News and seven Nickelodeon wordmarks combined identifiers. Used with permission.*

(or stated) means that ads and promos fail to reinforce each other. A different way of writing a company name appears to the casual eyes of disinterested viewers to represent a different company. Changing colors and motions do not alter a basic design, but shifting to a different layout or lettering does. Without question, *a key principle of successful media communication is* **reinforcement**. The same message needs to be repeated to have an impact.

Nonetheless, logos must evolve over time. What seems cutting edge at one time often looks dated a decade or two later. Box 5.8 shows the evolving pattern of a public television station's logo across the five decades from the 1960s to the present time. Each logo had advantages when it was introduced and disadvantages by the time it was changed.

5.7 *Telemundo and Tennis Channel logos. Used with permission of Telemundo Network Group LLC and permission of Steve Bellamy, The Tennis Channel.*

5.8

WTIU, 1960s

Is an official representative of the Indiana University Radio and Television Services in the capacity of

Expiration Date _____

Dir of Radio—TV Services

Joint educational TV and FM logos, used in 1960s

Positives: Before WTIU-TV went on the air as a broadcast station, it existed as an in-house educational station and had a sister FM station. The two stations were promoted together to associate them, build familiarity for the two names, and place them in the university context (note the university's name along one side). The center design suggests a smile as well as TV screen and (perhaps) antennas. *Negatives*: The design incorporates too many words for television use; it is more suited to print reproduction. Moreover, the need to co-promote the two stations diminished over time.

WTIU 30, 1970s

WTIU Channel 30
Bloomington, IN

First broadcast logo, used in 1970s

Positives: The logo incorporates the familiar State of Indiana outline (familiar to locals, anyway), along with the name of the city of license. The design emphasizes the channel number (30) over the calls (WTIU), and the lettering is bold and would show up on television. Also, the outline around the 30 suggests a TV screen.

Negatives: The 30, however, is crowded inside the screen shape. The visual scale of the 30 differs so much from the smaller scale of the WTIU Channel 30 that the eye tends to pass over the lower part of the message. The design's square overall shape favors printed materials (guides, newspapers) over television.

WTIU, 1980s

Channel 30/Bloomington, IN

Modernized broadcast logo, used in 1980s

Positives: At the time, this way of writing WTIU was a modern-looking wordmark. The thin font seems contemporary and distinctive. The complete logo continues to associate the station with the local community and identify itself as Channel 30.

Negatives: By the 1980s, most locals were getting their television stations via cable (on Channel 5 for WTIU) and thus the 30 was no longer a meaningful channel identifier (currently, the station has 13 different channel locations — appearing on 3, 5, 6, 7, 10, 11, 12, 13, 15, 18, 21, 26, and 32 in nearby cabled communities — a promotional nightmare).

WTIU, 1990s

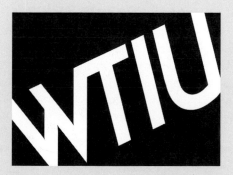

Dynamic broadcast logo, used in 1990s

Positives: Now the identifier has become a logo rather than a wordmark and is more video-friendly. It has taken a regional approach by dropping mention of just one city, acknowledging that the signal travels into several adjacent towns. The logo has once again become bold in black-and-white, but lends itself to variations in colors and works well in large size as well as shrunk down into a bug.

Negatives: The stylized letters are cut off at both ends, giving a slight tendency to pull eye off the page, especially at the W end. The sole associations with television (rather than radio or some commercial product) are the shape of the background and the prominence of the T in WTIU. Because the background has no outlining frame, the logo does not read "television" loudly, and the shape of TV screens was about to change.

WTIU, 2004

Co-branding logo, used after 2004

Positives: The association of the calls with the easily-recognized PBS logo makes the public nature of the station clear. (PBS has only recently permitted this type of co-branding.) The TV screen shape in the background reinforces the station as television (rather than any other medium) and emphasizes its unique calls (the TIU part — unique because the calls for all U.S. broadcast stations begin with either W or K). Moreover, the dark screen's diagonal slant adds dynamic energy. This logo can readily be used in multiple colors or black-and-white and large or small.

Negatives: The horizontal and linear shape of the logo will make the bug occupy considerable screen space as an overlay. In that case, the PBS logo might be dropped. Also, the screen shape will need to be elongated soon. All WTIU logos used with permission.

Signatures and Jingles

When used on the air, logos and wordmarks are often animated and accompanied by a **soundbed** (an associated set of sound effects or phrase of music). The elaborated version of the network, station, or service's on-air identifier is called a **signature**. An effective signature is thus an enhanced version of a two-dimensional logo or wordmark incorporating motion and sound (and perhaps the illusion of three-dimensionality) that simultaneously triggers recall of the basic logo or wordmark.

Radio stations use signatures in which jingles identify both music and non-music station formats. Although the word "jingle" makes most people think of light little tunes, in the industry, companies that create and produce station jingles utilize a huge range of musical types and sound effects. Such companies offer original sound bites to characterize a station playing a lot of hip-hop or urban country or oldies or beautiful music or even sports or news. These jingles/effects are combined with a specific station's identifier to create a sound signature, unique to that station or at least that market. (Visual designs and jingles can be resold in other markets after a contract expires.)

REINFORCEMENT, REPETITION, AND CONGRUENCE

Once management decides on a logo or wordmark and theme, it needs to be embodied in virtually every piece of the daily on-air and print promotion of the station or network. **Reinforcement** comes from **repetition**, such as replaying the same promo over and over on different days or in different programs. At the same time, reinforcement requires **congruence**, the attribute of saying or showing something always in the same way. The wordmark for the name Disney, for example, always appears in exactly the same visual form, whether the reference is to The Disney Channel, a Disney movie, Disney Toon, or some other Disney subsidiary.

CBC in Canada uses a logo made of half-circles arranged in a diamond shape with a solid circle in the center to identify the overall service (see 5.9). At the same time, the network uses variations for particular programming sequences that trigger immediate association with the main logo. Figure 5.9 shows the main CBC logo for the Canadian network and the clever variation for CBC's children's programming.

Advertising research has shown repeatedly that seeing or hearing a single message rarely gets through to anyone; absorbing just one message rarely changes behavior. *The traditional rule of thumb is that it takes at least three repetitions to affect behavior.* That means the same invitation to watch a program needs to air repeatedly to have a chance to increase viewing. It also means that signatures must be consistent to have optimum impact.

Moreover, all the various tools of promotion for a single station or network should have close consistency; they should trigger a sense of similarity, even if the media are different. *Congruence in look and sound among different promotional materials is essential to reinforce a promotional message.* Whether used on letterheads

5.9 a, b *CBC logo and Kids' CBC logo. Used with permission.*

and envelopes; trucks; bumper stickers; billboards or cab tops; in on-air promos or online websites; or in guides, magazines, or newspapers, a logo (or wordmark) should remain the *same in design* in order that the identifier communicate the *same identity*.

And the idea extends beyond logos to the whole "look" of a station in its on-air and print materials. Generally, promos benefit from being part of campaigns that have an overall artistic design — a look and sound that ties every promotional piece together. As has been pointed out, logos can differ in color and size, without losing congruence, but maximizing similarity is especially important for new niche cable channels, renamed radio stations, and other new media services. (MTV and Nickelodeon have fun with their promotion, but one never fails to recognize their logos!)

ON-AIR AND ONLINE TOOLS

In addition to identifiers, on-air promotion borrows techniques and tools from advertising practices but modifies them to suit the needs of persuasion to view or listen or advertise — activities that differ from buying products in stores. These tools range from varied-length visual and auditory messages of traditional airtime to website pages that use the evolving elements of logos and promotional clips in new ways (see Chapter 8, New Media Promotion).

Classic Elements

Formally, a **promo** is a short preproduced on-air spot that usually urges viewers to tune in to a particular episode of a show. Over the years, television network promos have been shortened from 60 seconds to 30 or 15 or even 10 seconds because airtime is so valuable and limited. One 30-second promo can be devoted to a single program or subdivided to promote several programs, a tactic that works well when most of the programs are well-known to audiences. A promotional **tease** is a brief live spot intended to lure viewers to a newscast or talk show. A news tease usually shows an anchor narrating the night's highlighted story in a sentence or two while showing the most vivid and attention-getting visuals and sound elements of the story (fires and sirens, bombs exploding, key sound bites from recognizable public figures). A talk-show tease probably shows the host asking a guest a tricky or intriguing or startling question, but does not include the response. The trick to successful scripts for teases is not to tell what has happened but to lure viewers to the newscast or talk show to find out what happened.

Typically located toward the end of a promo or tease, or recited over end credits, a **tag** is a line that gives the crucial information of *where* and *when* the program or newscast can be seen (key message). A tag that lacks prominence undermines the impact of the promo. A **bumper** is a very short message intended to "bump" viewers or listeners into the next segment or program. Common bumpers are auditory or combined visual and sounds. The illustration in 5.10 from the Fine Living cable channel is a visual *bumper* (also sometimes called a **billboard** when several upcoming programs in the same evening are listed). Note the great size of the "Next" and "Then" but low contrast in comparison to the high contrast of the actual program titles.

Historically, the information in bumpers often was stuck at the end of preproduced and reused spots and, in the early years of television and radio, was merely a vocal line saying something like "Stay tuned for the next episode of X." But promotion has become more sophisticated, and bumpers and tags more often are incorporated within promos and repeated both visually and auditorily in ways that are highly salient so that viewers cannot miss the messages.

Changing Graphics

The nonlinear, **cyberspace style** is the current look in on-screen graphics. Often called "TV as web pages," the style refers to multifaceted screens that bombard viewers with boxes, scrolls, divided screens, inserted boxes, and moving design elements, resembling the information-rich environment of websites.

Text information in **overlay graphics** (superimposed informational and promotional elements) began appearing on top of network prime-time programs

starting in 2004, initially to signal some news event. NBC affiliates, for example, use Namedropper XL to drop lower-third graphics into network promos, so they can include local identifiers and times.

Unlike bugs that usually appear in the right-hand corner of screens, overlay graphics can appear anywhere on the screen where the background is suitable (if the graphic is small and solid) or, if transparent, can be superimposed on large portions of the screen without hiding the program action. Credited to Bloomberg Television and Canada's City TV, on television the overlay process began with the addition of bugs, continued with crawls, banners, and tickers, and expanded to lower-third graphics and then to animated overlay titling.

Banners are fixed-appearing portions of the screen that are more like headlines in newspapers. On the web, many banners consist solely of advertising messages, but on television they are usually news or promotional messages. Most incorporate small logos and other small elements, such as clock faces or bugs around the edges, while the center portion has regularly cycling or replaced text. While it would be most unusual to see a banner on a traditional sitcom or drama, some reality programs make use of them for program-related information.

Tickers are listings of stock and bond prices that scroll across the bottom of television or computer screens. The same term also refers to digital (or analog) clocks that count down until the next program or some other event starts.

Occupying roughly the same amount of screen space as banners, **crawls** are text messages that scroll across the bottom of the television screen. Long used on sports channels for statistics and scores, on business channels for stock prices and market indicators, news channels for brief headlines and updates, and on any program for emergency weather warnings, they can also be used for promotional messages. To keep viewers constantly updated, for example, continuous crawls appeared on all programming on the television networks immediately following the 9/11 terrorist attacks in 2001. Every major news source except ABC News began using them, and many continued for a week or longer.

News crawls are sometimes called **headline banners** to differentiate them somewhat from the mix of double-crawls and flipping text traditionally used by CNN News. None of the Big Three networks use crawls during their regular

5.10 *Fine Living's Next, Then bumpers. Used with permission.*

nightly newscasts or other regularly-scheduled programs, but they can be quickly revived for breaking news events. Some local newscasts and CNN, MSNBC, and FOX News Channel have continued using crawls during their newscasts. When some ran right over commercial spots, they generated loud complaints from advertisers, so channels now stop the crawls during commercial breaks, sometimes ending abruptly in mid-sentence.

Crawls do provide an option for promotional information as well as informational headlines, taking on tagging and bumping functions. On entertainment channels, crawls tend to be used just for breaking news events or serious weather announcements (placed by affiliates, not the networks). They have become so widely used that the comedy channels mock them, such as on VH1's *Jump Start* and Comedy Central's *The Daily Show with Jon Stewart*. Many viewers find them distracting, especially if not personally relevant. When they fall on top of bugs and titles, they cover the networks' key promotional information.

Lower-third overlays have multiple functions, some of which are wholly promotional: If text messages, they provide something for viewers to read when not interested in the current story, or they can supplement the visually produced story, like web pages do, giving a bit more depth or detail. If they explicitly promote upcoming programs, they substitute for time-consuming promos. All this occurs on screens that are heavily designed nowadays during both programs and promotional messages.

Pop-Up Advance Titling

Pop-ups of upcoming program titles have most altered the look of the TV screen. Audiences have become used to seeing crawls and informational bars at the bottom of screens, at least on certain channels. The newest thing, **automated advance titling** (a large title bug for the upcoming program), now dominates the screen's lower left corner during portions of entertainment shows. This overlay technique was adapted from other uses to promote upcoming shows by flashing the name of the upcoming program near the bottom of the screen. Called **snipes** or **superbugs**, these pop-up messages combine animation and sound effects to capture viewers' attention. They do not supplant customary bumpers, which occur between programs or over credits, because snipes are superimposed on the program viewers are actually watching, and the identical snipe usually reappears several times in a half-hour. Computer-generated and scheduled snipes give the time and name of the upcoming program and are regularly used now by the major broadcast and major cable networks. For example, Oh! Oxygen used the vigorously animated superbug of the glittering *Mr. Romance* lead shown in 5.11 within the immediately preceding program (in this case, another *Mr. Romance* episode) to signal that a different episode of the series was coming next.

From the programmer's point of view, such titling often takes the place of a "Next" promo, saving many seconds of airtime for program content (or, more likely, for commercials). For detailed instructions related to snipes on co-op advertising, look ahead to 6.4. Some snipes need only show a familiar face or other element to identify an upcoming program. Bravo's award-winning graphics for *Queer Eye for the Straight Guy* are widely recognized for their innovative design, which are partly revealed in the still frame of *Queer Eye*'s snipe in 5.12, an image that pops up several times in the preceding program.

Especially when animated rather than still, some older viewers — but not younger ones — claim that such titling distracts from the current program's dialogue or interferes by overlaying some important part of the action on older

5.11 *Superbug for Mr. Romance on Oh! Oxygen. Used with permission.*

5.12 *Frame showing Bravo's snipe for* Queer Eye for the Straight Guy. *Used with permission.*

shows. Newly-produced series have compensated for this by placing most of the plot action in the upper two-thirds of the screen, leaving the lower-third for bugs, titles, crawls, snipes, and so on, but older series and movies may have action in the bottom third of the screen. Unlike bugs, which are small and often semi-transparent and generally stay still in their corners, automatic advance titling comes and goes, is often colorfully animated, and may even flash across large portions of the screen momentarily, thus insisting on immediate attention and drawing viewers' eyes away from the current program. Sometimes annoying, advance titles pop up and flash to draw attention (they snipe at the viewer, much like a sniper shoots brief bursts at targets). They are given a little history in Chapter 6.[2]

All such new computerized overlay graphics — the computerized bugs, snipes, crawls, banners, and tickers — take away parts of television or computer screens. Most are not transparent, so they hide portions of programming and discourage the use of subtitling (such as for the hearing impaired). The entire screen has become more crowded, complex, and multilayered in recent years, incorporating more logos, overlay boxes, pop-up titles, and multiple crawls traveling at different speeds or rolling vertically while another slides past horizontally. Viewers who use the Internet regularly have learned to multitask and expect active television screens that resemble web pages.

BASIC MESSAGE FORMS

From their producers' perspective, promos, print ads, and websites have two components: the message — its form and content — and the artistic design. As already noted, in creating promotional messages, it is essential to distinguish between **tune-in** and **image** promotion. However, other distinctions are essential to speak in the insider's vocabulary of promotion.

Message Format

The term **generic** (or general) promotion can refer to promotion about station or network images or about programs, but the point is that generic promos or ads are not tied to any particular episode or any particular airdate (as 5.3 is). A radio or TV spot that urges viewers to "Watch *Rosie O'Donnell* every day at 4:00 on Channel 6" is generic. In contrast, a **specific** promo will urge viewers to "Catch the Judge breaking his gavel today at 4:30 on Channel 8." Much of radio promotion, when not tied to contests, is generic because it promotes the overall format of the station. Outdoor billboards and bumper stickers, for example, claiming that a station airs "all the hits, all the time" or "all the news, all the time" are generic promotion. Look back at 1.4 for an example of a generic television program ad (for the beloved — or derided — White Sox, depending on whether one is a Sox or Cubs fan).

Because a specific promo (also called an **episodic** or **tune-in spot**) is tied to a particular episode (or movie or game) to be shown on a specified date, it can be used for only a short time. In contrast, generic messages are for a whole program (or whole station or service) and can be reused over a long period of time. A specific or tune-in spot might say, "Watch X do Y to Z tonight" or perhaps something a bit more clever. Look back at 3.2 for an example of a specific ad for *Joey, Will & Grace*, and *The Apprentice*. Guide and newspaper ads usually are specific and serve only for one day. *Experts agree that specific promotion for programs is much more likely to be effective on broadcast television and should be utilized whenever possible.* Although wise promotion managers will devote most of their activity to producing and scheduling specific promotion, having a few generics tucked away for emergencies makes sense. Once in a great while, a brief power outage, a camera malfunction, or some other technical disruption can be turned from a (promotional) disaster by hauling out a stash of generics for the shows.

Message Structure

Another distinction in television spots concerns the number of programs associated in a promo or ad. The networks create many **singles** (promoting just *one* TV program) for their new fall series, and local stations acquiring new syndicated shows usually promote them in singles until most of the audience has a chance to become familiar with their presence and location and time. News, entertainment, and sport specials also are promoted in singles much of the time. Singles tend to be highly produced, involving about as much time and budget as some commercials.

As already mentioned, familiar programs and dayparts often are promoted within **multiple spots** or **stack ads**, advertising two or more shows, which is a less costly format for program promotion (look again at 3.2). An evening's 2-hour lineup of four situation comedies can appear in one multiple, perhaps ending with a billboard listing the titles and times of each show in order of appearance on the air. Such multiples serve to promote the various shows, link them together, and teach the audience what time they appear. This is especially a useful tactic in the fall for the networks. Another tactic is to link a new show with an established hit by pairing them in a **double** (a multiple of just two shows). Such doubles are a form of co-branding perhaps, supposedly transferring some of the audience's positive feeling about the popular show to the unknown program. The promo producer is more likely to generate the linkage if the shows exhibit some similarity (of actors or plot) and use the same style of promotional design.

Multiples are the primary way much of the audience learns the order and times of programs, especially in the fall when television network (and station) schedules change. Indeed, the traditional scheduling of promos throughout a daypart follows the order of the program lineup and thus painlessly teaches the audience when shows will appear. As illustrated in Chapter 3, stack ads in program guides, newspapers, and magazines can include photographs, titles, and air-times for several programs succeeding each other on a network. Network co-op ads combining the 11:00 p.m. late news after two or more network programs convey the order of the lineup and visually link the local program to the network programs. The goal of multiples and stack ads is to promote the flow of programming to minimize tune-out.

Unique Selling Points

Rosser Reeves, an advertising genius of the 1950s and 1960s, coined the phrase *unique selling proposition* (USP), which has since embedded itself in the practice of advertising and promotion. A **USP**, generally translated nowadays as "unique selling point," refers to something that can be said about a program (or station or network) that cannot readily be claimed about its competitors. For example, when a cable network occupies a very narrow niche, it is logical to proclaim its unique

Lifetime®
Television for Women™

5.13   *Lifetime wordmark with a USP. The Lifetime logo is the exclusive property of Lifetime Entertainment and is used with permission.*

content in its promotion. The broadcast networks (and broad-appeal cable networks like USA and TNT) try to offer something for everyone, so their claims generally are tied to individual programs or blocks of shows. Networks with narrower goals pick out some other element as a USP. As 5.13 shows, the Lifetime television network specifies its target audience of women in its theme line.[3]

A television station can promote the fact that it is the only station in its market with a 10:00 newscast, or the only one carrying a recent off-network hit, or the only one with the most advanced weather radar. Radio stations usually hold up their formats as USPs: "WXXX, the station with the hottest hits" or "the station for soul-country," and so on.

Finding that USP and embodying it in promotion is one key to successful promotion. Ideally, a theme should state a station's overall USP, and every promo about any program should emphasize what is special about that program: "WXXX, always first with the news" and "Watch *Friends*, with the relationships you treasure."

Benefits

A related, and sometimes identical idea in practice, is the concept of a *benefit*. Because the best promotion is consumer driven, not product driven, an effective piece of promotion usually tells viewers or listeners (or buyers) what they will get out of tuning in to the promoted program (the **benefit**). What they will get, typically, is something relatively mundane, such as an opportunity to laugh a lot (as at David Letterman), an opportunity to be first to know what's happening in the city (as with a local newscast), or an opportunity to hear the hits before listeners to competing stations (or so a station may claim). These are crucial ideas for creating promotion.

Whatever the alleged benefit, telling viewers what they will get out of watching (or listeners from listening) answers the not-very-hidden question of "why *should* I [do what you want]?" Merely telling viewers that "this show is the greatest" is an example of telling what the product's value is to the station, hardly a matter of interest to consumers. They want to know what benefit they will get from viewing the show.

Similarly, promotion in trade magazines, as was illustrated in Chapter 3, has to tell stations what the benefits of buying a particular syndicated program can be, usually related to audience size (higher ratings than the competition). Promotional messages directed toward advertisers also report some aspect of ratings or audience composition (more younger viewers) in order to convince advertisers of the benefits of buying time in a show.

DESIGN CONTENT ELEMENTS

Artists and psychologists have long studied the movement of the human eye as it scans a two-dimensional design. While artists often sought complexity and impact, psychologists wanted to understand cognition and the behavior of the brain. Decades of study in this area have led to elaborate eye-tracking equipment for research, but the designer of promotion can use simpler methods in implementing messages. The first lesson from history is that organization matters. *The layout of the elements in any design is crucial to the movement of the eye and thus to what is seen and not seen by the reader or viewer.* Factors such as the relative size of elements, the colors of elements, the contrast between background and foreground or lettering, the amount of white space, and the vectors incorporated into a design profoundly affect what is seen and thus what has at least a chance of impacting the viewer's behavior.

Size, Color, and Contrast

It is pretty obvious that bigger elements on a TV screen or in a print ad are more likely to capture attention than small elements. Designers often designate larger items as foreground and smaller as background elements, though this distinction makes little sense when speaking of something as small, for example, as a bumper sticker or a baseball cap. Nonetheless, the rule of size clearly holds: *Bigger probably snares more attention than smaller.*

It also is obvious that *bright, strong colors attract attention more than dull ones and that particular colors have meaning in some contexts.* Americans associate red and green with one holiday, red, white, and blue with another; orange tends to appeal more to young males than to women, while pinks and pastels have clear gender associations. Loud and neon colors tend to appeal to young people while more conservative color pairings probably "read" older audience. What a designer chooses depends on the audience to be attracted, influenced by such other factors as which color combinations competitors already use and which ones have historical associations with the particular station or network.

Another well-known principle is that colors contrasting poorly with their background cannot attract attention. Maximal contrast occurs between such pairings as white/black and yellow/navy. Further, a light element (such as a word or logo) on a dark background looks larger than a dark element on a light background. Larger may be better or may contribute to crowding, so which to choose and what elements deserve high contrast and which can be minimized with lower contrast are the designer's decisions. They have to be based on such principles such as emphasizing the key message and targeting the right audience. In general, however, it is safe to say that *the larger or more colorful one item is in relation to the other elements in the ad or on the screen, the more powerful is its positive or negative effect.*

Vectors in Designs

Solid masses of white spaces (or black spaces, for that matter) can be used by the message designers to steer viewers' eyes in particular directions, but the most useful concept for understanding how the eye tracks, and thus how to *control* how the eye tracks, may be vectors. As explained by scholars of video design such as Herbert Zettl, based on the work of scholars of two-dimensional print such as Arnheim and others, a **vector** is a direction of force. Because all elements on a TV screen or in a print advertisement are presumed to be present on purpose (not by accident as in real life), any appearance of a vector influences how the viewer's eye moves. And all designs have vectors (or otherwise consist of totally blank screens or pages).

Fundamentally, vectors have three directions in two-dimensional spaces (such as television and print): *horizontal, vertical,* and *diagonal.* A set of three scribbled lines inside some framed shape (like a TV screen) on a piece of paper or chalkboard will easily demonstrate their relative strengths (see 5.14). In attracting your eye's attention, you can see that a horizontal line is weaker than a vertical line, and a vertical line is weaker than a diagonal line, though the effects are minimized when one line bisects others.

The relative strength of vectors is a visual phenomenon that is constantly utilized by promotion designers when creating on-air promos and print ads. The dominance of diagonals can be recognized in the common tactic of slanting a

5.14 *Simple graphic vectors (horizontal, vertical, diagonal, and combined).*

radio or TV station's identifier in logos and on billboards and bumper stickers. Slanting one word (or line) out of many gives that word a kind of dynamism or "off-centeredness" that grabs attention. The third and fourth examples in 5.14 show the impact of a little slant in such a mundane thing as a skinny line.

Another distinction important to understanding how vectors function is that they come in three main types, usually called *graphic* (or line) vectors, *index* (or pointing) vectors, and *motion* vectors. **Graphic vectors** have the appearance of horizontal, vertical, or diagonal lines, such as already shown in 5.14, although they may occur in the background and be broken or interfered with by foreground lines. Or graphic vectors may constitute most or all of the forces in an entire advertisement. Consider, for example, a billboard consisting of a logo and a few lines of print in various lettering fonts. Each line of print is a separate horizontal (or diagonal) graphic vector. The logo also is a graphic vector, but it probably is not horizontal. It usually has one main directional thrust that is more or less diagonal.

Most vectors in print ads (and on the air) are graphic, but occasionally one has the characteristics of an **index vector**: It points. Clearly, an arrow or pointing finger aims the viewer's attention in a specific direction. The screens in 5.15 illustrate index vectors with different directions of force — horizontal, vertical, and diagonal. It is easy to see how the diagonal index vector rivets one's attention, and it would even do so if there were other elements on the same screen.

Pointing vectors set up the expectation that what is at the end of the index vector is important. The eyes in a face and the nose on the human profile are thought to point, as well as fingers and arrows, and many other design constructions that may not be easy to name. For example, a band of color in a rainbow that narrows at one end may be seen to point toward something, a sloping arm in a photograph may seem to point either up or down, or a contrasting necktie or a partly revealed white shirt inside a dark jacket sometimes appears to point like an arrow to some other part of an advertisement. Ideally, designers use index vectors to force the viewer's eye to the key message — the where and when of the program.

The third type of vector comes from motion, and as all television and movie viewers will recognize, **motion vectors** are far more potent in capturing attention than any kind of line or arrow on a screen, and motion gives on-air video a big advantage over any printed message. The energy of motion confers most of what

5.15 *Examples of index vectors.*

makes television such a powerful communications medium. However, motion vectors can be horizontal and thus relatively weak (but still stronger than any graphic and index vectors), they can be vertical and dominate over any horizontal motions, or they can be diagonal (or come toward the viewer, thus also enlarging in size) and overpower the rest of what is on the screen.

While motion vectors are always stronger than index vectors, which are in turn stronger than graphic vectors, inside each ad or spot the motion (or index or graphic) can be predominantly horizontal, vertical, or diagonal and thus have varying degrees of strength. Analyzing a promo for a television sitcom (for example, *Everybody Loves Raymond*) or drama (for example, one for *Law & Order* or *CSI*) in terms of vectors will show how the star achieves overwhelming prominence — even in an appearance lasting just seconds.

It is important to understand that every promo, every ad, and every web page has vectors. They may be simple or complex, weak or strong, reinforced or minor, but they are there. The fewer the items on the screen or in an ad, the more powerfully the few vectors present affect the viewers' and readers' eyes.

Aspect Ratio of the Frame

Moreover, vectors function differently in designs of different shapes. A screen, page, sign, or any outlined shape functions as a frame. Some conceptions of a particular design will not serve in different media, because their frames have different **aspect ratios**. Magazine pages normally are oriented vertically; they are taller than they are wide. TV screens, in contrast, are horizontally oriented and wider than they are tall. Older television screens have a ratio of 3 units high to 4 units wide; high-definition screens are proportioned in 9 units high by 16 wide, irrespective of their number of inches.

Billboards, on the other hand, are even more horizontal and rectangular but variable in proportions; some are less thin than others, but none is as nearly square as an older TV screen's shape. Contrast the typical billboard with the typical bumper sticker; the latter is wholly horizontal (and skinny), usually in a one to four ratio. The standard bumper sticker is 3 inches high by 12 inches long, a very different proportion than that of billboards (more commonly a 1 to 1.5 ratio). The important point about aspect ratio is that the placement of the elements in each medium must vary, just to fit in or fill up the space, and thus the vectors become altered. *Changing relative shapes changes what the message conveys.*

Negative Edge Effects

Another related concept in two-dimensional design is the **edge effect**. This term refers to the tug *out-of-the-frame* created by placing any item too close to (or touching) an edge. The rabbits in 5.16 illustrate the difference between placing a

5.16　*Example of the edge effect.*

block of type or a logo (or a rabbit) too close to the screen or ad edge or, for comparison, positioning it well away from the edge. (The hypothetical block of writing in 5.16 is shown with a rectangular shape, but it could be any size or shape.) Moreover, the closer the elements are to each other in an ad, the more they seem to relate to each other; when too far apart, they seem unrelated, and the eye does not travel easily from one to the other.

The principle is that an item near a frame edge creates a vector that pulls the eye away from the rest of the content and off the frame. The purpose of a piece of promotion normally is to emphasize the essential message, but the presence of a negative edge effect completely distracts the reader or viewer and pulls the eye away from the essential message. Also, *items close to each other relate.*

Keeping the preceding guidelines in mind, try the exercise in Box 5.17.

5.17　Creative Exercise

As an exercise, prepare the following 12 items on a white background:

- A logo in three sizes
- A theme in three sizes
- A profiled face in three sizes
- Several lines of type in three different sizes

Cut out all 12 items. Then draw the outlines of a billboard, a bumper sticker, and a magazine advertisement. Arrange any 4 of your 12 items within each of three shapes. Discuss the changes in types and strengths of vectors and any edge effects that occur with different positions of the elements.

DESIGNING FOR THE MEDIUM

In the 1980s, MTV had an enormous impact on commercial artwork for advertising and consequently for promotion. Its first effect was to greatly speed up the pace of commercials (and promos), increasing the amount of content in short periods of time. Widespread adoption of fast-paced messages contributed to shortened lengths for video commercials and promos (from 30 seconds to 15 and 10 seconds), and digitalization further shortened some promotion to a matter of seconds. In the 1990s, websites had an equivalent impact on design. Automated titles began appearing on the screen just for about 3 to 5 seconds in repeating schedules independent of program content. Promotion managers have found that brief images of a familiar character with star power are enough to remind viewers to watch a favorite show. Thus three phenomena — the increased pace of content, the need to occupy less of saleable time, and digitalization of television and radio — have combined to shorten many promos, and indeed, to change the nature of network promotion away from preproduced 30-second promos to 2-second snipes.

Video and Sound Design Considerations

The overall speeding-up has also affected sound on television. Where once there was leisure for scripted storytelling in promos excerpted from programs or movies, now very brief video and audio "clips" are specially produced for promotional purposes. While the term *clips* once meant segments literally "clipped" out of film footage or taken from the videotape, many are now created solely for promotion, and the same shots do not happen in the actual series or movie. Audio is also remixed to capture sounds characterizing an episode to fit into titling sections and promos (tantalizing listeners with slivers of what is coming).

Digitalization has also had a huge impact on radio sounds. Enormous libraries of sound effects fit on a single CD, and music can be transferred virtually instantaneously to (registered and paying) users via the Internet rather than mailed out. Thus, the promo producer — for television or radio — has access to far more individual songs, more varied background music, and many more special effects for promotional use, as discussed in Chapter 4. In consequence, as with video, more complex manipulations of sounds now appear in promotional spots.

At the same time, digitalization allows the producer to generate speeded up or slowed down sounds. Playing a familiar sound or tune at high speed (or very low speed) to tease listeners has long been common in radio games and contests, but it has become a subtle promotional technique. Fitting more of a music sequence into a briefer-than-real-time spot means more messages (commercial and promotional) can appear in that time, making speed a digital tool. Indeed, to capture attention, when they lack unexpectedness, promotional sounds often adopt greater volume and speed. *Promotional sound bites and sound signatures use advanced sound manipulations to break through radio's clutter but still need a high rate of repetition to reinforce their key promotional messages.*

Print Design Considerations

Ads in newspapers need to be large enough to grab attention. Too small is the kiss of death, as is too gray. High contrast, using large sections of solid black or white (or even gray) tends to stand out from the welter of other advertising and news text. Indeed, designers of print ads sometimes shift to **reversal printing** (white lettering and images on a black background as opposed to the more common black letters on white) to draw attention in a program guide or newspaper environment. Shape can be useful, too. Although most newspaper ads are vertical rectangles, ESPN often employs strips across the bottom of sports pages as a way of reaching readers in nonstandardized spaces. Such ads run the full width of the newspaper's page and are wide enough to contain the key message as well as artwork, so they catch the reader's attention.

In *TV Guide*, full-page ads attract the eye and can be powerful promotion. Very small ads, however, can be effective, provided the promotion manager gives the audience time to learn to recognize the source of the messages, and no other media competitor uses the same size and style. TBS, for example, long promoted in very small ads in program guides, using the smallest size sold. It standardized on tiny vertical rectangles and stuck with one shape and a narrow range of design for enough years that readers could easily identify a TBS ad. *Sticking to a single design format, using extremes of size and shape, and creating in high contrast can help a station's (or network's) message emerge from the clutter of printed messages.*

Website Design Considerations

Industry experience has revealed some guidelines for effective promotion via the Internet, many of which are discussed in Chapter 8. For starters, a site's first frames should be composed as carefully as on-air promo and print ads to attract online users and to convey the station's or network's desired image. The design should avoid long lists of links because they readily can take the user *away* from the primary message and in some cases, catapult the user away from the site.

Instead, an effective site begins with the service's logo or wordmark, reinforced by a theme or signature sound, and then supplies pictorial links to pages that each open with a variant on the station's overall image promotion (for example, see *www.wrtv.com*). Detailed aspects of the station or service, such as talent bios, merchandise for purchase, company history, and so on should be buried because, as Chapter 8 points out, on media websites visitors want to be entertained and, to a lesser extent, informed about their entertainment. From the standpoint of effective promotion, no matter where the user goes, the identifier and theme should stand out, and only after going a long way into a site should a user be invited to link away from the current service (to a network, another station, a producer, a sports team, and so on).

Just like with on-air and print campaigns, an effective website strives for congruence of color, typeface (fonts), graphics, and sound with the station's or network's overall promotion. *No matter how an Internet user scrolls or jumps through a media website, the logo, theme, and "feel of the service" should be constantly on-screen.*

CRITERIA FOR LIKELY EFFECTIVENESS

The principles of design articulated in this chapter are guidelines for promotion. Knowing the principles can't spark extraordinary creativity, but following these guidelines can help in the daily process of creating and implementing on-air, print, and web promotion that effectively reaches the target audience. *But promotion always is a guessing game*: A promotion manager/producer must commit to a design style and message and schedule positions for spots (or in publications or to signage for ads) in advance of knowing whether the promotional messages will work. Pretesting of campaigns is relatively rare below the network level, and even then, positive tests do not guarantee effectiveness. Ratings improvements or weaknesses that might have been addressed in promotion are revealed only some days, weeks, or months later.

The guidelines summarized in 5.18 merely suggest what to do and what to avoid; they are no sure thing, because promotion remains part art and part science (and the money and time for adequate science rarely is available). Nonetheless, they are the sum of many experts' long experience and will rarely take the novice in the wrong direction.

5.18   Guidelines for Promotion

1. Keep promotional designs KISS.
2. Control every aspect of the screen or ad.
3. Grab readers' and viewers' attention because it won't be given casually.
4. Use vectors and sound to focus on the key message.
5. Adopt a logo or wordmark and theme, and stick to them in all promotion.
6. Achieve reinforcement through congruence and frequent repetition.
7. Remember that on-air reaches only current viewers or listeners, while external media reaches new people.
8. Use specifics more often than generics for programs.
9. Use multiples, stack ads, and shared IDs only for programs familiar to the audience.
10. Schedule the heaviest load of series promos and ads close in time to the airdate.
11. Incorporate a USP and a benefit in most promos and ads.
12. Avoid the edge effect.
13. Protect promos and ads from cluttered environments when possible.
14. Employ styles of design that precisely target the audience wanted.
15. Aim for effectiveness not awards.

SELECTED READINGS AND VIDEOS

Alten, S. R. (2005). *Audio in Media*, 7th ed. Belmont, CA: Wadsworth.

Insight Media. (2001). *Introduction to Design: Principles* (video), 24 min.

Insight Media. (2001). *Introduction to Design: Elements* (video), 24 min.

Insight Media. (2001). *Design: The Elements* (video), 19 min.

Insight Media. (2002). *The Marketing Mix Explained* (video/DVD), 25 min.

Insight Media. (1999). *Principles of Layout and Design: The Eye of the Beholder* (video), 30 min.

Insight Media. (2004). *Print Media* (video), 20 min.

Insight Media. (2004). *Positioning: How Advertisers Shape Perceptions* (video/DVD), 21 min.

McClellan, S., and Kerschbaumer, K. (2001). Tickers and Bugs: Has TV Gotten Way Too Graphic? *Broadcasting & Cable*, December 3, 2001. Retrieved online October 5, 2004 at *www.broadcastingcable/article/CA184668, html?display=cover.*

Walker, J. R., and Eastman, S. T. (2003). On-Air Promotional Effectiveness for Programs of Different Genres, Familiarity, and Audience Demographics. *Journal of Broadcasting & Electronic Media, 47* (4), 628–637.

Zettl, H. (2005). *Sight Sound Motion: Applied Media Aesthetics*, 4th ed. Belmont, CA: Wadsworth.

NOTES

1. In 1918, the Red Sox won their 5th World Series, the most by any team up to that year, aided by Babe Ruth, the best pitcher *and* slugger in baseball (or so fans say). In 1920 the Sox owner traded him (a/k/a "The Bambino") to the Yankees, where Ruth became an enduring legend. For the next 86 years, Boston never won another World Series, while the Yankees won 26, easily the best record in baseball. Long-suffering Red Sox fans referred to the subsequent drought as "The Curse of the Bambino," or simply, "The Curse."

2. Snipes have long been used in the print media, and the term was adopted by television for both print and on-air; see the print snipe in 6.3.

3. Although Oh! Oxygen, Home & Garden Television, and SOAP generally compete for women viewers, too, Lifetime's claim is not invalidated; its USP is that all the network's programming specifically serves women's interests and women's issues.

CHAPTER 6

Network Television Promotion

Douglas A. Ferguson

The number-one program on television in 1987 was *The Cosby Show,* watched by 44 percent of the viewers. By 2005, the number-one show was *CSI: Crime Scene Investigation,* which captured only 23 percent of the audience. The decline occurred because the combined cable networks have sufficiently nibbled away viewers to attract more prime-time audience than the big four broadcast networks (ABC, CBS, FOX, NBC) combined. Just as the major Detroit automakers lost market share to foreign cars, the major broadcast networks now struggle against cable's dominance. The other commercial broadcast networks (UPN, the WB, Pax, Telemundo, Univision) vie for the same audiences. This chapter examines broadcast network promotion, although cable network promotion, discussed in Chapter 7, bears some similarity.

Promotion of a broadcast network involves nearly all the tools of contemporary mass communications, plus an assist from newer interactive technologies often tied to the Internet. The most visible (and most effective) tool is **on-air promotion**—that is, the body of commercial announcements that networks put on their own air to induce people to watch their programs. As with local stations, the secondary tools are advertising messages in magazines, newspapers, radio, outdoor, and websites, as well as skywriting, cell messaging, and any other imaginable form of paid communication. The other standard tools of promotion — sales promotion and publicity — are certainly important, but at the network level, presentations and artistic design also play major parts in promotion.

As outlined in Chapter 4, departmental structures vary from network to network. Moreover, the internal organizational structures evolve, especially with regard to overall marketing and image branding. What does not change, however, is the basic goal of network advertising and promotion departments — *to maximize audience sampling.* The means for achieving this objective are on-air promotion and advertising incorporated in an annual cycle of network promotional events. A set of assumptions about audience behavior underlies this promotional calendar.

THE MARKETING APPROACH

Because of ever-increasing competition, broadcast network promotion requires a total marketing approach. Building an audience starts with the first announcement that a new show will be going on the air. The first phase, the **publicity buildup**, includes such events as the photo sessions for the picture service that publicity departments provide to newspapers and web publishers, talk show exposure, and plugs on radio — all the free things that announce new programs. The next chronological phase is the **on-air campaign** that starts two, three, or four weeks in advance of the air date, depending on the project. An on-air campaign starts about ten days in advance of the **premiere**, although brief hints (in promos) of what is to come may be scattered throughout the summer. Thus, the very first announcement is the beginning of a campaign that reaches a climax with the premiere of the show and then continues in an ongoing pattern for as long as the show remains on the air.

Assumptions about Audiences

The uniqueness of television is that the four full-time networks (ABC, CBS, FOX, and NBC) and the part-time networks (UPN and the WB) compete with each other using very similar products. Therefore, each network seeks to make its programs even more intriguing to viewers than its competitors' programs, and especially more interesting than shows on the encroaching cable networks. *Each network's objective is to be sure that the audience learns what programs are offered and to endow each with some unique appeal.* If that appeal coincides with what the viewers want, they will watch. If the program's appeal fails to relate to viewers' interests or needs, the bad news for the networks is that they have lots of other choices.

The function of advertising and promotion in television is to let audiences know what is on the air in an interesting, efficient, and memorable way. *On-air campaigns should define the nature of individual programs, identify the casts of the programs, and make clear when the programs are on the air.* Those are the three basic questions that need to be answered for viewers: the *what, who,* and *when* of network promotion. (Unlike with local channels as described in Channel 5, the *where* of a network program is normally self-evident in on-air promotion, often requiring only a small logo.)

Most people make an almost instantaneous judgment when exposed to a new program idea (the *what*). Subconsciously viewers react emotionally and almost immediately to questions like "Does that appeal to me? Do I have an interest in it?" In that moment, for better or worse, most viewing decisions are made.

Finally, promotion tells the viewer *when* the program is scheduled. In the case of a special time, a network promo emphasizes "one hour earlier (later)" to remind the loyal audience and attract new viewers. When a prime-time program changes its day, the standard tactic is to air more than an increased number of promos exclaiming "new night," often enlisting the show's cast to speak directly to the camera in customized promos. The CBS *TV Guide* ad in 6.1 shows *King of Queens* and *Yes, Dear*, identifying them with large titles, easily recognizable faces of the leads, and the all-important *when* in this case, because the shows' day and time changed.

6.1 *CBS's* King of Queens *and* Yes, Dear *TV Guide ad. Used with permission.*

Overnight Ratings and Marketing

Overnight ratings measure the effects of network promotion in major population areas. When a show debuts on a Monday, the networks have a strong indication of its popularity by Tuesday morning. By the second week of a new program, there has been time to increase the amounts of on-air, print, and radio promotion for a promising show. *But not all shows can be equally promoted.* Program promotion is akin to refilling the empty shelves in a retail store. Merchants need to choose how they will invest promotional dollars and how to rearrange the shelves to display products that are not moving. The difference is that the "not movers" get only a few weeks to get an audience or else network attention shifts to promoting shows that are indeed "moving," especially those that have the potential of becoming hits. *Valuable promotional time and effort is not wasted on shows likely to be canceled.*

The adoption of **peoplemeters** made audience measurement more complex, not only for programmers but also for promotion people. Although the original metering system counted only heads, the peoplemeters put demographic data at the industry's fingertips, and some demographic segments are more sought after than others. Because this additional information is available on a daily basis and used heavily by broadcast and multichannel competitors, promotional campaigns have become even more tightly tailored to specific tastes than in the past, and promos are constantly revised and improved based on the peoplemeter ratings. It is no longer sufficient to be number one in all households; networks need to reach the particular demographic groups desired by particular advertisers. Shows have to "move" with the right audiences.

Research for Marketing New Series

At the network level, promotional strategies and tactics are discussed constantly with the research department, and research staff members sit in on a good deal of promotional planning for new series. Research can identify a particular show's strongest appeals, which are useful information for producing effective promos. It can also isolate the best ways of reaching specific audiences, leading to maximally effective scheduling of specific spots in different time periods.

On-air promos and print advertising are always created with narrowly-defined demographic groups in mind. For example, FOX's 2004 campaign for *Arrested Development* targeted people who were less than 30 years old. ABC's 2004 campaign for *My Wife & Kids* targeted TV viewers who were preteenagers. CBS's 2005 fall season campaign targeted customers of the high-end retailer Williams-Sonoma, distributing a fall preview DVD in stores, catalogs, and packages.

Programs also are promoted by region when necessary. If a network's research department finds that a series is not doing well in a certain part of the country, promotional campaigns immediately can be designed with appropriate content and directed specifically to that region through the use of radio, newspapers, and local on-air support from the network's affiliates. If, on the other hand, a show is not doing well with a specific audience segment on a national basis (if, for example, all of a sudden, fewer women watch because of something the competition is doing), nationwide on-air and print promotion can be redirected toward that audience group.

Research is also used in testing approaches to promotion and can be especially helpful in testing campaign ideas and in developing formats for print advertising. Network promotion staffs often consider as many as 20 or 30 different design ideas and copy approaches for just a single new series. Eventually, five or six concepts may be field tested with focus groups in five, six, or seven different markets around the country. Finally, one is adopted for the upcoming fall (or midseason) campaign. The time and dollar investment in preparing promotion at the network level is staggering.

The Daily Downside

With demand approaching 7,000 spots a year per network, little time is left for testing daily on-air promotion for ongoing programs. Certain basics come from experience, however. *Finding something in an episode that is promotable is relatively simple after talking with the people who make the show — mainly because one criterion for choosing prime-time shows is that they be easily promotable.* Network promotion departments maintain day-to-day, hour-to-hour, minute-to-minute liaison with network entertainment divisions, news divisions, sports divisions, and the producers who are making the programs. Liaison between producers and promoters is essential to the marketing of any product and, despite the annoyance factor, especially crucial for the effective marketing of television programs.

Promotional creativity comes in the "how" of promos and ads. Do designers show audiences a clip? Do they have the stars talk about the show? Do they edit in fast cuts, animate, slow down, or speed up? Do they use split screens, multilayering, or morphing? All kinds of techniques are possible, and research, when available, can identify which techniques to emphasize in appealing to different demographic groups. But because research is not always available, designers with track records of innovative and effective promotion get the big salaries.

EVOLVING NETWORK ON-AIR

Of all the ways to promote a show, on-air continues to be the key to attracting viewers. Research from Frank Magid indicates that 9 of 10 viewers still depend on on-air promos to learn what's new, and two-thirds point to television as the most important source for information about what to watch on TV.[1]

For decades, the only type of television promotion that viewers saw on the air was a 30-second piece of video (a **clip**) with an announcer saying enticing things about the show (in **voice-over**). Few promos were more sophisticated in the 1960s and 1970s, although sometimes the dialogue in the clip came through so that viewers might hear a joke, a scream, or the screeching of tires. After all, most new network shows were sampled by at least one-third of the viewers (there were just three networks then), and few alternatives existed. Because everyone learned the characters and concepts, even of shows they opted not to watch, simple "reminder" promos were all that were needed.

Clips to Shoots

In the 1980s, the networks began editing clips in the manner of movie trailers, snipping a piece from here and a piece from there and pulling them together in such a way that they communicated the essence of the show in an entertaining or exciting way using actual dialogue. Because of facilities and technical problems, however, production was limited to 300 or 400 spots per year for prime time and a few other dayparts.

The standard approach to promo-making soon dictated the use of clips from programs, but starting in the 1990s, the networks began the big-budget promos era. Nowadays, fully one-third of network spots utilize original **live shoots**. In other words, tougher competition forced prime-time promos to be produced like commercials, using original material and big budgets. Although about 80 percent of promos for introducing new programs continue to employ actual scenes (or special versions of them), many key marketing points are now being made by means of specially scripted and taped spots produced in tandem with the actual program.

The daily bread and butter of broadcast network episodic promotion for established, ongoing programs, however, continues to draw on clips. Promos for situation comedies, for example, nearly always consist of a clip containing a joke within the dialogue, accompanied by a voice-over that identifies the show and time. Nonetheless, all the broadcast and cable networks doggedly seek original ideas that push out the boundaries of both style and content in promos and ads. The creative challenge for on-air is to discover, write, and produce original promotional concepts that motivate people who have not seen a show (often 95 percent of viewers) to sample it. At the same time, promos at the national level have to fight through their busy environments. They need to compete effectively with advertisers' big-budget commercials for viewers' attention. *When a promo succeeds in standing out from surrounding clutter, it is said to be a **breakthrough** spot and will certainly win awards.*

Split Screens to Snipes

Split-screens are an innovation of the 1990s that has become commonplace in which promos share the screen with a program's closing credits. Before this technique was developed, audiences were expected to sit through every show's closing credits with only a voice-over to announce the next show. (The ends of TV programs seemed as endless as the closes of movies in theaters.) The other benefit of split-screen promos is that they do not extract time from advertising inventory. Also, the advent of **seamless programming** (no break in the action between adjacent shows) led to innovative uses of short, compelling promos to pass the viewers quickly from one show to the next, with minimal distraction from either closing or opening show titles.

The latest innovation in on-air promotion is the **snipe** (also spelled *snype* and called *automatic advance titling* in Chapter 5), which caught on quickly at both broadcast and cable networks. Originally meant as an overlaying identifier in a print advertisement (an element pasted on paper), screen-version snipes flash the name of upcoming programs at the bottom of the screen in the middle of the shows currently being watched. As illustrated in 5.11 for Oh! Oxygen and 5.12 for Bravo, snipes are efforts to capture viewers' attention for a couple of seconds. A flashing name is often combined with motion and an animated figure or video of a star's face.

The animated automatic titling idea was likely borrowed from *pop-up* advertising on the Internet, and although some web users dislike invasive messages, perhaps because the web was initially noncommercial, typical television viewers may be more resilient to bugs and snipes invading the screen than their Internet counterparts. Banner and box overlays have long characterized newscasts, and viewers may take entertainment snipes in stride because broadcast television has always been commercial. Younger viewers especially can process multiple sources of information (like several lower-screen text crawls and pop-ups during programming), because they learned to multitask web pages with iPods in their ears while still in their teen years.

Research from Frank Magid Associates pins most of the dislike of bugs and snipes to over-55 viewers. NBC initially estimated that 20 percent of viewers objected to snipes but began scaling back the number of such interruptions in late 2004, just at the time when several cable networks began regularly airing snipes. As the number of TiVo-like commercial-skipping devices increases, it will be interesting to see how frantic the schedulers of on-air promotion need to become.

Cross-Promotion and Frequency

The networks are also pushing the envelope on **cross-program promotion**. In 2004, ABC started its telecast of *Monday Night Football* with a promotional stunt for its hit show *Desperate Housewives*, in which a housewife character removed her towel to entice a football player to miss the game. The stunt backfired, attracting FCC complaints and bad public relations, but still serves as an example of how some broadcast channels have become "desperate networks." (On the other hand, *Monday Night Football* has moved to ESPN.)

Choosing the place to cross-promote and deciding how often to cross-promote are the network promotion executives' responsibilities, and two principles guide them. First, *promos for new shows are best located in well-established programs*, especially those whose core audience represents potential viewers of the new show. Second, *those shows for which a network has the highest hopes should receive the most frequent cross-promotion*. When the spinoff *CSI: New York* was introduced, CBS placed its promos in *CSI: Crime Scene Investigation* and *CSI: Miami*, as well as in other dramatic series. But the quantity of spots did not need to be extraordinary because the new show's concept would be immediately familiar to likely viewers — those who regularly watch the other *CSI* series. In the case of the hit show *Desperate Housewives*, placement was less than usually crucial because ABC sought to attract mass audiences rather than smaller demographic groups, and the show had no immediate look-alikes in prime time. It is difficult to over-promote a new hit show, especially if the network has gone through lean times (as was ABC's case for many years before the 2004–2005 season).

Some executive producers of new programs are more savvy than others and spend energy working network executives to secure more promo time. No matter what networks do, executive producers are often disappointed with the amount of on-air promotion they get. Many unhappy producers assign assistants to videotape prime-time schedules so they find out exactly how many and when spots for their seemingly low-rated shows aired.

Credibility and Creativity

Placement and frequency are only two of the factors that make promos effective. For example, a promo that does not accurately convey the show itself sets viewers up for confusion when they tune in to watch. Collaboration among a show's producers and the network's programming and promotion executives can help craft a show's promo message accurately. Insiders say collaboration not only helps to get more promos on the air (because more executives are invested in the show's success), but it ensures that the creator's vision comes through in the promotion.[2]

Network promotion executives have recognized the need to reach out to creative resources outside their own departments for fresh ideas and new skills. In conference presentations and panels, Chuck Blore, head of his own creative services company and veteran writer-producer of television and radio promotion, has often called promos that simply provide program information "part of the wallpaper of television." His own award-winning spots exhibit that elusive but essential element of memorability that makes them stand out. Perhaps the most famous of these is the "Remarkable Mouth" series (in which an extreme close-up of a woman's beautiful mouth seemingly speaks with multiple male voices), an idea that has been widely imitated and adapted. He has explained the creative solution as adopting the viewer's perspective rather than the advertiser's. Effective television promotion seems to work on an emotional level through the devices of humor, warmth, or drama. Innovative promotion benefits the broadcaster through heightened viewer awareness of the promotional message. For the public, the rewards are promos with the values of entertainment.

THE BRANDING APPROACH

The most effective use of promos is when the network can organize an image campaign around a thematic symbol, and if the concept adheres firmly to the programs (or service) it becomes **branding**. A single evening or an entire service can be branded by giving it a characterizing audio/video message that stays with the audience and becomes a widely-known and stable mental image. Catchy jingles helped NBC generate excitement in several "Must-See-TV" promos in the late-1990s, for example, succeeding in branding Thursday evenings with the "must see" label. Students of promotion can view other examples from past network campaigns at the *www.tv-ark.org.uk/international/us_index.html* website.

By 2004, NBC had become the Network of the Olympics, a brand that had previously greatly benefited ABC's promotional efforts when it held the title in the 1970s and 1980s. NBC Universal spent $4.3 billion for its contract to carry the Games through 2012 and has used its singular long-term position as "The Olympic Network" to brand the network itself and as a vehicle for promoting its prime-time lineup before and during the biennial Games. Especially in 2004 and continuing toward the 2008 and 2012 Summer Games, promos for NBC's new prime-time shows adopted the Olympic symbol and the tagline of "Network of the Olympics."

Branding refers to a symbol association, not merely a theme. It is a metaphor borrowed from cattle ranching — the rancher stamps the butts of its cows with a brand. This is like a network "painting everything yellow" (ABC in the 1990s) or NBC labeling everything with the word "Olympics." When a network consciously decides to call itself "The Network of Yellow" or "The Network of the Olympics" in every promo for all kinds of shows (even for sitcoms) and in all its printed publicity and advertising and on every page of its website, the network is making a branding decision. But not all branding efforts work. CBS has made many lackluster efforts to change its image over the years but only succeeded in 2005 when it had a franchise program (the hit *CSI*) to back up its claims of being "a network for hits" and a network "for all viewers." Brands can be reinforced in themes and taglines once the symbolic association has occurred, but using a theme sporadically is no guarantee of successful branding.

NBC was so dedicated to this branding approach that they created a character, Gary the Lifeguard (from the U.S. Olympic Swim Team), to pop up all over the other Olympic game events to promote NBC's fall prime-time shows. NBC proclaimed the introduction of this so-called "viral" character to be a network "first."[3]

PROMO SCHEDULING

Television executives have long recognized the existence of demographic differences in viewing patterns. For example, the Monday to Friday daytime audience is mostly women, while prime-time audiences are whole families. But daypart differences became less important as some demographic groups migrated to specialized channels, and the traditional networks seemed to have been left with the broad 18–54 age group. Although cable clearly swallowed up certain groups (children, sports fans, teens), network shows also differentiated, becoming recognized for appealing primarily to subgroups within a demographic group.

In editing and producing promotional spots for various time periods, both the *content* (appeal) and the *scheduling* of spots have become critical functions. Nowadays, the networks produce an ever-increasing number of targeted spots for single programs, rather than continuing to run a few generic spots all over the schedule. For on-air, they use tools such as cross-promoting and packaging spots in related groups, and for external media, they share the promotional burden with their affiliates.

Cross-Plugs

At the networks, a **cross-plug** is a specific promo for the next show inserted within the preceding show or a spot for the next episode of the same show inserted in the previous episode. (As previously pointed out, there are additional types of cross-promotion.) A **vertical cross-plug** is for the next time period; a **horizontal cross-plug** is for the next night (or next week if scheduling is weekly). According to industry research, the highest number of sets-in-use is at 9:00 p.m. *The strategy behind vertical network cross-plugging is to begin building toward that peak audience at the start of prime time.* Thus, the goal of network cross-plugging is to guarantee maximum audience flow from 8:00 to 8:30 to 9:00 p.m. and on through the rest of prime time. Cross-plugs to encourage audience flow have become standard practice at all broadcast and cable networks and most stations.

Multiple Spots

Multiple spots contain stacked promotion for more than one program, usually several series scheduled sequentially on the same evening (the usual exceptions are movies, which get promoted far ahead; see Eastman, Schwartz, & Cai, 2005). Because the time to air promos is always limited, networks have to promote their series selectively. *The more competitive the network television business becomes, the more important on-air promotion becomes, and every program acquires its own priority rank.* One solution to having limited time is to promote groups of shows inside a single spot, instead of creating one 30-second spot merely advertising one show. In the early 1980s, the stacking practice was extended until, finally, an entire night's lineup was often included in a single spot. When the evening included many half-hour shows, multiples usually were poor promotion because they overburdened the audience. Viewers can absorb only a limited amount of information in 30 seconds.

A multiple spot works best when dealing with a few easily identifiable (established and familiar) programs in a station schedule, but it can create overload on a night in which two or three out of five or six are new shows or specials. The mind cannot absorb sufficient information in 23 seconds (the usable amount in most 30-second promos), thus the promos' information fails to be stored in ways that might trigger future viewing behavior. However, no reliable research findings exist on exactly how much information people can absorb: Can they learn about six old shows in 30 seconds? Is just three old and new the practical limit? The ideal number of shows to include in a multiple spot remains a judgment call. *Typically, 30-second multiple spots today (or their print counterparts, **stack ads**) promote from two to four network shows plus one local show.*

Co-op Advertising

Some commercial broadcast and cable networks offer co-op advertising programs to their affiliates in which the network supplies the materials and pays half the cost of the ad. The type of co-op print promotion ABC used in 2005 is illustrated in 6.2. *Grey's Anatomy* appears in the top half, and the local affiliate (in this case WRTV 6) places its own ad in the lower half (choosing to promote Stormteam 6 and a new weather technology called True View).

Nowadays, the networks maintain special websites for affiliates, and local promotion managers create their own stack ads and multiple spots from the array of video clips and stills that the network provides. The networks want affiliated stations to advertise network programming in any measured local medium at specified times (such as in the fall). Stations decide what media serve their needs best in their own markets.

Co-op advertising typically is a 50–50 arrangement wherein some networks return 50 cents per dollar spent by affiliated stations. A fixed amount is generally

6.2   *Co-op ad from ABC and affiliate WRTV (Grey's Anatomy and Stormteam 6). Used with permission.*

allotted to each of the 211 markets, and each affiliate is in charge of that budget. Affiliates usually can spend it at any time of the year and for any program within the prime-time schedule, but priority recommendations are supplied by the networks. *The rule of thumb is that the most popular shows don't need the affiliates' help once they are established, and the weakest shows won't benefit from help, so most co-op dollars are spent promoting the "almost hits" in the prime-time schedule.* However, stronger competition has generated more need for maintaining the visibility of even major successes.

On occasion, the networks pick up even more than half the cost of co-op promotion for pivotal programs in hopes of having additional promotion boost audiences during ratings periods. Affiliates may sometimes choose to promote hit network shows in conjunction with their own shows in order to have the "hit" bolster the status of the local program. CBS offers co-ops to its affiliates for such hits as *Survivor* and *CSI*, allowing their stature to "rub off on" local station programs by association. Figure 6.3 illustrates the co-op before and after a local addition.

6.3　*CBS's horizontal co-op for* Survivor, CSI, *and* Without a Trace: *Before and after the local promotion for* CBS 2 News at 11. *Used with permission.*

Although network co-ops are primarily for prime-time programs, occasionally the networks offer **news co-ops,** as mentioned in Chapter 3, and encourage advertising that jointly promotes local newscasts adjacent to network news programs. The networks, of course, want the strongest possible lead-ins to prime time and their newscasts. Frequently, early-evening local and network news are promoted in the same stack ad or multiple spot. Also, an affiliate's 7:30 p.m. access show and the first show in the network schedule usually can be effectively promoted as a unit.

Pairing the last prime-time show, ending at 10:59 p.m., with the local late newscast sometimes can be useful. The networks sometimes pay only half the cost of the network portion of the ad, however, not half the total cost of the ad. Co-op strategy is becoming even more important as the television marketplace becomes more competitive. *Network strategy is to maximize advertising support even in the smaller markets,* but not all networks offer co-op plans nowadays. A typical plan is outlined in 6.4.

6.4   *Typical network co-op advertising program.*

Eligibility

Only network affiliates participating in a qualifying swap program.

Co-Op Periods

Feb Sweeps (4 weeks)
May Sweeps (4 weeks)
Fall Launch: (mid-September through first week in October)
November Sweeps: (4 weeks)

Eligible Programs

Network: Prime time ONLY.
Affiliate: All locally broadcast programs.

Eligible Media

Radio and cable only, during the 4 co-op periods. See attached details for eligibility. Cable approval will be handled on a case-by-case basis.

Reimbursement

The determinant of the reimbursement percentage is the kind of local program the station combines with the network's radio or cable spot.

Radio: Buy :60 radio spots and combine the network-supplied :30 radio spot with a :30 radio spot for local news and the station is reimbursed at a rate of 50% of the cost of the :60. Combine the network :30 with a syndicated show and the station is reimbursed at a rate of 40%. Spanish or predominantly Spanish-language radio stations are not eligible for co-op unless pre-approved.

(Continued)

6.4 (*Continued*)

Cable: Buy :30 cable spots and combine the network-supplied :15 spot with a :15 spot for local news and the station is reimbursed at a rate of 50% of the cost of the :30. Combine the network :15 with a syndicated show and the station is reimbursed at a rate of 40% (same rules apply when splitting :60 cable spots). Cable co-op will be approved on a case-by-case basis, provided the affiliate can meet specific guidelines.

Affidavits of performance for radio and cable are required with reimbursement request forms. Affidavits must clearly indicate the network in the product/flight information.

Budgets

Budget levels will be based upon the affiliate's request, the plans the station submits, the station's performance, available funds, and timing. Funds are not limitless. The sooner the affiliate submits its budget planning forms, the better chance it has of receiving the amount requested. Please remember that "Budget Planning and Request Forms" are required.

Fixed Reconciliation Deadlines

- 1st quarter is due May 6.
- 2nd quarter is due August 5.
- 3rd quarter is due December 2.
- 4th quarter is due March 1.

Application

Application forms for Feb. co-op will be sent by mid-December, to all stations electing to participate in a swap program. By mid-December, the station should receive confirmation of its swap participation and co-op budget approval for the next year.

Occasionally, some broadcast networks even *pay* affiliates in larger markets to run network promotion during their high-rated early fringe, news, and access programs. ABC began this practice in 1989, and other networks followed, but it is practiced only sporadically and only for particular programs.

FALL CAMPAIGNS

Fall campaigns ostensibly are intended to achieve one primary goal — *to get the greatest number of people to sample as many of a network's prime-time shows as possible*. New shows have the highest priority for promotion; returning shows in new time periods have second priority in the fall. Made-for-TV movies also may have high priority at the broadcast networks because they represent "event" programming and occupy a large amount of an evening, although theatrical-release movies are less common in prime time nowadays as most films have migrated to basic and pay cable.[4] Shows that return in their previous time slots have fourth priority. *A show's time priority generally determines how many different promos are produced about it and how they are scheduled.*

Network dramas typically get more promotion than do comedies during a season. George Schweitzer, President of CBS Marketing Group, says:

> "With comedies, you don't want to wear out the jokes. There is less material to work with [than with dramas]. But there are many different ways to sell or promote dramas. There are the characters, there are the plots."[5]

Networks begin prioritizing shows right after the "upfront" meetings in the spring with advertisers and affiliates, deciding which programs will get the biggest fall promo campaigns. Then, about 8 to 12 weeks leading up to the fall debut of the shows, the networks unleash scores of promos on behalf of the new series. *Most networks run a total of 100 to 120 spots — 15, 20, and 30 seconds in length — in support of each of its top new fall shows.* That adds up to a total of about 60 minutes of promotion during prime time before a show debuts, normally amounting to 600 to 800 total household rating points (GRPs) in building to the show's debut.

Fall campaigns involve certain tangibles for broadcast stations. Starting in the summer, the broadcast networks make their on-air promotional materials available to affiliates. All the fall promos, graphics, animation, and music go to the stations via private Internet. The affiliates have to save and edit them and then fit them into local needs. Stations get this at no charge. In addition, the broadcast and cable networks send money for joint cooperative advertising between the network and the station, and co-ops usually promote network prime-time programs. The ad for *Fear Factor* in 6.5 is an example of NBC's 2004–2005 season promotion. Each affiliate will add the correct local time for the show and can add its own access program.

Networks also supply stills and video for use in **shared IDs**. Stations insert their own identifiers in promos and ads that promote network programs to show local viewers where to find the programs. The networks also produce radio spots, prerecorded and supplemented with scripts for local live **tag** copy. They send posters featuring new shows and photographs of personalities starring in network shows. Moreover, promotion experts are available to help individual stations. During the summer, a 30-minute videotape or DVD dealing with each network's programs is distributed free to affiliates to use in local sales promotion. The thematic opening and closing of that video serve as the basis for station spots to tie in with the network's generic approach to the fall campaign.

Promotion is a 52-week-a-year operation (especially for FOX which tends to introduce new shows continuously). National television ratings occur year round, and marketing and promotion budgets must be continuous. Even so, promotion

6.5   *NBC co-op for* Fear Factor. *Used with permission.*

peaks in the third and fourth quarters (fall and Christmas) and peaks again in the first quarter (mid-January through February) with the promotion of new "second season" programs. But frequent preemptions of the regular schedule for specials and movies, and introductions of new programs at anytime in the year, mean there is no such thing as a slack time. Every period is measured nationally by research companies and examined under a microscope by the industry. Nevertheless, the broadcast networks continue to create their glitzy fall campaigns, aimed as much at exciting the affiliates at their annual meetings and attracting advertisers as at building audiences.

While promotion is a key ingredient in the success of a show, other factors, including the quality of the writing, overall execution, and schedule placement, are also critical in its success. Even so, shows without initial sampling are often doomed to failure. Once in a while, a series struggling along with just minimal success is saved for a few months or another season because some programmers feel the show needs time to grow. Promoting is analogous to gardening: Sufficient watering is essential but too much can be deadly. *When the network decides to ax under-performing shows, those programs that received extra-heavy promotion may depart much sooner than those that received average or below-average promotional support.*

NETWORK WEBSITES

As is well known, the broadcast networks maintain highly sophisticated websites for the purpose of promoting their programs, marketing tie-in merchandise, and getting feedback from viewers. The CBS (*www.cbs.com*), NBC (*www.nbc.com*), FOX (*www.fox.com*), and ABC (*www.abc.com*) sites originally provided a "go to" box on their main pages so that users could visit their local affiliates, but most local affiliates now provide their own sophisticated web pages.

The dominant theme on all network websites is programming. The banner ad in 6.6 for *Medium* on NBC's website isolates the star's eyes to catch the reader's eyes and squeezes in all the key message elements that would normally appear in a brief on-air promo or guide ad: day, time, "all new," and the show's twist ("concept") of the lead being able "to see inside the criminal mind." In addition to learning about programs, the web visitor can watch promos, purchase merchandise, and link to news and sports.

Banner advertising also exists on some network sites to cross-promote other websites. The FOX site, for example, links its users to the many co-owned Fox sites: Fox News, Fox Sports, FX cable channel, Fox Box (4Kids.com), and the main 20th Century Fox movie studio site (*www.foxmovies.com*).

The content on the Big Four's websites is quite similar but laid out differently, and the page layouts undergo continual revision. *The common thread among the network websites is an effort to promote the current night's program lineup.* Various buttons and click boxes also allow users to obtain more information about a favorite show, enter a contest, download the new-season schedule, or participate in chat groups and forums. Some networks have special sites dedicated to particular shows and personalities. CBS reruns the latest Top 10 list from David Letterman; ABC links users to its popular daytime soap operas; NBC promotes Jay Leno and Conan O'Brien; and FOX displays full-motion promos for its top prime-time shows like *24*.

6.6 *Banner ad for NBC's* Medium. *Used with permission.*

Although network websites serve to acquire and retain viewers as well as sell things, their most important function is to obtain immediate **feedback**, as discussed in Chapter 8. Most promotion and marketing discussed in this book is "one-way" communication — from network to viewers. Websites add another dimension by combining high-impact graphics and information with the ability to connect with viewers. The web provides users with information and entertainment and provides the network with responses to their programming.

The major networks cooperate with DVR makers like TiVo to provide easier ways to sample programming and long-form promos, even without a computer connection. For those who do have broadband connections, sites like AOL TV allow viewers to get season passes to shows and meet other fans of the programs in chat rooms.

OTHER MEDIA

Print, radio, websites, and other special promotions are secondary in importance to network on-air promos. Still, benefits are to be derived from the judicious use of outside advertising in at least some of the 211 television markets. The development of programming from newer networks, the rise of cable viewing, and time lost to web surfing and video games have dramatically reduced the size of the total network audience, making it necessary for the networks to seek additional means to reach potential viewers. The Big Six networks each spent $15–20 million on off-air promotion during the Fall 2003 campaign. Jason Haikara of FOX says, "We cannot rely solely on on-air advertising anymore."[6]

Guides

In television promotion's infancy, newspaper and magazine advertising enabled the stations and networks to reach an audience eager to learn about the medium. Experts quickly discovered that such advertising of television programs served a dual function: First, it promoted the programs, and second, it unexpectedly created a general interest in the medium among viewers and potential advertisers. But as television's reach grew across the country and newspapers' reach shrank (and readership aged), the television networks turned more and more to their own medium, to radio, to cable, and to a greater use of such listing publications as *TV Guide*, because they provide more intense reader involvement. One problem is that *TV Guide*'s readership tends to be older and female, but like newspaper TV supplements, guides stay near the TV set and are thus handy when viewers are not already committed to watching a particular program.

TV Guide and its competitors are ideal for reminding about favorite shows, informing about advertising changes in day and time, and touting specials, such as the *Saturday Night Live* five-year retrospective illustrated in 6.7. Notice that NBC has five affiliated stations in the geographic area that this particular *TV Guide* issue reaches. Also, the ad includes three recently adopted practices: naming the lead-in program, giving an advisory, and supplying the network's URL.

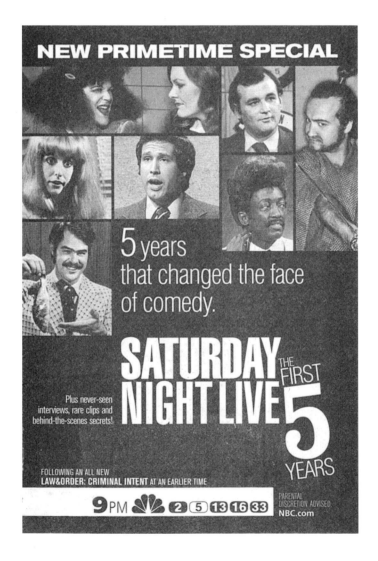

6.7 SNL *"First Five Years"* TV Guide *ad. Used with permission.*

Although listings for broadcast services once dominated guide pages, coverage of huge numbers of cable networks nowadays has made cable programs more salient, concomitantly reducing the visibility of network listings. A sign of the near future, electronic program guides (EPGs) have replaced printed listings for digital cable viewers. Currently about 40 percent of cable subscribers and 100 percent of satellite subscribers have digital service, and both groups together account for over half of all U.S. viewers.

For more routine guide and newspaper advertising, the networks also upload **slicks** (named for the glossy paper on which they used to be printed), which are generic print ads to be adapted by affiliates into local stacked ads and tune-in ads for newspapers and program guides. Radio's immediacy provides an invaluable reinforcement of such printed ads. Moreover, broadcast networks have added cable to their promotional mix, and at the same time, cable networks advertise on the commercial broadcast networks, at least on the co-owned ones.

Tie-Ins

*The networks also seek promotional **tie-ins** (joint promotional/advertising efforts) with other mass marketers in order to create new avenues for program promotion.* Reaching out, with the help of Sears, K-Mart, Coca Cola, and others, became the hallmark of 1990s broadcasting promotion. CBS was the first to announce national tie-ins with TWA and American Airlines for in-flight advertising programs, and it tied in with the K-Mart Corporation for a national contest, as illustrated in 6.8. The joint television-retailer promotion was built around a viewers' contest on the network, backed by multimedia promotions inside the huge string of 2,200 K-Mart stores and in print advertising. It was estimated that the 1994 fall program schedule for CBS received monthly exposure to more than 76 million K-Mart customers within the stores and even more through the chain's own advertising efforts

In 2002, CBS offered a free DVD to Blockbuster customers to promote the network's new fall programming. In 2003, CBS offered another "sneak peek" DVD but worked out a deal where GMC paid for all costs in exchange for the opportunity to show off its new trucks.

Other networks have followed CBS's lead. NBC purchased big screen pre-movie promos at Regal Cinemas to promote its Olympic coverage. FOX promoted its first-season shows using tie-ins with AOL and Ford, in one case offering first-run videos on the AOL Music Showcase website and, in another case, presenting a commercial-free episode of *The O.C.*, sponsored by Ford. To promote its *American Idol* series, FOX partnered with Ford, Coca-Cola, AT&T, Old Navy, Herbal Essence, Subway, and Nokia, offering up show host Ryan Seacrest as a sponsor spokesperson. Finally, the

6.8 *CBS/K-Mart prizes. Used with permission.*

WB struck a deal with K-Mart in 2004 to put the stars of the network's new series in clothing from the retailer in exchange for print ads, billboards, and in-store promos (particularly in the electronics department).

Each network is on the lookout for new domestic distribution systems for its marketing messages. The aim of these efforts is to increase sampling of new and returning prime-time programs. *External promotion has become necessary because the effectiveness of traditional network on-air declines as audience size decreases*. The impact of TV-retailer campaigns will come down to how well the media are used. All promotional things being equal, creativity (that most immeasurable of dimensions) probably will determine the success of future tie-in campaigns.

Radio

As readership flattens or declines for major daily newspapers, the networks have begun to move a good deal of their national advertising to radio, especially for co-op buys on stations in the local affiliate's market. The networks recognize that promotional information is best delivered in the late afternoon, when the audience may be deciding what to watch that evening on television. The demise of afternoon newspapers (supplanted by morning dailies) has led to more reliance on afternoon drive-time spot announcements on the radio to remind listeners about the evening's prime-time lineup.

Radio is particularly useful in attracting attention to new programs targeted at specific audiences. Unlike some media, radio is a medium where the advertising target is clear and recognized from the music format because each format was designed to appeal to a particular group. Networks and their affiliates can selectively enhance the audience sampling of appropriate programs with well-placed promos on radio stations that reach part of the desired target audience.

NETWORK NEWS PROMOTION

News viewers change their attitudes and therefore their viewing habits very slowly and often reluctantly. *News ratings on a national level change through the course of years rather than in weeks as with entertainment programs*. When consistently repeated over long periods of time, the verbal and graphic messages in news promotion make lasting impressions that strongly influence viewers' choice of newscasts.

When the three major broadcast networks saw changes at their anchor desks in 2005, they pulled out the big guns to get their new anchors established as the network voices. Brian Williams, for example, replaced Tom Brokaw on *NBC Nightly News*, and 6.9 illustrates the image the network created for him. Standard promotional practice is to assure the public that a news organization and its personalities are reliable, competent, and knowledgeable. How that impression is transmitted is the result of creative imagination. The dramatically lighted ad for Williams, which appeared in newspapers and magazines, goes even further. It signals such characteristics as professionalism (small pictures at the top), experience and commitment (the text), mixed with compassion and perhaps a touch of wry wit (his expression), with a touch of informality (the shirtsleeves with a necktie).

6.9 *Brian Williams on* NBC Nightly News. *Used with permission.*

The same means used to promote entertainment shows also are available for news promotion (on-air, newspaper and magazine advertising, radio, billboard), but specialized magazines, news-oriented radio stations, and sections of the newspaper other than the television listing page may be particularly useful for reaching news viewers. Moreover, the far-in-advance closing dates for national magazines (*TV Guide* needs its ad materials three weeks before publication) force the networks to use radio and newspapers rather than guides to achieve national exposure for topical news promotions.

In on-air promotion of news, tying the national and local newscasts into a unified campaign can be useful to both the network and affiliates. *The network encourages flow into its evening news; the affiliate gets rub-off prestige from the association for its local news team.* In addition to the spots they produce for their own programs, the networks make special promos that showcase local news personalities alongside network news personalities. In print advertising, cooperative ventures that join the local and national news programs have become the norm. In some cases, the network provides special advertising materials free to stations for local integration. More commonly, the network pays half the media costs for ads that feature a combination of local and network news (**news co-ops**).

In general, network news campaigns tend to be less than memorable. There's so much risk of offending regular viewers that few imaginative campaign ideas get realized. In any event, the number of viewers who rely on the nightly news programs had declined from 60 percent in 1994 to 34 percent by 2004. Cable news accounts for almost 38 percent, showing that more people (72 percent) rely on television for their news than before, but not news from the broadcast networks. In fact, of those between the ages of 18 and 29 surveyed in 2004, young viewers reported that they got almost as much news about politics from TV comedy shows like *Saturday Night Live* as they do from newspapers. And the number of web logs (**blogs**) that competed with news sources had grown from 23 in 1999 to over 4 million by 2004.

The advent of CNN and the more-recent 24-hour news channels (and more-watched in the case of Fox News) has had a devastating effect on the size of network news audiences, but the evening newscasts remain the flagships of each major network, and the absence of an evening newscast condemns a network to less than equal status. *One key advantage of having a news division is that it helps promote the entertainment division.* Positive interaction occurs when morning talk shows (network or local) create news features about some prime-time program or series. Similarly, stories about entertainment stars and events have immediate effects on ratings when they pop up on such shows as *60 Minutes, 20/20,* and *Dateline,* which are produced by the network news divisions.

PROMOTIONAL TECHNIQUES AND STRATEGIES

All kinds of promotional techniques are available: clipping comic bits, cartoon and graphic animating, scientific demonstrating or documenting, star and public endorsing, and others. Advertisers use them all on the air every night in commercials. *The question is whether the techniques of television advertising are applicable to program promotion.*

Traditionally, few people, even in the television industry, have thought of promos in the same terms as television commercials. The advertising industry has tended to denigrate TV promos by comparison with TV commercials, and commercials long seemed to have an environment and prestige of their own. However, the pressures of competition (and the advent of remote controls and digital devices) gradually pushed network television promotion operations to become as sophisticated as commercial production houses. Network promotion now means dealing 24 hours a day with fully-produced visual images, replacing each image in ongoing cycles while maintaining congruence and a central network image. At the same time, it is essential to make every on-air promo entertaining because viewers get bored easily.

Promotional impact has to be instantaneous, and immediate memorability is the key to tune-in promotion, because television occupies only ephemeral moments in time. Once a program goes by, there is no second shot for promoting it. A network's image is the sum of all its parts — its promotion as well as its programming — and the technical and aesthetic qualities of changing on-air and print promotion are central to the creation of those images.

Despite the need for constant innovation, there have been classic exceptions to the transience of promotional work. Certain graphic images have emerged from the mass of promotional patterns and become permanently embedded in world culture. These include the Olympic rings, the traditional Christian cross and Muslim crescent, and a very few others. Among them are the CBS eye, the ABC circle, the NBC peacock, and the FOX spotlight, illustrated in 6.10. Like the BBC and one or two others, these black and white logos are the classic, standard images of television media, long recognizable around the world. Nonetheless, each has considerable versatility, and as fashions in visual design change, they can be adapted by being colored in different hues, animated or put in motion, and combined with a variety of themes in any language. These images stand for the dominant forces in television and always seem contemporary.

The Big Four networks have adjusted to the challenge of cable by buying 57 percent control of all competing cable networks in 2005 (as compared with owning only 18 percent of competing cable networks in 1993), but few cable networks have achieved such world recognition for their images as the major broadcast networks.[7] Univision strives to join this group as the fifth major

6.10 *Big Four network logos. Used with permission.*

American network, but does not yet have the same level of instant world recognition. Broadcasters' on-going struggle to maintain and grow broadcast audiences against the onslaught of specialty channels is the real story.

SELECTED READINGS AND WEBSITES

Eastman, S. T., and Ferguson, D. A. (2006). *Media Programming: Strategies and Practices*, 7th ed. Belmont, CA: Wadsworth.

Eastman, S. T., Schwartz, N. D., and Cai, X. (2005). Promoting movies on television. *Journal of Applied Communication Research, 33*(2), 139–158.

Journal of Broadcasting & Electronic Media, Broadcast Education Association, 1955 to date.

Webster, J. G., Phalen, P. E., and Lichty, L. W. (2006). *Ratings Analysis: The Theory and Practice of Audience Research*, 3rd ed. Mahwah, NJ: Erlbaum.

tv.yahoo.com
tv.zap2it.com
www.abc.com
www.cbs.com
www.clicktv.com
www.fox.com
www.gist.com
www.nbc.com
www.paxtv.com
www.telemundo.com
www.thewb.com
www.tvpicks.net
www.univision.com
www.upn.com

NOTES

1. Eggerton, J. "IPG Surfing Is Next Big Wave," *Broadcasting & Cable*, June 25, 2004. Retrieved online from *www.broadcastingcable.com/article/CA430656*.
2. Friedman, W. "Shows Crave Juice from On-Air Promos," *TV Week*, March 21, 2005. Retrieved online from *www.tvweek.com/article.cms?articleId=27535*.
3. Albiniak, P. "The Name of the Games Is Promotion," *Broadcasting & Cable*, August 9, 2004. Retrieved online from *www.broadcastingcable.com/article/CA443523*.
4. Except for ABC, which is owned by Disney and thus able to show classic Disney films.
5. Friedman, W. "Shows Crave Juice from On-Air Promos," *TV Week*, March 21, 2005. Retrieved online from *www.tvweek.com/article.cms?articleId=27535*.
6. Cohen, L. "Coming to a Store Near You: Network TV promo," *Video Age International*, 24:3 (May 2004).
7. Hearn, T. "MSOs: 'Big Four' Nets Abusing Power," *Multichannel News*, March 2, 2005. Retrieved online at *www.multichannel.com/article/CA507914.html*.

CHAPTER 7

Cable Marketing and Promotion

Robert A. Klein

This chapter focuses on the cable television industry, although many of the strategies and tactics are equally applicable to direct-to-home satellite (DBS). Indeed, they are applicable to all systems delivering *multichannel television*. Still, the word *cable* communicates quite well the idea of multichannel service, at least in the minds of viewers, advertisers, regulators, and investors.

THE OLD AND THE NEW

As of the turn of the century, the cable industry was solidly established with more than 90% of all U.S. television households subscribing to nearly 10,000 systems. Most systems had completed (or were in the process of installing) advanced digital converter boxes, generally with digital video recording capability (**DVRs** to their users). Cable network viewership continues to increase at the expense of traditional broadcast networks and their affiliates, with nearly 200 channels collectively attracting more than half the total viewing audience. Since 2000, for example, the cable networks' combined audience share in prime time has been greater than the combined share of the four biggest broadcast networks. And cable's share continues to grow. Cable advertising revenue has also increased as advertisers acknowledge the impact of the medium. *Heavy competition from DBS and telephone companies has been a powerful dynamic forcing much of the cable industry to substantially increase its marketing and promotional efforts.*

Expansion and Concentration

Government regulation supposedly aimed at restricting cable business practices actually opened the door to new opportunities for cable growth and profitability in the 1990s. Industry concentration multiplied as companies like Time Warner and Viacom expanded their network offerings and multiple system operators (**MSOs**) merged, sold off, and swapped systems to achieve greater regional concentration and operational efficiency. Advances in fiber optics, digital compression and transmission, and other innovations fueled cable economic expansion and gave cable a greater proportion of the viewing audience.

Nonetheless, with over 200 national cable networks and pay-per-view services competing for system carriage and new services being offered all the time, launching new channels has become more challenging than ever, and launches on **basic tiers** are almost impossible. With the large MSOs controlling primary access to the audience, no network can survive without substantial MSO commitment or, more commonly, an MSO ownership position (**equity**). Therefore, operating cable program networks independent of conglomerate ownership grows less and less viable.

Nationally, close to 100 percent of all homes are passed by cable so operators no longer need to be preoccupied with initial cable construction. Their emphasis now is on upgrading existing systems and installing advanced digital boxes to allow the creation of broadband networks. **Broadband networks** (combining fiber optics and digital delivery) are able to deliver digital television, video-on-demand programming (**VOD**), music, DVR, voice and telephony, and high-speed modem service, along with traditional cable service (basic, premium, and pay-per-view).

Promotion's Role

Marketing is the engine behind cable's growth and its ability to adapt in this era of extraordinary change. Cable focuses on strategically manipulating the "4Ps" of marketing: pricing, product (programming), placement (distribution), and promotion. Promotion, the topic of interest, comes in six types:

- network and national trade sales promotion and advertising
- system acquisition and retention advertising
- new product marketing
- direct sales
- public relations
- program tune-in

Of these six, **tune-in** promotion gets a heavy emphasis at both the network and systems levels. Indeed, a much greater financial commitment has enabled

7.1   *A frame from Discovery Channel's tune-in promo for* Lost Beasts. *Used with permission.*

cable on-air spots from the larger networks to become equal and in many cases superior in production quality and innovation to traditional broadcast promos. For example, the frame from a promo for *Lost Beasts* in 7.1 illustrates Discovery Channel's eye-catching letter-box format (subsequent frames supply the day and time messages).

CONSUMER MARKETING BY CABLE SYSTEMS

Most local cable systems are owned by MSOs that control dozens of systems, even hundreds, from a central headquarters. To achieve **economies of scale** in purchasing and production, marketing materials from central or regional offices often minimize local identification. For example, many promotional materials for Comcast-owned systems show the parent corporation's name and an 800 number but do not identify the local system. Other MSOs take a more bottom-up approach to their marketing. In general, companies like Time Warner and Cox Communications handle their cable marketing in a decentralized fashion with local systems taking responsibility for their own marketing efforts. Still, even these parent companies provide local systems with corporate image campaigns and customized cross-channel, tune-in promotion as well as major promotion campaigns for new services like high-speed modems and **VoIP** (Voice Over Internet Protocol, or Internet telephone service). They also distribute anti-satellite messages for their systems to air that the systems usually tag locally.

Cable system operators' marketing goals include acquiring and retaining subscribers (by keeping them satisfied), rolling out new services, and establishing a brand image. To accomplish these goals system operators undertake seven tasks: They must persuade nonsubscribers to take service, encourage upgrades, reduce **churn** (turnover among subscribers), build brand image, manage subscriber perceptions, introduce new services, and encourage viewing of cable-only channels.

Acquiring Subscribers and Upgrades

Given the high percentage of homes passed and rate of subscribership, attracting new subscribers is not the marketing focus it once was. Nevertheless, paid television, radio, newspaper, magazine, and outdoor advertising are used to reach potential subscribers. Personal selling by representatives going door-to-door is used to launch a system in some newly-constructed residential areas (**new builds**) and for marketing new product tiers and advanced telecommunications services such as digital TV, Internet access, and phone service. Direct mail and telemarketing also are useful for **remarketing** basic service — reselling to households that chose not to subscribe during previous marketing efforts — and for gaining upgrades to expanded basic and premium channel packages. The primary tactic here is **bundling**, packaging offers of digital channels or high-speed Internet access and phone service at an appealing package price.

By the early 2000s, cable operators had developed cross-marketing programs with long-distance telephone services that offered discounts to subscribers in selected markets. Such **cooperative ventures** give the long-distance companies the opportunity to maintain or gain market share. For example, leading operators Comcast and Cox have had partnerships with Sprint, the number three long-distance company. At times, Comcast subscribers who took Sprint's long-distance service got a discount on a premium movie channel package or their basic or basic-plus cable bills. Cox customers have been offered reductions in their overall monthly cable bills equal to 10 percent of their long-distance bill.

Cable's main competition today comes from the satellite services, Direct TV and DISH Network. These DBS services have the advantage of national distribution, and by combining national and local marketing and advertising, they have successfully lured away millions of cable subscribers. Consequently, many MSOs moved away from mass-market advertising on television, radio, and newspapers to a targeted approach.

*The key to targeting for cable is **database marketing** — using an enhanced, in-house database to reach potential customers through direct mail and telemarketing.* System operators are supplementing their own database enhancement efforts with the PRIZM cluster system. It identifies blocks in their subscriber areas by demographics and permits tailored direct-mail appeals to residents' likely viewing interests. This reduces costs and increases response rates. To a large extent, precision targeting is driven by the roll-out of digital television and advanced telecommunications services in existing service areas. Cable's digital technology returns enormous amounts of viewing data of value to system marketing and to advertisers and agencies. Time Warner Cable of New York City rolled out its DTV (Digital Television) system upgrade (a lineup of many new cable channels plus high-speed Internet and digital phone service) using database-driven direct mail and telemarketing. Figure 7.2 illustrates one of its highly-targeted new resident mailers.

For marketing purposes, nonsubscribers are commonly divided into two groups: former subscribers (**formers**) and those who have never subscribed (**nevers**). Formers often are easy to convince to re-subscribe when they have moved to a new location, and many, in fact, will telephone the cable company to subscribe without prompting.

Former pays are basic subscribers who **downgraded** (meaning they canceled one or more pay channels). Cable system direct mail and telemarketing can be effective at persuading them once again to **upgrade**, perhaps to a different pay channel. The offer made to former pays typically is at a discounted trial rate or for a multi-pay channel package.

Nevers, those people who have not previously subscribed to cable television, also can be divided into two groups. The first consists of young people just starting their own households. Their parents probably had cable, or they may have had cable in a college setting, and they are ready to subscribe if they can afford the monthly payments. In fact, young people typically view cable service as an indispensable utility like power, telephone, and gas services. The second group consists of those people who, for a variety of reasons, have consistently refused cable service. Although this group is shrinking in number, some people still refuse cable because the off-air broadcasts in their area are reasonably plentiful and signal reception is of good quality. Others, especially those in rural areas, may have purchased satellite dishes before their communities were wired for cable. And still others may look unfavorably on television in general or simply are unable to afford cable service. Even the most skillful marketers will find these consumers' objections difficult to overcome. Special offers that include a free trial period as illustrated in 7.3 can be effective with a small percentage of nevers but are most useful in luring formers to upgrade.

Marketing plans that target just one subgroup of formers, nevers, or downgraders (for upgrades) have a greater likelihood of success than broad, multipurpose advertising. Cable operators should be cautious, however, not to **overmarket** by persuading consumers to subscribe to more than they can afford or really want. Overmarketing usually results in unwanted churn, which is discussed next.

7.2 *Welcome Home print ad. Courtesy Time Warner Cable.*

Catch it while you can!

Offer expires April 30th.

DTV–Digital Television from Time Warner Cable delivers more entertainment for every member of your family, with a broad range of children's programming, everything the sports fan needs to stay in the action, and enough movies for a film festival every night of the week.

• Access to more than **250 channels**, including **Boomerang, Toon Disney, Fox Soccer Channel, ESPNews, Sundance Channel** and **TCM** • **13 FREE DTV On Demand channels**, including **AOL Music On Demand** • Access to cable-exclusive services like **Movies On Demand** and **Premiums On Demand**—watch what you want, when you want!

Movies On Demand–Channel 1000
No time to run to the video store? All the movies you want are at your fingertips. Just tune to Channel 1000, browse our movie library, and order anytime with the push of a button.

Now anything's possible... **TIME WARNER** CABLE

TIME WARNER CABLE
2 Industrial Drive, Middletown, NY 10941

PRSRT STD
US Postage
PAID
Time Warner
Cable

FREE upgrade to **DTV**
Order any premium channel you don't currently receive and your first month is **FREE!**

Plus, get a 30-Day Free Trial of Premiums On Demand. Call **1.800.OKCable**

7.3 *More Entertainment postcard advertisement. Courtesy Time Warner Cable.*

Subscriber Retention and Churn

These days, *subscriber retention and upgrades are more of a priority for cable operators than subscriber acquisition.* Of particular concern to system operators is the outward migration of their subscribers: Research shows that more than one-third of DBS subscribers switched to DBS from cable. And these lost subscribers usually sign up for the highly-profitable premium services like pay-per-view movies: About two-thirds of DBS subscribers purchase pay-per-view movies, compared to less than 10 percent of cable subscribers generally. Promotional appeals from competing national DBS services and some local phone companies resonate with cable subscribers long frustrated by their lack of choice, poor service, or the high price of a cable provider. Currently, about 20 percent of multichannel subscribers take DBS services, and projections point to continued subscriber growth for the satellite services.

To minimize migration and reduce churn, successful cable marketers customize their promotional materials, provide convenience, and encourage channel sampling. **Customization** of print, broadcast, cross-channel promotion, and specialty advertising materials with the name of the local system helps to establish an image. Having a recognized image is essential to building loyalty. Distributing channel lineup cards makes a digital system more useful to subscribers and encourages sampling of cable-only channels. Lineup cards not only help subscribers recognize the value of their cable service, they also provide welcome convenience when accessing 250 to 300 channels.

Cable-only program guides are another convenience element that enables subscribers to maximize their use of cable service. Guides may be printed or electronic, generic or customized, and however they appear, they increase the efficiency of cable use. Printed guides, such as *TV Guide*, typically provide channel-by-channel listings of programs, feature stories, and photographs. Guides also may contain local advertising for businesses in the community, providing a small revenue stream. Generic guides list the programs of only the most widely-distributed cable networks (such as ESPN, CNN, Discovery Channel, TBS), while customized guides are tailored for a single cable system listing all or most of the channels that system offers. Nonetheless, because of the high cost, fewer and fewer systems mail small program guides to all subscribers each month without charge, and less than a handful — such as Disney and A&E — offer elaborate magazine guides for a monthly charge.

Larger systems usually have electronic guides, but as the number of channels has grown, the slow scroll on such services as the TV Guide Channel has become increasingly cumbersome for subscribers to use. Preview channels and built-in digital program guides are useful in assisting subscribers to learn about new premium channels and VOD offerings. The most advanced guide services are built into the cable box. They provide information about programs at the touch of a remote-control button: An "info" request shows a program's running time, elapsed time, and show synopsis. Various buttons control pay-per-view (**PPV**) purchases along with an increasing number of new interactive features. Typically, the "last" button activates DVR functions.

Building Brand Image

Initially, most major MSOs made some effort to brand their systems in order to develop positive images in subscribers' minds. Some were notably more successful than others. Changes in the marketplace during the 1990s — negative subscriber attitudes, government pressure, and emerging competition — convinced operators that traditional efforts to build name recognition and reduce churn needed to evolve. The old methods morphed into full-scale branding campaigns that trumpeted the dramatic increase in numbers of channels and claimed improved customer service, meanwhile carrying a strong anti-satellite thrust.

The video rental business also competes with cable. In one clever campaign (see 7.4), Time Warner positioned itself by pointing out advantages of on-demand movies over video rentals. The top item is part of a magazine ad, the middle part of a bill stuffer, and the bottom the front of a postcard.

Brand-building has emerged as an essential strategy for retaining subscribers by increasing satisfaction and loyalty. In cable, brand-building programs articulate an image based on the communication of one or more messages about market leadership, customer service, reliability, and new technologies. Nowadays, brand-image efforts have become full-blown multimedia campaigns that may include a name change, logo development or facelift, new creative message and slogan, print and broadcast advertising, outdoor billboards, direct mail, coupons, and joint promotions: big budget, but big impact.

Cox Communications, formerly known as Cox Cable, unfolded several brand-image campaigns in recent years. Cox currently focuses on strengthening customer relationships and leveraging its strong company image across new product launches, such as Internet connections. TV spots that run on cable channels promote Cox as a leader in technology, customer service, and reliability with the slogan "Expect the best."

Image marketing by MSOs aims to foster loyalty among customers. Comcast's efforts include television and direct response advertising, coupons in statement stuffers, joint promotions, and a frequent-buyer continuity program. Subscribers receive coupons good for discounts at such chains as Red Lobster, Holiday Inn, and Circuit City. The frequent-buyer plan rewards subscribers, based on the amount of programming they buy, with points good for the purchase of airline mileage and phone card minutes. The underlying strategy is to add value to Comcast service.

**"I hate parking at the video store...
Now I just park on the sofa."**

**time for an easier way to
enjoy movies at home**

Sick of video store hassles? ◗ **Movies On Demand with iCONTROL**℠
from Time Warner Cable gives you the power to select great movies at
home <u>instantly</u> with the simple touch of a button on your digital remote
control! It's perfect for spontaneous, stress-free entertainment.

**"No late return fees, no video
store hassles. Just movie fun,
right at home. I love it."**

**time for ◗ Movies On Demand
with iCONTROL**℠

**"Going to the video store with
kids is such a hassle,
<u>I'm</u> the one who feels like crying."**

**time for a better way to enjoy
movies at home**

TIME WARNER
CABLE
Now anything's possible.

7.4 *Movies-On-Demand print ads. Courtesy Time Warner Cable.*

Sponsorships are also a key part of cable operators' brand-building efforts. For instance, Comcast sponsored *The Cable Guy*, starring Jim Carrey, despite the film's negative take on the cable industry. Comcast was the title sponsor of the film's Hollywood premiere and showed the opening-night party live on its systems. Comcast also hosted local premieres in 45 markets, gaining positive associations with its name, especially among Carrey fans.

Managing Subscriber Perceptions

Another key task for the cable industry and its operators is to manage consumer perceptions and address negative perceptions already held by subscribers. Because several previous attempts were unsuccessful in improving cable's national image, the industry's main trade association, National Cable Television Association (**NCTA**), took on the task in the 1990s by developing a marketing effort called "The Future is on Cable" that stressed an on-time service guarantee. Major system operators got on the bandwagon and tailored supplementary promotion of their own. Time Warner of New York, for example, created a gently humorous campaign with the tagline "We just might surprise you" to exploit the ingrained cynicism of New Yorkers. Ads depicted locals barely reacting to dramatic world occurrences but being astonished by the timely delivery of cable service. Cox Communications ran a straightforward six-month campaign with the tagline "First in reliability, service, and technology."

Because consumers are highly rate sensitive, most system operators attempt to strategically market and time rate hikes to avoid tarnishing their developing — but still vulnerable — brand images. MSO tactics for **cushioning rate increases** include creating packets of news releases, Q&A sheets, letters to franchise authorities, and point-of-purchase brochures, sending the packets to local systems months in advance of the actual rate increases. Another tactic is to use notification letters to compare cost and product advantages of cable service over DBS. Still another way to soften the impact of rate hikes is to provide discounts on premium services and to bundle the increases in expanded basic prices with new products.

Marketing New Services

Offering cable modem service that provides high-speed Internet access to subscribers, and rolling out telephone services presents operators with interesting new marketing challenges in building awareness and then competitive positioning. Time Warner's Road Runner is, perhaps, the best-known Internet access service, and its roll-out illustrates the typical stages in marketing new cable products.

Initially, promotion for Road Runner included simple education and awareness ads, promotional spots and infomercials, and strategically placed demonstration kiosks. To build a customer base quickly, Road Runner then offered cable operators two integrated marketing campaigns. Both themes positioned Road Runner competitively against other access providers and exploited customer frustration with slow service and long download times. The "It's a Crime to Waste Time" campaign included TV, radio, and print advertising. The "You Don't Have to Take It Anymore" effort launched with an outdoor teaser campaign followed by cable TV, radio, print, and such collateral materials as the doorhanger in 7.5.

Next, Road Runner created topical spots about its features to be inserted into local system **avails** (unsold commercial positions on networks and local channels). In addition, website promotion targeted computer users with up-to-the-minute information about the service. In the competitive world of high-speed modem services, both interface design and websites are crucial tools in marketing and promotional strategy. Finally, going beyond traditional promotional tactics, Time Warner wired every school in its high-speed markets and provided each with a free computer to help educate the next generation of high-speed Internet users.

7.5 *Road Runner theme doorhanger. Used with permission.*

PROGRAM PROMOTION

Cable systems and networks promote both their own and each other's programs. **Tune-in promotion** by cable networks is self-promotion using promos that encourage viewers of a cable channel to stay tuned or come back later for a particular

7.6 *TBS, CNN, TNT, and Headline News logos. Used with permission.*

program. **Cross-channel promotion** refers to scheduling promos for cable-only channels in unsold or dedicated spots on other channels. Time-Warner-owned networks, for example, cross-promote their own programs on other-owned-networks: Promos for TBS, Headline News, and CNN regularly appear on TNT and vice versa (see logos for these Time Warner networks in 7.6). This practice has two advantages: It enhances subscribers' perceptions of the value of cable service, a vital element of retention, and it also boosts the ratings of the promoted cable networks, making them more desirable as carriers of spot advertising. Time Warner's cable systems also promote non-owned programs as well, specifically those new digital networks and programs that, if promoted, are likely to attract the most viewing.

Changing System Promotion

Cable marketers generally agree that 20–25 percent of local system spots should be devoted to system promotion. The term **system promotion** includes tune-in as well as ads showcasing improved customer service, system upgrades, anti-satellite messages, repair and maintenance service, and local public service. And with increasing channel capacity, the inventory available for promotional spots increases.

Going beyond traditional cross-channel promotion of just program airtimes, cable operators have adopted marketing practices that draw viewers to their specific program lineups. Comcast implemented one of the more aggressive efforts with daily spots promoting "What's on Comcast Tonight" that aired nationally on all the thousands of Comcast systems. The spots promoted two different shows each day and ran on the eight highest-rated basic networks (such as USA, ESPN, TBS, TNT, A&E, ABC Family, Lifetime, Discovery) from mid-afternoon to about 10 p.m. The promos were oriented toward program genres and featured, for example, sports one day and movies the next.

7.7 *Two frames of promo for VH1. Used with permission.*

The Value of Insertion Technology

Effectively promoting dozens of cable channels is a logistically complex task, requiring adequate budgets and dedicated promotion staff or outside suppliers. **Insertion capability** is having the technical equipment necessary for placing local spots in the positions intended for them on the major basic-cable networks. Then a system can cover up a cable network's own promos and other filler with locally-originated promos (or commercial advertising messages). Systems with insertion capability also can take network promos from the satellite feed and run them after adding local identification and tags for day, time, and channel information, making them as slick as anything broadcasters do.

More and more of the nearly 10,000 cable systems now have insertion equipment, but the newer problem is that systems cover up different times on different channels. Until recently, little accountability existed. Although most local cable systems insert cross-promotional spots in unsold local time, that arrangement is haphazard, and the networks then do not know when, where, or how much cross-promotion they are getting. Intriguing on-air promos for VH1, such as illustrated by two frames in 7.7, are appealing cross-promotional messages, but tracking their use around the country has been iffy. Digital technology, however, is resolving this problem because it allows viewing decisions to be tracked in great detail. The data about who-is-watching-what then become valuable tools for both consumer marketing (to target tune-in spots) and advertising sales (to help advertisers and agencies evaluate where to place their buys).

SALES PROMOTION BY CABLE SYSTEMS

Most cable networks are of the basic, ad-carrying variety, as opposed to such monthly subscription services as HBO and Showtime and PPV channels, none of which carry advertising at this time. Local cable systems must compete with radio, television, and newspapers for precious local and national spot advertising dollars.

Operators typically handle the sale of advertising in one of four ways. Some of the largest systems employ a regional or national sales representative firm (a **rep**) to sell their spot time. Many systems instead have their own sales staffs to sell time. Some, mostly in middle-sized markets, use a local advertising agency (a **turnkey arrangement**) to sell their time in the local market. In addition to having a professional sales team, interconnects have emerged as key to growth in national advertising. An **interconnect** is a cable connection or microwave/satellite relay among systems (two or many more) in one geographic area to simultaneously distribute the same commercial signals. Having this technology allows cable systems to sell ads on a multi-system or marketwide basis and requires negotiation of just a single contract. Hence, the audiences of the collection of systems might be equal to or greater than that of a local broadcast station, and thus the commercial time is much more salable to advertisers than before interconnects came along.

Interconnects now exist in hundreds of cable markets across the United States and represent systems that reach subscriber audiences numbering from the tens-of-thousands in smaller markets to millions in the largest markets. In one market, interconnect ad sales are often handled cooperatively or by a dominant system or an MSO in the market. Such centralization has been highly effective in shifting ad budgets away from print and radio and toward cable.

The Materials

Regardless of how cable systems sell their local advertising time, professionally produced sales materials are needed to convince advertisers to buy time. In persuading advertisers to buy time, cable operators use the same kinds of geographic coverage maps, displays of demographics for the system's subscriber base, lists of audience ratings and demographics for (cable) networks, and colorful information on key programs as illustrated for stations in Chapter 4.

In some cases, the MSO supplies branded promotional information to the system, sales rep, or interconnect, which inserts locally relevant audience information and then prepares the final printed materials and video presentations to use in sales calls. Without such MSO services, local systems must generate such materials themselves.

Tie-Ins, Events, and Co-Branding

Among the most popular marketing practices that help local operators sell advertising are promotional tie-ins, event promotions, and co-branding efforts — variations on the same tools used to promote to cable viewers. These marketing tactics leverage the success of cable networks on behalf of their affiliates.

System operators exploit network programming to target specific ad client categories with promotional **tie-ins** — contractual links between two companies for the purposes of promoting both. For example, Adlink, the Los Angeles interconnect, worked with the Food Network to create a series called "Food Bites" to capture the interest of a major food advertiser. Food Bites is a short vignette series offering food preparation tips such as how to make vegetables attractive to kids. The idea is that an advertiser becomes the exclusive sponsor of such a mini-series inserted between longer programs. Similarly, CNBC produced a series on tax tips that can be sponsored by local financial advertisers. The New York Interconnect, for example, sold tie-ins to Chase Manhattan Bank. In a joint branding effort that began in 2005, NBC joined forces with Mazda to promote its new fall schedule; the cars both starred in some shows and were prizes in the network's sweepstakes.

Operators and interconnects have increased their **event promotion** (extra promotion for special occasions) to sell ad time. In one case, Comcast Cable of Philadelphia boosted its sales on Nickelodeon by partnering with the network to create "Nick at Nite at the 76ers," a promotion designed to draw families to a professional basketball game and turn the spotlight on such Nick characters as Ren and Stimpy. Comcast also participates in mall promotions with Nick's animated characters and has seen sales of its cable ad time to children's advertisers climb steadily.

Another benefit of mall promotions and special events to system operators is the opportunity to generate advertising revenue beyond the airtime sold while also increasing live community presence. Some events allow operators to extend the credit they receive from carrying a marquee attraction. Affiliates associated with the MTV Music Awards, for example, generated $3.5 million in extra revenue through a localized merchandising program. And E! Entertainment Television provided affiliates with Hollywood Party-in-a-Bag kits, enabling them to tie into its coverage of major award ceremonies.

Co-branded events (double-sponsored) also can be effective in raising an operator's local profile. For instance, some cable operators have co-branded their systems with the Food Network's "Cooking Across America" tour. These were one-day tour events that featured well-known chefs offering cooking tips to consumers. System operators sold tickets to the events, offered advertisers sponsorships, and enjoyed the positive publicity that association with the events generated. Other widely-recognized co-branded programs include A&E's efforts surrounding *Biography*'s tenth anniversary, History Channel's plans for its signature program *In Search of History*, Lifetime's **cause marketing** campaigns for breast cancer awareness, and USA's cause marketing campaigns to "Erase the Hate." The exposure that operators, advertisers, and networks gain from co-branding extends beyond event signage, cross-channel, and on-air spots. Operators get extensive off-channel promotional exposure from statement stuffers, retail point-of-sale displays, cable office displays, and sweepstakes entry forms, all showing their names and logos well as those of the advertiser.

MARKETING BY CABLE NETWORKS

Cable networks' marketing expenditures grew dramatically throughout the 1990s and early 2000s. Expanded marketing activity by basic networks reflects the realization that substantial ratings gains are achievable and that competition extends beyond cable-to-cable competition into vying with the broadcast networks. Pay networks spend an even larger percentage of their revenues on marketing to viewers than basic networks because pay channels rely entirely on subscription revenues. HBO continues to be the pace setter, promoting its original movies, series, and mini-series with print, outdoor, transit, and on-air promotions equal to or surpassing the traditional TV networks.

At one time, basic and pay services carried recognizably divergent program content. Increasingly, as the cable audience has grown, basic channels have diversified into made-for-cable movies, originals series, and variety specials, while pay channels now schedule sports and entertainment series. Therefore, all cable networks share the marketing challenge of competing against each other as well as broadcasters for viewers, against each other for ad dollars, and against each other for cable system affiliates. Additional competitive problems for MSOs and systems come from being available both on satellite as well as terrestrial cable systems.

Brand Building in Basic Niches

In a highly competitive programming environment, building a brand image becomes fundamental to the success of all cable networks, and the key to building a cable network's brand is identifying a viable niche and developing a distinct, positive image based on programming and promotion. Indeed, *strategies created to compete effectively against other networks depend on differentiating a network from its competitors*. To develop a niche and achieve **differentiation**, cable networks create sophisticated, integrated brand-building programs.

Integrated marketing requires effective interweaving of all marketing efforts, relying on design congruence and reinforcement (as described in Chapter 5). Achieving integration demands consistent communication of a message across an array of promotional vehicles and media over time. The goal is to establish, then reinforce, an image for the network among the already-established channels. A niche is developed by going after an audience defined demographically, psychographically, or behaviorally that remains unserved by the established networks or, more commonly today, by challenging the existing services for their audiences.

The foundation of cable networks' branding efforts is the creation of distinctive logos or signatures and advertising with identifiable themes or taglines. As explained in Chapter 5, **logos** are distinctive trademarks that identify a network and are key elements of a network's signature (sometimes written in a distinctive type style called **wordmarks**). Cable network logos often are acronyms of their full names, such as TNT, QVC, and HBO. Several cable networks, especially relative latecomers, rely on signatures placed inside or underneath their acronyms. The History Channel underscores its "H" logo with "Where the Past Comes Alive," making apparent the highly-differentiated nature of its content. Some network acronyms take advantage of the recognizability of their parent company's symbol, such as the ever-present NBC peacock in the CNBC and MSNBC logos. As the result of long-term consistent use, some logos such as CNN and MTV have become instantly recognizable around the world. As suggested by the images in 7.8, MTV has deliberately broken the usual consistency rules by varying the treatment and colors of its logo and, in on-air IDs, altering the animated motion to give its identifier a nontraditional slant that appeals to younger audiences.

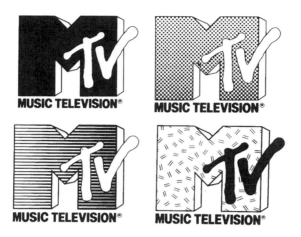

7.8 *Four MTV logos. Used with permission of MTV Networks.*

One notable characteristic of the digital age is the extension of brand names, especially by the major cable networks. **Line extensions** are the creation of new networks under an existing brand and logo, and they serve to position branded companies for a future of abundance (as opposed to the relative scarcity of the past). For example, the ESPN brand is one of the strongest among cable networks, and line extensions of the brand now include ESPN2, ESPNU, and ESPNEWS on cable and ESPNET Sports Zone on the Internet. CNN and its sister networks CNNfn, CNN/SI, and CNNI clearly represent this trend. (Some of these brand extensions stuck, and some, however, faded away.)

Over time, logos and taglines should be updated to reflect programming changes. For its first-ever advertising campaign aimed at promoting the USA brand, USA (whose emphasis at launch was more on sports) reworked its logo to better reflect its later programming, first focusing on its "national-ness" with a waving flag and then on originally-produced entertainment programming. Later, the slogan for USA became "The Cure for the Common Show." The Disney Channel also underwent a makeover. With its switch from premium to basic, more original productions were blended into its programming lineup, and the Disney Channel was positioned as "a place where families feel connected with information and entertainment."

As described in Chapter 5, many services have adopted campaign themes or taglines and paired them with their logos or signatures in their promotional materials. A **tagline** is a phrase intended to better define a network's offerings and clarify its position relative to competitors. For example, the VH1 logo has been paired with "Music First." The A&E tagline "Time Well Spent" was later combined with "Escape the Ordinary." In 7.9, a newcomer, the here! Channel, announces

7.9 *here! cable network promotion. Used with permission.*

itself as "So much more than straight TV." TNT, initially a network that offered something-for-everybody, has now narrowed its niche to "TNT, We Know Drama." Other networks combine a logo, signature, and tagline. The Discovery Channel's signature and picture of planet Earth are combined with themes like "Entertain Your Brain." The Animal Planet signature and profile of an elephant reaching for planet Earth are linked with the tag "All Animals. All the Time."

Cable networks' integrated marketing now typically extends beyond logos and taglines in advertising. Innovative marketing tactics include in-store merchandising, sport and event sponsorships, program guides, newsletters, network seals of approval, DVDs, CD-ROMs, and websites.

Comedy Central has utilized an integrated marketing program with the particular goal of distinguishing the network from competitors that also target the 18- to 49-year-old male audience. Adapted from its affiliate campaign "Save World Sanity," the consumer effort included spot cable buys in 11 markets, and print and radio ads for image and tune-in messages. Among the more imaginative aspects of the campaign were a series of stunts in six suburban markets by "Jackson," the central character of the campaign. He visited these markets in a Comedy Central customized 1972 Chevrolet El Camino, and (supposedly) went on a three-market "wild posting" spree applying posters to blank walls in such places as urban construction sites.

Many other examples of the creativity and sophistication of cable network branding efforts exist. Lifetime sponsors a woman Indy race car driver, and its website is designed to support the network's brand with content that includes practical information on women's health, parenting, sports, and fitness. The Discovery Channel owns a chain of retail stores (including the former Nature Company outlets), where such merchandise as dinosaur fossil kits and telescopes are sold. The stores' environments and merchandise support interest in Discovery programming, while the channel's programs create interest in the merchandise. The Discovery Channel also heightened its profile when it partnered with Coca-Cola in a pavilion at the 1996 Summer Olympics in Atlanta.

MTV has its MTV Video and Movie Awards and theatrical motion pictures based on its programming. The Sci-Fi Channel markets such image-consistent merchandise as computer trivia games and images of key characters in its signature programs, in part though boutiques in Spencer Gifts stores. Nickelodeon publishes *Nickelodeon Magazine*, with a circulation of 500,000-plus. And product licensing agreements with Mattel further extend the Nickelodeon brand into viewers' lives.

Brand Building by Pay Services

Brand-building campaigns for pay services differ somewhat from those developed by basic networks, but not significantly. Logos, signatures, and taglines anchor the brand identities if consistently used in widespread promotion. But, because pay services are not dependent on advertisers for revenues, much of the product merchandising and co-branding activity characterizing basic networks is unnecessary for pay channels.

HBO has built widespread recognition of its logo with taglines like, "It's not TV. It's HBO." This theme, capitalizing on the network's award-winning original programming, was shrewdly designed to set HBO apart as a programmer by emphasizing that the network adds value to the viewing experience. In addition, to maintain its competitive edge, HBO airs **prestige branding spots** (ones that demonstrate an industry leader's achievements) to provide an umbrella over its high-budgeted advertising campaigns for individual movies, mini-series, and series. HBO's prestige spots usually recap major awards or feature great moments from movies, series, and specials that it has carried or will carry. Even run-of-the-mill series promotion from HBO is usually eye-catching (see the gold nugget in 7.10 distributed widely to promote the new season of *Deadwood*).

7.10   *HBO's "gold" nugget campaign for* Deadwood. *Used with permission from Home Box Office.*

In an on-going effort to emerge from HBO's shadow, Showtime has employed cutting-edge brand marketing to re-brand itself in support of its edgier programming fare. Its recently redesigned logo emphasizes the letters *Sho* by placing them inside a spotlight, because *SHO* is how Showtime appears in program guides across the country. The theme for the campaign, "No limits," has appeal for television enthusiasts looking for programming that pushes the boundaries of traditional television. The ads were scheduled on broadcast and cable networks, on radio, and in consumer magazines and trade publications as well as extensively on Showtime's own air. Posters, direct mail, and telemarketing also supported the campaign.

PPV has evolved well beyond the days when subscribers had to be taught a complex ordering process in order to view a handful of movies at specific times. With the evolution of digital technology, VOD has begun gradually replacing the old PPV with an increasing array of movies and program offerings, some for pay, and a lot more for free (**FVOD**). In recent years, the traditional suppliers of PPV programming to cable, Viewers Choice and Request, merged to become ON DEMAND thus giving up any significant marketing identity partnered to the older names.

In the meantime, DBS has also been able to offer many more choices, some with **exclusivity** such as "Season Pass" sports, which helped them achieve a much higher buy rate. Such exclusive offerings partly account for satellite's ability to lure away substantial numbers of cable subscribers. Both cable and DBS feature movie trailers, schedules, and descriptions on preview channels, and many cable systems have dedicated a channel to VOD ordering, start times, and cost information. Depending on the resources of the local system, local newspaper, radio, and television ads may be used to promote the daily schedule or special events.

Boosting Ratings

Basic and pay cable networks all encourage viewers to watch their programs through daily tune-in advertising on the air, and print ads in program guides. Cable networks have adopted most of the strategies of their broadcast counterparts, including network IDs, on-screen billboarding of upcoming programs during program breaks, and pop-up **snipes** for upcoming shows, as previously illustrated for Oh! Oxygen in 5.11 and Bravo in 5.12. They also utilize high-quality 30- and 60-second topical promos (**specifics**) for episodes of stripped series, for guests on daily talk programs, and for specials, as well as **generic** spots to reinforce their identities and viewing of long-running popular programs. To direct viewers to their shows more effectively, pay networks and some basic networks supply consumers with program guides listing only their programs. For example, HBO distributes statement stuffer-sized guides for HBO and Cinemax. When permitted, cable networks also purchase advertising time on the national broadcast networks to reach as wide an audience as possible in an effort to bolster ratings. However, the big networks increasingly are refusing ads from direct competitors.

Promoting to Advertisers and Affiliates

Because all basic cable networks (except C-SPAN) are advertiser supported, selling a network to advertisers has always been an essential marketing activity, but it becomes even more crucial when newer networks relinquish per-month subscriber revenues as a condition of MSO carriage. The promotional tactics most commonly used by networks for reaching advertisers are trade advertising and personal selling, both used by broadcast networks, and multimedia package and bundling deals, an option for owners of several cable networks. Advertising in industry publications like *Advertising Age* and *Ad Week* is one way to reach advertisers and such agency decision-makers as media planners and buyers.

However, the most important point of contact for any cable network is the sales pitch. As the major cable networks have matured, often extending into several branded networks, they have revamped their approaches to advertising sales. Multimedia sales presentations that communicate demographic and programming information about several networks are becoming the norm, just as they are for major movie distributors and television program syndicators.

CNN's laptop sales presentation (familiarly known as The Powerpoint) incorporates full-motion video to present CNN's whole portfolio of network offerings such as CNN, Headline News, CNN International, CNN Airport, and other offshoots such as CNN/SI. Sales staff can tailor a presentation by moving with a mouse between their offerings and other sections such as lifestyle and features and sponsorships. Comedy Central has used a novel technique, an interactive trivia quiz on demographic details of the network, which plays up the strengths of the network's programming and audience. For each correct answer, a piece of the Comedy Central logo, which appears to cover a naked couple, falls away. The disk has been sent to media buyers and planners and also is used in sales presentations.

Bundling advertising opportunities is an effective, product-based strategy for boosting advertising sales. Cable brands with multiple networks (such as MTV, ESPN, Discovery, Nickelodeon, and CNN) can offer advertisers package deals for buys across their networks. This strategy can be extended into **cross-platform multimedia buys** by including the networks' websites, magazines, and co-branded sponsorships. Cable networks also can offer attractive multimedia packages by partnering with other media such as network radio, major market newspapers, national magazines, and syndicated television. All this is aggressively supported by cable's national sales promotion organization, Cable Advertising Bureau (**CAB**), which tirelessly promotes cable as an advertising medium and sponsors an annual national conference to showcase industry progress for advertisers and agencies.

Trade advertising is also designed to interest cable operators in affiliating with a cable network. It runs in such publications as *Multichannel News* and *CableFax* (which is now more e-mail than fax). The Hallmark Channel has run an ongoing series of trade ads featuring a theme ("Where success stories come to life") that is a variation of its overall consumer branding theme ("Where great stories come to life"). The ad in 7.11 illustrates addressing potential affiliates using this theme.

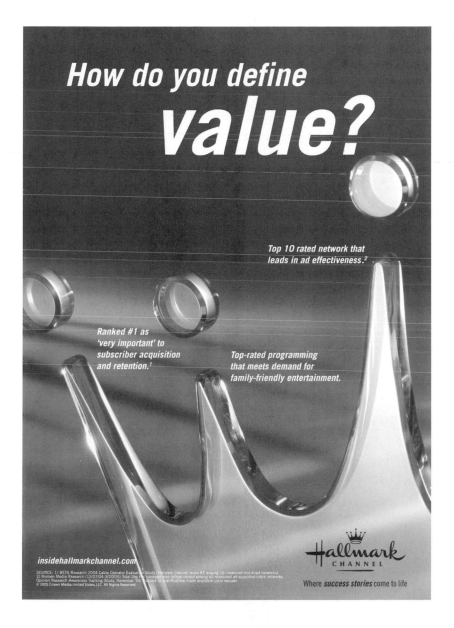

7.11   *Trade ad targeting cable operators by Hallmark Channel. Used with permission.*

Many cable networks that have been around for years continually try to increase the number of cable systems carrying them, because more affiliates means a larger audience which leads to stronger advertising sales. The networks use a combination of such **incentives** as reduced subscriber fees for a period of time, more avails for local sales, and/or periodic big-budget national campaigns that differentiate the channel and support local tune-in promotion. Without offers of equity or packaging with co-owned channels, the stand-alone networks must offer lavish economic incentives to operators as well as generate audience demand to get picked up by the major systems.

NETWORK LAUNCH STRATEGIES

Similarly, new networks must offer systems different content and economic value. The strategies employed to **launch** basic and pay cable services altered over time. Once, new pay networks concentrated primarily on audience promotion tactics to increase viewing, and basic networks focused on trade promotion, convincing cable operators to provide carriage for new channels. Today, most service launches employ elements of both audience and trade strategies to sell operators on carriage and spur viewer interest in and requests for the channel.

Growing the Pay Audience

Few truly new premium network launches have been attempted in the past decade. In fact, the number of premium channels has declined somewhat. Instead, existing premium services such as HBO, Showtime, and Encore have multiplexed their programming for digital systems and DBS services (HBO creating HBO Plus and HBO Signature, for example). When new premium networks are launched, they are usually part of an MSO-hyped digital-only package that is used to motivate subscribers to upgrade. Discounts and multi-pay channel packages routinely are offered to stimulate acceptance of the premium channel.

Capturing Basic Affiliates

Basic network launches became more challenging as the number of new channel concepts grew from a few dozen to hundreds, and competition for carriage continues to be intense. Before and during launch time, acquiring cable affiliates is by far the greatest marketing priority. *Without affiliate systems providing a significant number of cable subscribers to reach, a network is in no position to attract advertisers.* The carriage challenge is especially great for the few remaining independent networks not owned by such leading MSOs as Comcast and Time Warner, or such entertainment conglomerates as Disney and Viacom, or represented in affiliate sales by companies with muscle like FOX and Discovery. Nonetheless, even well-known brand names, logos, and generous incentives for affiliates can carry a network only so far. *To generate interest in a new channel, the essentials are high-quality programming with finely targeted appeal, supported by a strong affiliate sales organization, supported by big-budget consumer promotion and powerful trade marketing.*

The most fundamental marketing tool for any new network is the product itself. The programming must be **brandable** (differentiated) and compelling to viewers. System operators must perceive that subscriber interest exists. For many newer networks, such as Home & Garden Television (HGTV), Outdoor Life, and Animal Planet, brandability means having lots of original programming. Fox's FX did not gain traction until it began to offer such distinctive original series as *Nip/Tuck*, which it seasons with occasional original movies and off-network reruns and sports. For the NFL Sports Network, brandability means highlights and entire rebroadcasts of classic and recent sporting events. In the ever-expanding universe of cable networks, the channel's niche must be apparent to viewers and nonviewers, including advertisers and operators.

Pull and Push in Launch

To **pull** a new network onto cable systems, networks advertise in both consumer magazines and the trade press to increase viewership and thus distribution. "I Want My MTV," was pure pull. M2, a line extension of the MTV brand, uses advertising on MTV to spur viewer requests to cable operators to pick up the new channel. MTV Espanol uses appeals to Hispanic viewers. Nick at Nite's TV Land has targeted consumers with cross-promotions on Nickelodeon and other MTV networks' sister channels. Since its launch, The History Channel has consistently advertised to viewers on its sister channel A&E and other cable networks. Nonetheless, forcing distribution on cable systems by means of consumer advertising, as with the classic "I Want My MTV," is impossible now for less well-known brands.

Network **push** efforts during launch target potential affiliates with trade advertising, strong affiliate sales, partnerships with MSOs, and equity offerings (ownership shares). Affiliate incentives such as upfront carriage fees, discounts or waivers of the subscriber fee, and expanded local ads are now used more aggressively than ever.

ZDTV exemplified a struggling independent network dedicated to programming about computers, created by publisher Ziff-Davis. After a long fight to survive, it was sold and re-named TECH TV. The new owners used taglines like "Your Computer Channel," teased readers with references to "Wireheads. Geeks. Techies. Jillionaires.," and promotional ads invited inquiries from potential affiliates. It didn't work. Now in still another identity change and with new owners, the channel has been renamed G4 and re-programmed around video gaming. And it continues to struggle.

Incentives for Carriage

Partnerships with MSOs and equity offerings continue to be used by cable networks to gain carriage by affiliates. In fact, as illustrated in Chapter 1, a sizeable percentage of cable networks are owned, at least in part, by Time Warner and Comcast. When launching the Fox News Channel, owner Rupert Murdoch offered TCI, a former giant among MSOs, the option of buying 20 percent of Fox News as an inducement to carry the channel. One supposes that the option, growing more valuable with the channel's success, passed subsequently to AT&T and then to Comcast as the TCI's ownership changed hands.

In addition, the use of such affiliate incentives as upfront carriage fees has escalated substantially. The turning point was when News Corp. launched Fox News Channel to compete against CNN and MSNBC. News Corp. began paying cable operators $10 for each subscriber they delivered to Fox! It is now extremely difficult for a new network to gain widespread carriage on cable systems without offering generous incentives.

REMARKETING

Remarketing is the reselling of basic or pay services to subscribers. Networks usually promote the unique nature of their programming using a theme line that is a **USP**, as already described. Another approach is to promote the special nature of specific programs, as when Sci-Fi or HBO calls some content "exclusive" or "original."

The pay networks and local operators want to persuade households to subscribe to the digital platform and take one or more pay channels (becoming a *one-pay* or *multi-pay* subscriber). Called **upgrading** when households already take the basic service package, both the networks and operators have an incentive to market pay channels extensively because the monthly revenue from pay subscribers gets split between the local system and network. The six pay network logos shown in 7.12 commonly sponsor telephone sales campaigns offering package deals; for example, "two pays for the price of one" (for a limited time) for HBO and Cinemax or Showtime and The Movie Channel, or a Starz/Encore package, in standard television, digital, or high definition.

The major basic and pay networks also supply large amounts of free camera-ready advertising to their affiliates for insertion in local newspapers and magazines, enclosures in monthly bills (**bill stuffers**), and inclusion in plastic bags left on the doorsteps of nonsubscriber homes (**door hangers**). In addition, they supply

7.12 *The logos of the six major pay networks. Used with permission.*

customized **direct mailers** and "last chance" postcards targeting nonsubscribers to large cable systems. Small systems receive noncustomized materials. HBO and Showtime also supply cable operators with **point-of-purchase displays** (signs for the operators' lobbies) for free or a low charge. Generic advertising **slicks** (camera-ready pictures and copy) for print media and billboards leave space for tagging with the local system's name and telephone number. Many small, ready-for-distribution pamphlets and threefolds for statement stuffers, however, promote a network without leaving space for local system customization, thus they do nothing to brand the operators as the suppliers of this "network programming." Nowadays, most cable networks also supply generic and some topical TV and radio spots for local system insertion, as well as spots for cooperative advertising or tradeouts with broadcast stations.

As operators try to interest subscribers in paying for new channels, they rely mostly on digital marketing upgrades of basic and premium services. Time Warner Cable, for example, markets several different packages, at several price points, combining new channels with existing services.

DBS MARKETING

The main DBS services in the United States, DirecTV and DISH, are serious — even threatening — competitors to cable system operators. Initially, these satellite services attracted primarily rural households where cable service was not available, but research now shows that DBS has lured away millions of former and existing cable subscribers, especially the highly desirable multi-pay channel subscribers. The marketing situation for DBS services differs from that of cable system operators who are essentially local entities. Because DBS service is available nationally, promotional efforts to attract subscribers can be centralized and nationwide.

Most visible today are the network television spots and print ads that point up cable's weaknesses in order to convince consumers to move to satellite service. DirecTV and DISH have big budget advertising campaigns to create consumer awareness and interest, and they use three message strategies. In their advertising materials, they tout their crystal-clear digital video and audio, enormous selections of programming, and special sports and movie packages. DirecTV has been especially aggressive at positioning itself as superior to cable. Since its purchase by News Corp., DirecTV has also speeded up its transition into such new technologies as interactive TV (ITV), thus creating new product advantages over cable.

As with cable, **incentives** in the form of discounts, allowances for PPV movies, and free programming packages are offered to consumers who subscribe to services within a given time period or take premium program packages. Because the dishes and set-top receivers are sold through consumer electronic retailers such as Radio Shack, in-store demonstrations can also be used to interest consumers. DirecTV has also employed standard public relations techniques, such as sponsoring local events and charities, to create a positive public image.

Some cable operators have responded to the DBS threat with anti-DBS commercials that draw consumers' attention to major weaknesses of DBS — hidden costs, weather-interrupted service — and in many markets, the absence of local broadcast stations. In some places, subscribers cannot receive local television stations unless they switch out of DBS to a regular antenna. In another tactic, cable spots depict DBS as too complicated for consumers to install and offering merely the same programming as cable.

CABLE MARKETING IN THE COMING DECADE

The cable industry has successfully addressed many of the marketing demands of the past decade. Now the digital age allows for the further proliferation of channels and advanced telecommunication services, technological convergence of television and the computer, and the new dynamic of electronic (e-)commerce. With advances in on-demand, interactivity, and video Wi-Fi, *the industry is moving ever closer to a time when the consumer will be able to watch whatever they want to watch whenever they want to watch it and wherever they want to watch it.* These changes, plus the ongoing threat of big-budget competition from phone companies and others, will continue to challenge the industry's marketing prowess and elevate the importance of promotion.

As the marketplace and competitive landscape change, cable marketing and promotion have grown in scope, sophistication, and importance. Cable promotes itself within the industry at the annual NCTA conference and the **CTAM** (Cable and Telecommunications Association for Marketing), CAB gatherings, and at **PROMAX** (Promotion and Marketing Executives in the Media). At NCTA, bevies of star appearances, merchandise giveaways, and extravagant multiscreen video promotions are aimed at maintaining momentum for the established networks, creating an irresistible buzz for new ones, or promoting new technology.

Defining and differentiating the cable industry's mass of programming and service choices will preoccupy cable marketers as the decade progresses. And as information society consumers become more sophisticated, greater use of the Internet, beginning with the application of websites as promotional vehicles for separate cable channels and local system operators, will provide new opportunities to interact with subscribers and prospects. E-commerce also has a huge, as yet unrealized, potential for promotional and merchandising innovation. Whether for use as promotional tools or as products to be marketed, new technologies will place fresh demands on cable marketers.

SELECTED READINGS AND WEBSITES

CableFax Magazine. Biannual. Potomac, MD: Access Intelligence Cable Group, 1989 to date.

Kapferer, J. N. (2004). *The New Strategic Brand Management: Creating and Sustaining Brand Equity Long Term*, 3rd ed. Herndon, VA: Kogan Page.

Multichannel News. Weekly trade magazine. New York: Reed Business Information, 1979 to date.

Television Week. Chicago, 1982 to date. *www.tvweek.com.*

Variety: Weekly Trade Newspaper of Stage and Film, Television, and the Recording Industries. New York and Hollywood: Reed Business Information, 1925 to date.

www.cinemax.com
www.cnn.com
www.ctam.com

www.directv.com
www.dishnetwork.com
www.foodtv.com
www.hbo.com
www.indemand.com
www.kleinand.com
www.ncta.com
www.playboy.com/pbtv
www.ppv.com
www.promax.tv
www.tnt.tv

CHAPTER 8

New Media Promotion

Steven Masiclat and Robert A. Klein

The media landscape is morphing in ways that go far beyond just the appearance of the Internet and the World Wide Web. In a *New York Times* article, Nielsen's chief of technology, Robert Luff, pointed out, "Television and media will change more in the next 3 or 5 years than it's changed in the past 50."[1] These anticipated changes are complex and multifaceted. Programs like the 30-minute situation comedy, which used to dominate prime-time television, have become just one of many kinds of video content. Talk to someone today about a program you just watched, and they won't be sure if you're talking about a standard TV episode, a **webisode** (episodic programs delivered via web technology), or a **mobisode** (short episodic programs delivered to mobile devices).

CHANGING EXPECTATIONS AND USAGE

Video entertainment is now available — on demand — on television sets, cell phones, **PDAs**, and new devices like SONY's **PSPs** (Play Station Portables). Music, video, and radio programs are appearing on iPods or other MP3 players. Wherever these new media programs are appearing, consumers are increasingly insistent that they control the experience. People aren't just watching and listening anymore; they're also interacting.

The promotional strategies and practices of traditional and new-media producers change when they use the Internet. A touch of humor doesn't hurt when targeting younger users; witness the online ad in 8.1 and the banners in 8.2 for

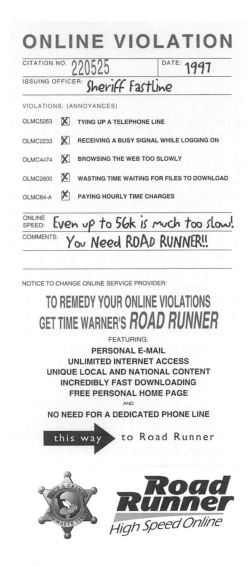

8.1 *"Online Violation" ad for Road Runner. Looney Tunes™ and © 2001 Warner Bros. Used with permission.*

Time Warner's Road Runner, a high-speed cable broadband service. Strategies alter still more radically when programming contents are distributed to devices such as cell phones, MP3 players, and palm-top computers; partly because of the limits of the technology but also because users' expectations and patterns of use are different.

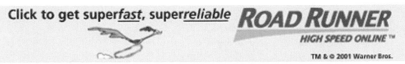

LOONEY TUNES TM & © 2001 Warner Bros.

LOONEY TUNES TM & © 2001 Warner Bros.

8.2　*Road Runner banners for Cable Broadband Service. Looney Tunes™ and © 2001 Warner Bros. Used with permission.*

INTERNET PROMOTION

Although promotion online has the potential for generating revenue, the ways it is realized blur distinctions among marketing, advertising, and merchandising. Online promotion may also have such additional goals as capturing space, tying up popular names, and establishing web-only identities.

Essentially, there are two types of online program promotion: *e-mail*, including html mail, and program-specific *websites*. These Internet-based communications perform the basic functions of all program promotion, while adding the unique dimension of immersive experiences. On an average day approximately 70 million American adults use the Internet, typically to read and send e-mail, get news, and access all kinds of information.

Sources of Web Promotional Content

The promotion-related content on the Internet comes from several different entities: Hollywood studios that produce movies and television, radio and TV networks and stations, independent filmmakers, webcasters, and podcasters. The various traditional entities (studios, broadcast and cable television networks, and radio stations) were first to make extended use of websites and streamed content for supplementation and enhancement of their main programming.

Beyond the traditional purposes of promotion — increasing viewing of specific television programs or listening to radio stations and branding of program sources — online promotion is generally intended to satisfy users' need for additional involvement with characters, plots, and performers, and these goals are gradually being extended to the newer media. In addition, the web can be used to promote reused/repurposed programming such as DVDs, packaged videos, and weekly reruns, as well as to deliver original-to-online programs. Thus, *the Internet and other new media serve to promote the content of traditional media as well as promote their own content.*

Principles of Promotion Online

The length of time users spend with the Internet contrasts with the amount of time they consume non-program content on television or radio. Although typical on-air television promos seldom last more than 30 seconds, broadcasters can only pray that viewers stay in front of the TV set and pay attention. In contrast, Internet users spend from 5 minutes to several hours with various kinds of program-related websites, including the promotion they carry. *The primary key to effective use of the Internet for promotion is taking advantage of users' time-spent-online.*

Clearly, the web differs from traditional television and radio in its essential interactivity. Until far more convergence of media occurs, the Internet has the unique characteristic of allowing users to select content in much more detail than merely choosing channels on a TV set. Users can order up content they want, rather like video-on-demand, except much of the available content is supplementary to programs rather than the programs themselves. *Effective promotion exploits the Internet's interactive nature by offering lots of choices.*

Moreover, typical computer users run four or more programs simultaneously whenever they turn on their computers. They probably open a web browser, perhaps a music player, and a chat window, as well as some productivity application such as a word processor or e-mail program. The company providing the web browser necessarily exerts control over much of the selection of sounds users hear, but typical users seek messages and sites that give the user maximum control over sound. By and large, predetermined automatic audio on websites and e-mails is widely perceived as intrusive. *For promotion, this suggests that tune-in messages must be brief and not dominated by automatic audio.*

Still another characteristic of the current Internet is that most major sites are maintained by large entities owning many media (and non-media) properties. Because the economics of the Internet are only beginning to mature, advertising revenues from outside sources tend to be small, and owners need to maximize income-producing activities to make online self-supporting. Thus, *effective promotional messages, from the perspective of owners, are those that incorporate links to paying activities and cross-promote other media businesses.*

Finally, *effective Internet promotion uses technologies and behaviors that are mindful of the context of usage.* For example, a producer wanting to promote a streaming video program via e-mail might decide to send a digital video preview or trailer as an e-mail attachment. In creating that digital video preview, the producer must ensure the file is small enough to load quickly on a client machine. In addition, forwarding a message to friends is a typical behavior in the context of dealing with e-mail. A producer would be wise to ensure promotional messages are constructed so they can be easily forwarded.

ADVANTAGES OF E-MAIL

One of the most important of the new kinds of activities made possible by the Internet, from the standpoint of a program promoter, is audience interaction with entertainment content. At its best, these interactions are unique for each audience member. The ability to easily deliver personalized communications in general (and promotion in particular) is the great strength of Internet communication. But to deliver interactive and immersive promotional messages, one must have the ability to gather and store information about the recipients, and the fundamental piece of required information is a valid e-mail address.

General and Personal E-Mail Promotion

E-mail promotion normally takes the form of alerts and newsletters. Viewers subscribe to these messages and in turn receive personalized messages for upcoming programs and series, related informational links and, quite often, opportunities to purchase program-inspired merchandise. The most effective e-mail is the **solicited** message; that is, the response that comes automatically when viewers have themselves added their names and addresses to a promotional database. When potential viewers subscribe to a promotion mailing list, they ensure the messages will be received.

Many subscribers will spend considerable time reading e-mail about individual programs, and for promoters, this pattern of **time-spent-online** (TSO) with promotional materials creates opportunities for linking to even more detail in a customized website. Typically, people reading their e-mail spend anywhere from 5 to 35 minutes interacting with promotional content. If that promotional e-mail contains links to sites or discussion groups where other interested fans of the programs congregate, that interaction can extend for hours.

The e-mail promotion from PBS shown in 8.3 included extended descriptions accompanied by **hyperlinks** (actually in red) that allow readers to move from this simplest of online promotions to a more complex form — the program-specific site. In this example, the design of the promotion should not be judged harshly. An important hallmark of personalization is the ability of audience members to tailor their messages to their preferred formats, and in this case, the recipient set an initial preference for text-only messages. If the recipient chose to, he could update the preferences stored in the producer's database and begin receiving more graphically complex messages.

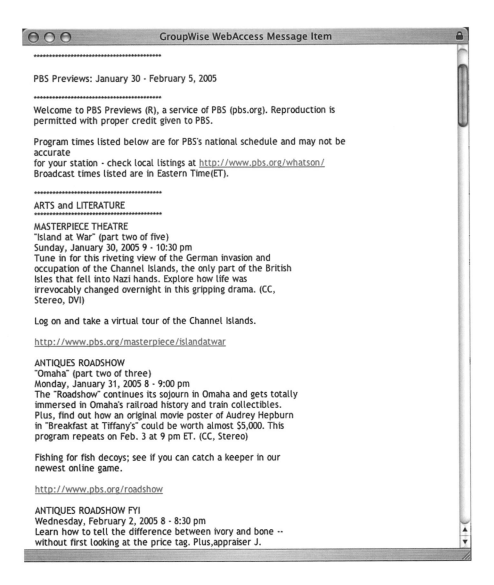

○ ○ ○   **GroupWise WebAccess Message Item**

••

PBS Previews: January 30 - February 5, 2005

••

Welcome to PBS Previews (R), a service of PBS (pbs.org). Reproduction is
permitted with proper credit given to PBS.

Program times listed below are for PBS's national schedule and may not be
accurate
for your station - check local listings at http://www.pbs.org/whatson/
Broadcast times listed are in Eastern Time(ET).

••

ARTS and LITERATURE
••

MASTERPIECE THEATRE
"Island at War" (part two of five)
Sunday, January 30, 2005 9 - 10:30 pm
Tune in for this riveting view of the German invasion and
occupation of the Channel Islands, the only part of the British
Isles that fell into Nazi hands. Explore how life was
irrevocably changed overnight in this gripping drama. (CC,
Stereo, DVI)

Log on and take a virtual tour of the Channel Islands.

http://www.pbs.org/masterpiece/islandatwar

ANTIQUES ROADSHOW
"Omaha" (part two of three)
Monday, January 31, 2005 8 - 9:00 pm
The "Roadshow" continues its sojourn in Omaha and gets totally
immersed in Omaha's railroad history and train collectibles.
Plus, find out how an original movie poster of Audrey Hepburn
in "Breakfast at Tiffany's" could be worth almost $5,000. This
program repeats on Feb. 3 at 9 pm ET. (CC, Stereo)

Fishing for fish decoys; see if you can catch a keeper in our
newest online game.

http://www.pbs.org/roadshow

ANTIQUES ROADSHOW FYI
Wednesday, February 2, 2005 8 - 8:30 pm
Learn how to tell the difference between ivory and bone --
without first looking at the price tag. Plus,appraiser J.

8.3 *PBS e-mail. Used with permission.*

The user-requested nature of e-mail promotion is another of its important aspects because most junk-mail filters permit recipient-requested mass messages to pass. To ensure that e-mail promotion is received, the sender usually asks each receiver to set a number of preferences and to authenticate the request for promotional e-mail. This authentication process prevents the interception of promotional e-mail by most spam filters.

More complex e-mail can include simple graphics, HTML, or even JavaScript inviting the receiver to submit information or participate in promotions such as sweepstakes and contests connected with programs. Companies have sprouted, like e-Prize shown in its ad in 8.4, offering both media and

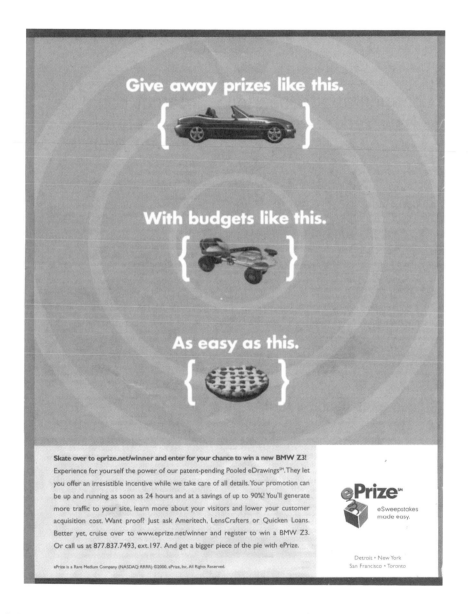

8.4   *E-Prize "Sweepstakes Made Easy." Used with permission.*

retailers ways to draw visitors to sites with sweepstakes (and the ad even offers the retailers considering purchase of an e-prize sweepstakes a chance to win a car themselves!).

Contests and other games can be very effective at gathering information about audiences, but only if the sender adheres to one of the most important principles of e-mail promotion: *Avoid sending unsolicited promotions to an e-mail inbox.* Unsolicited e-mail, or **spam**, is such a large problem that it has resulted in legislation meant to curb its spread. But more important to the promoter, unsolicited e-mail can create negative feelings about the source. Every site that solicits user information such as e-mail addresses should have a stated Privacy Policy that stipulates how personal information is to be used and to whom e-mail addresses might be sold. The Electronic Privacy Information Center has a comprehensive summary of the American public's attitudes toward online privacy and unsolicited e-mail (*www.epic.org/privacy/survey/*), and companies using e-mail as a means of program promotion are advised to follow the Center's guidelines strictly, or risk damaging their relationships with the online viewing public. Unwanted e-mail usually isn't seen as funny.

E-Newsletters

The **e-newsletter** (or **e-letter**) is a still more complex version of e-mail promotion, characterized by a higher degree of interactivity and a broader promotion agenda. Multiple programs, Internet-specific content, sponsored links, revenue-generating materials, and other co-owned network properties are typically promoted in e-newsletters.

FoodTV, parent of the Food Network, for example, uses its e-letter to promote four different programs, offer program DVDs for sale, and provide access to video programming and the network's recipe and cooking technique databases. In one promotional message alone, receivers have over 40 different interactions they can take, and some, such as invitations to view special Internet-only content, create new opportunities for extending the program brand and experience.

This form of promotion, where broadcast programs promote related web content and web promotions reference past programs, is particularly appropriate for instructional and informational programs because it exploits the strengths of each medium (television and the Internet) and avoids their weaknesses. The television program delivers information, but the emphasis is on making the instructions entertaining and on making the program brand and personality distinctive. The accompanying web media (always promoted in the television broadcast) delivers the less entertaining but more instructive program content in the most logical form (for example, printable instructions, recipe file cards, step-by-step digital video, and so on). Each medium is used to best effect, and together, they form a new symbiotic program form.

Every link in an e-newsletter has the potential to engage receivers in extended promotion cycles. It is up to the promotion producer to find the interactions that are most rewarding for consumers in each media "space."

Perhaps the ultimate in cross-property program promotion via an e-newsletter was sent by the Discovery Networks. The content shown in 8.5 represents just a fraction of a typical Discovery Dispatch.

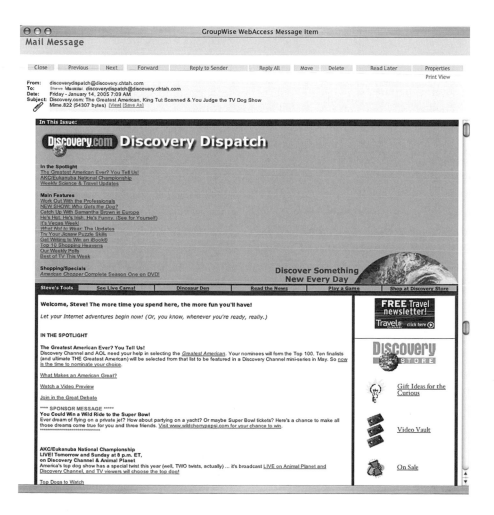

8.5 www.Discovery.com: *The Greatest American, King Tut Scanned, & You Judge the TV Dog Show. Used with permission.*

This e-newsletter demonstrates a highly developed understanding of the way audiences use the Internet. It contains over 200 opportunities for readers to interact with programs on the many channels owned by the Discovery Networks. But what distinguishes this e-newsletter is the high level of personalization that is both apparent and potentially available. Using links to databases, the message's producers provided opportunities to search databases on topics as varied as custom motorcycles, animal shows, fashion, travel, and science news. This particular newsletter is addressed to a unique recipient, and its contents are dynamically generated using a user "profile" stored in one of Discovery Corp.'s online databases. Such databases are part of the machinery that generates the website. The operating costs of building a promotion mailing list AND generating the promotion message AND updating the full set of websites are so low precisely because databases have replaced many middlemen.

The Discovery illustration in 8.5 is extremely effective because the message is tailored to deliver user-specified "favorite program reminders," alerts about new programs, and new Internet-specific content such as online games or live web cams that display content tied to programs. For example, when The Discovery Channel aired the program *Supervolcano!*, the Discovery.com website provided round-the-clock access to a web cam showing the Old Faithful geyser in Yellowstone National Park. This e-letter form immediately generates the potential for even more extended interactions. The user is able to shop for promotional merchandise, enter online contests and sweepstakes, and join an online chat group.

In keeping with one of the principles discussed earlier, subscribers are also encouraged to "forward" these e-newsletters to friends and family. *Using consumers to spread messages is an effective technique known as* **viral marketing**. Typically, a viral e-mail campaign uses interpersonal communication to spread messages much like a virus is spread from person to person. The premise is that people will trust the recommendations of the people in their personal network and are more likely to attend to, and act on, messages from those people. Viral marketing is especially effective for e-mail messages because it is easy for people to do (just click on a button to forward to a friend), and such messages automatically avoid the recipient's junk-mail filter.

E-mail and e-newsletters are powerful promotion tools but less than perfect. So much junk e-mail floods consumers that the effectiveness of promotional e-mail communications is diminishing. Almost everyone has had the experience of simply deleting large batches of e-mail because there was just too much of it clogging the inbox. Some new e-mail programs have **spam filters** that block a previously desired e-newsletter. Still, e-mail remains the single largest use of the Internet and thus will continue to be a powerful promotional tool for media companies for some years to come.

PROMOTIONAL INTERNET SITES

If you had told a broadcaster in the 1980s that you could create promotional commercials that people would actively search for, and that they would happily spend several minutes reading, watching, and listening to these promotions, you would have become an industry legend. That is essentially what program websites are, and their ubiquity is testament to their effectiveness.

Websites are the most complex and flexible means of Internet-based promotion for television and radio programs. They can be effective when well designed and constantly maintained. *The most important principle for effective site design is ensuring the website is informative and current.*

When people surf the Internet, they are actively seeking information and, in the case of media sites, entertainment. Thus, when consumers go to program sites, the networks and program producers must have the latest and best information available for audiences. In addition it must be presented in entertaining and effective formats. Properly constructed, websites are consumer-driven opportunities for program promotion of unprecedented value.

When creating a promotional site, producers must serve three distinct constituencies: They must provide clear and strong branding information to new or potential audience members; they must supply detailed program and broadcast information to casually interested viewers; and they must generate highly interactive and engaging experiences for the program's dedicated fans. Examples of such engaging and interactive features include:

- Participation in chat and message boards
- Entering contests to win program merchandise
- Providing links to "unofficial fan sites"
- In the case of some reality shows, providing viewers with the ability to influence them by voting for or against certain outcomes

Still another characteristic of effective program sites is that the *producers don't make it too easy to leave the site.* Certainly, big sites have many links but most are cross-promotion to other co-owned properties, not to sites outside the group. The effective use of visual and even auditory devices can draw attention to the variety of things the site offers, while avoiding distractions related to what's outside. Once users click away, they're gone. If they go to a cross-promoted site, fine, but not if they go outside the group's parameters.

Finally, and perhaps most crucial to corporate management, producers can use the program sites to gather demographic information about the people who watch their shows. Such information gathering can combine typical survey data (age, gender, income level) with questions about favorite episodes, favorite characters, or opinions about other programs created by the parent company. In turn, this information becomes the basis for customized promotion, advertising sales, and product sales.

Television Network Web Portals

The front screen of NBC's website, shown in 8.6, is a typical television network **portal** (web entrance). The **splash page** (first screen) uses a layout in which each object displayed is a link to program-specific pages in the site. Graphics on television network portals tend to feature large portraits of prime-time lead characters because they are the most widely and most rapidly recognized as symbols of particular programs. In this example, note how the images of the two pairs of *West Wing* and *Law & Order* characters are set off by the adjacent uncluttered box of text (listing that evening's lineup) and the smaller "screens" below. Also, the title treatment on the top two images matches the logos of the programs.

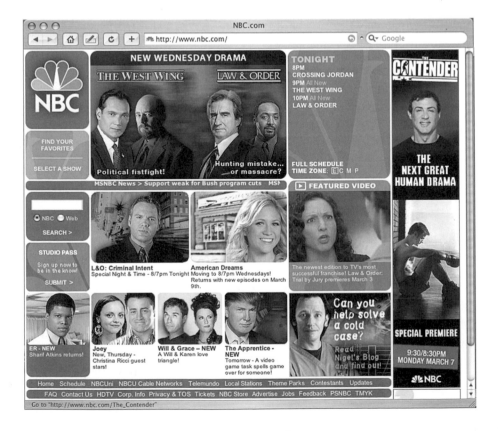

8.6   *NBC website portal,* www.NBC.com. *Used with permission.*

The search functions at the left of the page allow users either to browse a list of program titles to find their favorites or, alternatively, to enter a search term into a field to find more esoteric content. Below that, the site provides a link to NBC's "Studio Pass" section. This is the place where audience members can subscribe to e-newsletters by entering their names into databases on the NBC servers. NBC offers promotional updates and reminders in multiple forms, and audience members can receive these promotional and program reminders on their cell phones as well as via their e-mail accounts.

Every major broadcast network uses this same basic web portal approach. From the perspective of a typical user, a portal's most important characteristic is that it supports a quick and efficient search for specific program information. Thus, it fulfills the users' needs for the latest information as well as extended and detailed information.

Cable Network Sites

Sites for the various cable channels can be accessed by using a channel's on-air name (for example, *www.hbo.com* or *www.tnt.com*), and if a channel is group-owned, the URL for the parent company should also work. For example, the sites for the various Scripps properties — Food Network, HGTV, DIY Network, and Great American Country — can be accessed through the Scripps corporate site (*www.scripps.com*). The Scripps properties are examples of linked **sister sites** that cross-promote programs to audiences who might not encounter all of the parent company's properties. For example, the handyman who regularly watches DIYtv might never think of tuning his television to Great American Country, but a well-placed promotion might just alert him to a program of interest on the other cable channel.

Like the major networks, the home pages of *www.foodtv.com* have graphics at the page top that act like typical portal links. Just as with the traditional broadcasters' sites, visitors can click on links to go to program-specific pages for viewing times, program personalities, and upcoming episodes. In addition, by entering an e-mail address, visitors can receive reminders and alerts about specific programs. The site also provides links to the more interactive content by connecting visitors to the "community" of Food Network viewers. Other clickable objects provide visitors the opportunity to send messages and feedback to program producers and to the network.

Visitors can also interact with the site by using personalized content areas like the Recipe Box, a personal database where one can store favorite recipes. While functioning as a useful "virtual recipe file" for the consumer, this personalized content can also be studied by the network to determine a number of characteristics of their viewers, such as which programs engender the most downloads and what demographic characteristics and geographic locations the interested viewers have. This kind of information allows the sales departments to provide detailed audience descriptions to sponsors. Visitors also have the opportunity to buy merchandise tied to specific programs and personalities, including cookbooks, programs on DVD, and kitchen supplies like aprons and spatulas.

The *www.foodtv.com* site also provides links to instructional video that is available only on the website. Such short digital video files point to the future for television, computers, and the art of program promotion — one in which programs in specific time slots are only the start of longer, more immersive experiences.

Still another use for program websites run by cable companies is to market their other services. Time Warner Cable uses multiple means for marketing its comprehensive broadband service that incorporates high-speed Internet access with Internet phone service and fancy cable video, including on-demand and HDTV. Ads such as the one in 7.2 appear in newspapers and magazines, as well as on many Time Warner websites.

The richness and variety of activities available on these sites points to one of the problems of interactive media like websites: They get very cluttered, very quickly. Often, designers will try to make one or two of the clickable links stand out by animating them. Recent studies indicate that motion graphics on websites tend to be perceived as advertisements, and many computer users simply ignore them. *The design approach that seems to work best is to create consistent "interaction zones" where similar actions are grouped.* Thus, many sites have their navigational controls stacked along the left or right side of the web page. Designers of online promotions are advised to be somewhat conventional in their approaches. For example, text links should generally be underlined as this has come to be a standard way to visually signal the presence of a hyperlink.

Finally, one must avoid a cluttered promotion page, but uncluttered does not mean simple. In fact, the best websites are complex but very rigorously organized. *Clear, consistent, and conventional organization allows people to develop skill in manipulating and navigating through a website.* As people interact, they gradually learn the inherent organization of the site, and over time their manipulation of it becomes more and more expert.

Local Station Sites

While the sites for national networks and cable channels are rich with varied content, the sites for the local radio and TV stations are usually portals to specific and local content. Outside of the largest groups, stations seldom have the resources to create complex content, and they generally cannot afford the support staff needed to monitor and update web content. The usual result is a sameness in local television station sites. Visitors to these web pages see links to local news stories and little else.

These news story links may also promote particular news personalities, but there is no research to prove or disprove the promotional effectiveness of these types of links in building brands, improving images, or raising ratings. It is likely, however, that the absence of a station website would have negative repercussions for that station.

Radio websites also tend to suffer from similar patterns of implementation. Accessing their call letters (such as *www.wnbc.com*) provides some information about particular station's personalities, but other than the ability to send e-mail to the stations, rarely do radio station sites have innovative content that allows radio listeners to interact in the immersive ways occurring today in the larger television and cable channel sites. Innovation connected to radio (and television) is indeed out there, just hard to find — unless one looks in new places.

PROMOTING ORIGINAL INTERNET CONTENT

Program content on the Internet comes in a wide range of types. One might consider the newest versions of the highly popular dating services a unique kind of web programming. Personal interactive content, such as on *www.friendster.com* and *www.facebook.com*, blurs the line between services and programs. As always, plenty of pornography in video and stills appears online, although it is hardly an Internet-only program format. Several kinds of original online programming channels have recently emerged that reflect changes in home technology and a greater appreciation by media companies and individuals of the innovative things the web can accomplish.

Newspapers are among the most experienced of website users, having experimented early with putting the news online. One of the cleverest sites is run by the *San Francisco Chronicle*. Called *www.sfgate.com*, the site contains the day's headlines — both local and world — but tends to give them a light touch and surround serious stories with human interest, celebrity news, and extensive lists of what's going on around the Bay. Colorful and easy to read, such sites make it easy to understand why young people are deserting traditional printed newspapers for online versions of at least some of the same news. An ad that appeared in the printed San Francisco paper promoting its online site, *www.sfgate.com*, appears in 8.7.

Rerun Channels

Among the newest phenomena are the commercial rerun TV channels, such as one maintained by Yahoo (*www.tv.yahoo.com*). Others along this line are *www.reelclassics.com*, *www.tvplex.go.com/touchstone*, *www.titanicmovie.com*, and *www.sonypictures.com/tv/shows*.

8.7 *Sfgate newspaper ad. Used with permission.*

Some broadcast networks have placed repeat showings of key episodes on rerun sites for single showings to feed the needs of viewers who missed the premiere or other key episodes. This practice may become more common because it is unlikely to decrease on-air program ratings while it measurably satisfies some enthusiasts of particular programs.

Made-for-Online Channels

Another kind of commercial Internet-only programming is the **made-for-online** channel, which are few in number but potentially profitable because of their narrow specialization and appeal to specific advertisers, one of which is The Knot TV (*www.theknot.com*). The Knot is a 24-hour streaming video channel featuring wedding-related shows. One can speculate that package promotional deals with *Bride* magazine and others will cross-fertilize the online channel and the magazines and thus serve as a highly targeted promotion.

Short Online Movies

During the run up to the 2004 Presidential election, Americans learned about a new entertainment form—the **online mini-movie**—from a group of parody artists calling themselves JibJab. People all over America downloaded, watched, and then re-sent these short musical parodies featuring the caricatured Presidential candidates and their running mates. These short films were promoted in true Internet fashion. People sent e-mail with links to the films to their friends. Those friends sent the links to their friends, and in an exponential growth pattern, the word got around about these funny digital films. This promotion was so effective that it spawned a sequel, mentions on the major news networks, and a Hollywood production deal.

JibJab is just the proverbial tip of the online content iceberg. There are literally hundreds of sites offering short films (*www.atomfilms.com*) and animations (*www.shockwave.com*). These entertainment files are generally either created with an animation program called **Flash** (produced by the computer software company Macromedia), or they are digitized video stored as WindowsMedia or Quicktime Video files.

One popular **flash series** is the Ninjai cartoons (*www.ninjai.com*). This very graphic, animated, episodic story of a small ninja boy developed a cult following in the early 2000s, solely by word of mouth. People began putting links to the site up on their web pages, and soon the producers of the series, "the ninjai gang," had trouble paying for the server capacity to keep up with the online demand for the programs. Fans of the series waited almost three years for the first season of the series to finish and eagerly awaited word of subsequent episodes.

The popularity of short films will most likely lead to a standardized business in which producers allow a distributor exclusive access to their programs in return for a share of potential sponsorship profit. The JibJab producers are the first to move along this predicted path as they have signed a distribution deal with an Internet portal company (Yahoo!). If this deal heralds the future of online video production and distribution, the principles of program promotion discussed in this book will still apply. The Internet is a new distribution channel, but if producers want to earn a living creating digital content like flash series, they will still have to find a way to get someone to pay for the content.

WEBCASTING

The other front in Internet programming is the noncommercial side that signals a radical change in the sources of programming. Cheap digital audio and video recording and editing equipment and readily-available computer software now give any amateur the capabilities of a 1980 radio or television studio at very low cost. Non-professionals have plunged into making their own television shows. Although hobbyists who played at being broadcasters existed throughout the last century, they lacked access to national distribution. Not many people saw or heard these programs until the Internet and home broadband access made it possible for people with home recording and editing equipment to send their programs to anyone else with a computer. The result has been a steady increase in the availability of extreme niche programming.

Webcasts and **webisodes** (video **blogs** and amateur digital video programs sent out over the Internet) consist of everything from personal home movies to teenagers lip-synching Romanian pop music. These webcasts are just tossed out there to see if they find an audience (or to satisfy the hungers of the originators for publicity and fleeting fame).

How potential viewers learn about particular webcasts is an interesting question. Some webcasters have assembled directories of other webcast URLs, none of which claim to be complete. Indeed, the number of webcasts grows and shrinks so quickly, no service could keep up, especially not-for-profit ones run by volunteers. *Word of mouth and e-mail forwarding are probably the most used means of promotion, although, unlike commercially prepared promotional messages, the originator of a webcast has no control over promotion by private means* (talk and e-mail).

Still, this is an area that bears close watching because new and creative things are always happening. Two innovative examples are the **machinima** (video created from computer games) web series *Red vs. Blue* and *The Strangerhood.* Using the video games HALO2 and The Sims, and computers configured to capture the video signals just as cameras capture live action, producers Mike Burns, Geoff Fink, and Jason Saldaña have created a significant online following for their programs. These programs are so popular that *The Wall Street Journal* put them on its front page: *"When Art Imitates Videogames, you have 'Red vs. Blue'."*[2] Fans of both programs can download low- or high-resolution video clips, or buy full seasons of the shows on DVD. Until *The Wall Street Journal* article, their promotion was strictly word of mouth and forwarded e-mail links. It is reasonable to expect that there will be a good deal more of this kind of new media because the business model has proven viable.

PODCASTING

Radio has its own counterpart. To serve the rapidly increasing popularity of personal MP3 players, both established and independent radio producers are now creating digitally recorded "shows" that can be downloaded to such players as Apple computer's iPod and its MP3 cohorts. National Public Radio is easily the best known producer of audio-only podcasts because it makes a number of its long-running radio shows available for download.

The person most responsible for popularizing the podcast medium is Adam Curry, the former MTV veejay, who posts a podcast called *Adam Curry: Daily Source Code*. Millions of ordinary people are also creating podcasts of their own, and like the blogs that preceded them, these new forms of programming will evolve as researchers seek to understand how people will consume them — and how the producers expect to profit from them.

Currently, two grassroots sites that were built and are maintained by enthusiasts act as portals to these audio files: *www.podcast.net/* and *www.ipodder.org*. The grassroots nature of these podcast portals means that no cohesive strategy for promoting the contents exists as yet. The leaders in the podcasting movement are still working to define the standards for organizing and categorizing these sites, and the post in 8.8 from Adam Curry gives a sense of their efforts.

8.8   Adam Curry on Podcasting

"Posted by Adam Curry, 1/1/05 at 5:59:43 AM.
   What it is *http://www.ipodder.org/aboutTheDirectory#whatItIs*
   A decentralized, categorized directory of links to podcast feeds
   That said, the most common complaint is that the directory *only* contains links to the podcast feeds, technically known as the RSS-2.0 file with mp3 enclosures. This is usually accompanied by complaints about the lack of descriptions, samples and ratings for each podcast.
   All true if this were intended to be the definitive 'Podcast Portal' or something as equally dotcommie sounding.
   Anatomy of a podcast feed
   http://www.ipodder.org/aboutTheDirectory#anatomyOfAPodcastFeed
   What these commentaries are talking about is commonly referred to as 'meta data.' This is the information that tells you about an object, or in this case, a podcast.

(Continued)

The beauty is that almost anything you could wish for is contained in the actual podcast feeds themselves. In order for a podcast feed to be valid, it must contain certain information, and can contain lots of optional information. These are some important pieces of data that are found in every podcast feed:

- Title: The title of the podcast
- Link: A URL to a website, presumably the podcast's homepage
- Description: What is this podcast about?
- Language: Handy to know!
- Managing Editor: A bit of a misnomer for podcasting. Usually this will be the podcaster's name
- Directions: For a full list of all data fields and explanations go here.

Each link to a podcast in the directory is a single resource to all of the 'meta data' as described above. The URL to each podcast feed really is the gateway to the information.

It's a resource! *http://www.ipodder.org/aboutTheDirectory#itsAResource*

So why don't we parse each feed listed in the directory and present some of the wonderful nuggets of information in the iPodder.org directory? Well, first of all it would take time and significant effort to adapt the directory's software. That would be time not spent podcasting or working on new ideas and projects.

But perhaps more important is that this directory is a resource. In order to be effective, it must be simple and non competitive.

There is an XML version of the directory that is freely available to anyone to read and use. It is formatted in OPML, which makes it very easy to read, organize and edit in an outliner. The very nature of XML makes it incredibly easy for software to access this information for a multitude of uses.

Think of iPodder.org's XML directory as the stream that feeds the rivers to the open seas.

How it works *http://www.ipodder.org/aboutTheDirectory#howItWorks*

The iPodder.org directory is maintained by anyone who fills out a Submit Link form in any node of the directory.* This information is routed to whomever maintains that particular category in the directory, sometimes also known as a 'node.'

Here's where it gets really cool. The directory isn't built on a centralized database that contains all the data. Instead, it is a collection of OPML files that are linked together across the globe. Contributers maintain a 'node' in the directory, by maintaining links to podcasts in their category. If you can create an OPML file and host it on a webserver then you can contribute!

(Continued)

In fact, you can even create your own 'Top Level' directory and link other categories into it to make your own resource. In the decentralized directory model, nobody wins by locking others out.

*The iPodder.org directory also culls information from the Last 100 Podcasts page, located at *audio.weblogs.com*

How it is used *http://www.ipodder.org/aboutTheDirectory#howItIsUsed*

The information contained in the directory is used by software programmers and developers to feed their own directories, where they in turn can focus on rendering all the meta data into helpful information to base your podcast listening decisions on. Podcast Alley is a good example of this.

Most iPodder software uses the directory information to enable easy access to browsing categories and subscribing to podcasts. This leaves the development teams with more time to focus on features important to their users while new data just keeps on flowing though their applications.

Closing the loop *http://www.ipodder.org/aboutTheDirectory#closingTheLoop*

It really starts to get fun when developers return data based upon the directory information. The iPodderX software tracks most popular (most subscribed to in their software) podcasts and feeds this information back into the ipodder.org information flow. Like hooking your exhaust up to the carburetor intake. (The definition of turbo-charging!)

So far no other directories are providing a similar resource, which no doubt contains a mixture of the ipodder.org information and their own data, culled from submissions and other user input. Completely understandable of those who are in the business of attracting podcast listeners to their portal.

Partying together
http://www.ipodder.org/aboutTheDirectory partying#Together

When Users and Developers work together, the resulting party delivers software that gets used. It can create entire communities, as we've seen with podcasting.

Join us!

Feed the directory with links to podcasts, use the OPML in your software, help maintain a node, or just subscribe to the rss feed to be kept up to date on the latest podcasts as they are added. New additions are parsed to render the meta data on the ipodder.org homepage, Where Users and Developers Party Together!

• Adam Curry
http://www.ipodder.org/aboutTheDirectory#l2a16d82aeef81540b06697ab0b7df9aa

MOBISODES

In 2005, Fox Studio's Twentieth Television division began supplying Vodafone (Europe) and Verizon (U.S.) with one-minute **mobisodes** (mini-episodes intended for mobile media).[3] The first of these was of the FOX television series *24*, followed by one-minute original mobisodes of the serial dramas *Love and Hate* and *The Sunset Hotel*. Initiated as part of cross-promotional efforts by the wireless phone companies, the production and distribution of such mini-programs is intended as video device sales by positioning advanced phones as complete entertainment platforms.

This is likely to be a continuing pattern. Device manufacturers have, since the days of the early dotcom boom, known that content is a crucial contributor to the viability of any entertainment or information product. Building-in the ability to play various forms of programming enhances the value of new media devices, and subsidizing the production of new kinds of programming strengthens the perceived value of new devices. Moreover, *such cross-promotional activities create a vested interest on the part of device makers in successful promotion of the content and programs, a potential source of a great deal of money and clout.*

THE FUTURE BEYOND

Two of the most recently deployed technologies associated with television — VoIP telephony and DVRs — are convergence technologies that blur the line between the television, the telephone, and the computer. In fact, the February 2005 edition of *Popular Science* magazine had an article detailing how anyone could create his or her own MediaPC, a computer that connects to a subscriber's TV cable and digitally recorded programming. With just a few more software packages, MediaPC owners could e-mail those programs to friends and relatives, or perhaps to another MediaPC in another room. This is the ultimate convergence technology, a computer that tunes your channels, digitally records and stores your programs, and allows you to watch them on your time and in a place of your choosing. And this is the current reality of televised entertainment. Every cable MSO either has, or is planning to offer, broadband Internet service using the coaxial cables they have placed in people's homes.

The logical assumption is that every type of program will soon originate in as many locations as webcasts and podcasts do now — that people with broadband connections, digital video cameras, and broadband Internet connections will soon be using MediaPCs to distribute their content. In the world of a million choices, promotion becomes the heartbeat of a viable marketplace and perhaps of cultural change. Effective promotion is the main way consumers learn about what online content is available to watch, but the conventional practices of the past make up only part of the communication process; new promotion techniques are being created daily in an ever-changing media world.

SELECTED READINGS AND WEBSITES

Rainee, L., and Horrigan, J. (2005). *A Decade of Adoption: How the Internet has Woven Itself into American Life.* Report retrieved from *www.pewinternet.org/PPF/r/148/report_display.asp.*

Gertner, J. (2005). Our Ratings, Ourselves. *New York Times Sunday Magazine,* 10 April, pp. 34–41.

Masiclat, S. (2001). *Computer Usage Behaviors in the GenY Audience: A Study for Advance Internet and Syracuse.com.* Syracuse, New York: Syracuse University, October. Contact *masiclat@syr.edu* for a copy.

www.atomfilms.com
www.facebook.com
www.friendster.com
www.movielink.com
www.multichannel.com
www.shockwave.com
www.sonypictures.com/tv/shows.
www.titanicmovie.com
www.tvplex.go.com/touchstone
www.warnerbros.com/web/originals/

NOTES

1. Gertner, J. Our Ratings, Ourselves, *New York Times Sunday Magazine,* April 10, 2005. pp. 34–41.
2. Delany, K. C. *The Wall Street Journal,* April 9, 2005. Vol. CCXLIII, n. 70.
3. Online News release: Twentieth Television and Verizon Wireless Enter an Agreement On Direct-to-Mobile Series for New V CAST Service: *Twentieth Television to Produce 52 One-Minute "Mobisodes" of Two Original Soap Operas for Wireless Distribution with Verizon Wireless and Vodafone, www.news.vzw.com/news/2005/01/pr2005–01–24.html.*

CHAPTER 9

Promotion in Public Television and Radio

Robert K. Avery and Mary L. Dickson

Unlike commercial radio and television networks, the Public Broadcasting Service (PBS) and National Public Radio (NPR) are not centralized networks, but national systems of independent, locally-owned community voices. PBS and NPR are both partly government supported (unlike the other main noncommercial radio network, Public Radio International). All had to develop system-specific promotional strategies to protect their audience shares as they faced intensified competition from specialized cable, direct-broadcast channels, video on demand, and format-specific radio. An increased emphasis on sophisticated marketing and promotional strategies during the 1990s laid the groundwork for modest increases in audience size, and ultimately secured better funding both from viewers and listeners and from Congress for PBS and NPR.

THE ONGOING THREAT

Every time some members of Congress threaten to cut the federal portion of their funding, as senators and representatives do periodically, they claim that the commercial marketplace provides the same programming and services as public television and radio, and leave PBS and NPR in the unpleasant position of mounting nationwide self-defenses. So far, public broadcasting has been successful in responding to the duplication claim because the threats have repeatedly generated public outcry. Clear evidence of widespread grassroots support defining public television and radio as unique and essential comes from floods of letters and e-mails, reinforced by local financial donations and large institutional grants. The debate over federal funding for public broadcasting has been won not by those in the system, but by viewers and listeners convinced of its intrinsic value in their lives. Each time the question has arisen, the congressional voices have quieted, and federal funding has been renewed. Nonetheless, the threat continues to resurface, reminding public broadcasters of the continuing need to shape public attitudes by building and reinforcing strong brand identities.

Most recently, as the political climate changed in the early 2000s, public broadcasting came under attack once again, both from those on the right who charged a liberal bias in public affairs programming and from fiscal conservatives who, at a time of budgetary challenges, again questioned the relevancy of what were once accepted as public broadcasting's unique services. In response, NPR instituted a campaign addressed specifically to Congress in a series of ads published in the *National Journal*. The ads showcased different reasons why public radio is important and played up the impact of its listeners.[1] Addressing the Arizona congressional representatives, for example, an ad said "In Arizona, half a million constituents vote with their ears," meaning more than half a million voters listen to NPR. Another in the campaign was "Mississippi is fertile ground for NPR," speaking of public radio's in-depth coverage of news in the magnolia state. Still another political punch line was "Whether Ohioans go left or right, they always turn to NPR," and so on through the 50 states.

At mid-decade, viewers again rallied in support of public broadcasting and quieted congressional complaints by acknowledging the perceived value of PBS and NPR. Surveys conducted by various research organizations, including Roper Public Affairs & Media, have repeatedly shown that the public believes PBS programs are the most trusted on television. Despite bias claims, a 2003 nationwide study commissioned by the Corporation for Public Broadcasting (**CPB**) found that 79 percent of Americans do not believe that the news and information programming on public radio and public television have a liberal bias.

INSTITUTIONAL MARKETING

One driving goal of public broadcasting is to reinforce its value through strong **institutional promotion** — nationwide efforts on behalf of stations and the television and radio national networks. To survive, PBS and NPR have to go beyond providing high-quality programs; *they have to signal the value of those programs to viewers and listeners*, which, in turn, is expected to lead audiences to support those programs.

At the turn of the century, **brand management** became the buzzword in public television (PTV) because the growth of cable look-alikes — with the financial resources to extend their brands — had eroded PTV's brand image at the same time that the public system faced a federally-mandated transition to digital broadcasting. Not only was the world of a hundred or more channels a reality, but the media landscape was being further fragmented by technologies including the Internet, video and audio streaming, and video on demand — all of which had implications for how public broadcasting promotes and brands itself. To manage its valuable brand, PBS had to mount *unified national campaigns* that spelled out the value of public television as an institution and to institute *tune-in promotion* that reinforced the national campaigns.

Unified National Television Promotion

Some community-licensed stations achieved national status as regional production centers decades ago. WGBH, Boston; WNET, New York; WQED, Pittsburgh; WETA, Washington; WTTW, Chicago; and KCET, Los Angeles have long attracted underwriters that fund such major television series as *Nova, Masterpiece Theatre, Evening at Pops, The French Chef, National Geographic Specials*, and *Great Performances*. These core series have given public television a national identity, and such major underwriters as General Motors, Mobil, and Gulf recognized that if the programs they fund are not widely viewed, the productions are lost investments.

Although the dozen or so major producing stations clearly understand the importance of bringing an audience to their programs, their funds for program promotion are generally limited. Moreover, most of the 300+ other public-television stations in the country have still fewer dollars for promotion and so restrict their promotion to a small quantity of on-air promos, supplemented by occasional newspaper advertisements. Few stations have the resources or the marketing savvy to develop integrated institutional or image promotion campaigns. Because most stations also lack the resources to promote to any groups beyond their current viewers, their efforts tend toward **retention** not **acquisition**.

Because public broadcasters are generally a very independent lot who commit more than lip service to the concept of **localism**, they have traditionally scheduled programs as they thought best. Compounding the promotional problem, until the 1980s, PBS lacked any common national schedule, making successful national promotion virtually impossible. Any national tune-in advertising carried the tag, "check local listings for broadcast date and time," an ineffective means of driving viewers to programs. As communication scholar Thomas McCain once observed, "When you've seen one public television station, you've seen *one* public television station!"

A new era in public television's promotional efforts began when Lawrence Grossman became PBS president. Coming from the competitive ranks of commercial television, where fighting for a market share was critical, Grossman initiated strategies at both the network and station levels to counter-program commercial television stations. His greatest contribution was to institute a **common carriage schedule**, or the *core schedule*, during prime time from Sundays to Wednesdays. The results of common carriage were immediate and persuasive. *With a consistent evening program schedule, national advertising, and promotional campaigns, PBS was able to support the core programs in the major markets where they could enjoy high visibility and garner press attention.* Although the precise programs and time periods included in common carriage have changed, PBS has held to the strategy of enticing stations to participate in same-day common carriage by funding advertising in their local markets (an **incentive**).

Although the concept of **institutional positioning** was hardly new, it was close to revolutionary for a system built on the notion of "assumed virtue." In order to survive, PBS found it had to tell its story better, and reluctant stations had to buy into a unified branding message. But the rapid effects of common carriage on ratings and funding were powerful persuaders.

Much of PBS's success in positioning itself against specialized cable channels like The History Channel, Discovery, and A&E resulted from PBS's adopting such commercial network marketing strategies as **unified branding** (using the identical logos and themes in all promotional materials, publicity, and advertising). In the early 1990s, PBS began its strategy of hiring promotion directors straight from cable television, raising the sophistication of its acquisitive campaigns and retentive tune-in promotion.

Signaling Value

At the local level, stations across the country now focus attention on what makes public television not only different from commercial and cable stations, but valuable to the American public. *Signaling value is about positioning public television as a valuable resource; creating a strong, unified message; and then disseminating that message to all of public television's various constituencies such as viewers, funders, and legislators.*

To brand themselves as essential community institutions, one crucial element in getting stations was that PBS developed and disseminated professional development manuals to stations. These manuals provided practical methods for communicating the message to viewers that public stations bring such unique services as *locally produced programs* and *community outreach activities*. Station staffs are now trained in how to develop message points as the basic tools for communicating their value. **Message points** are positioning statements that specify **benefits** to audiences, not merely a bunch of changeable slogans or taglines. Once stations go through the process of articulating their positions and crafting dozens of message points that serve as "proofs" of that position, a process that is repeated periodically, they can use the manual's specific guidelines to integrate those positioning messages into all public communications — press releases, on-air announcements, brochures, speeches, letters, advertisements, development materials, and the station's program guide.

*The key to this station-wide strategy is the creation of several **boilerplate statements** in one or two sentences that signal the value of the station to the community served.* For example, in promoting its locally produced documentaries, KUED in Salt Lake City adopted the following statement: "KUED is the home to and creator of outstanding productions that preserve our unique legacy." Another message speaks to a diversity of programming serving a diversity of viewers, a theme that has been picked up across the country. In Utah, KUED speaks about "Celebrating Utah's Diverse Voices." In Indiana, diversity of programming and audiences was represented in a set of silhouettes shown in 9.1.

Integrating one of these messages into all public communications causes a station to speak with a single voice, regardless of the particular message or the target audience. Successful implementation depends on a shared vision by everyone on the station staff, so internal communication about the current message becomes vital. Moreover, increased **station buy-in** (compliance) has been the result of having local staff craft the on-air and print articulation of messages, even when they are part of a national strategy.

Ideally, each staff member, from tape room operators and front desk receptionists to general managers, are viewed as ambassadors who can deliver a station's messages. Department heads can lead their staffs in developing "proof of performance" objectives, along with identifying specific projects in programming, education, membership, underwriting, or outreach that can be leveraged to

9.1 *WTIU's tote bag promoting diversity in programming. Graphic by Milton Hamburger. Used with permission.*

deliver the station's institutional message. Through "Signaling Value" exercises, staff members learn to recognize and celebrate all station efforts that successfully signal value, and the local developmental process has become a rallying force for the separate departments at stations and a great method of team building.

One classic example concerns a janitor named Victor at WEDU in Tampa, Florida. When he happened to watch a performance featuring a relatively unknown musician named Yanni, he had the idea that the musician could excite public television viewers who might turn that excitement into financial support. At his station, he persuaded programming and membership to produce a Yanni pledge special. The rest is pledge history. Then-station-manager Stephen Rogers called it "our greatest success," meaning not the pledge dollars but the **participatory empowerment** that the signaling value exercise had given all staff members. His "Victor Factor" became a legend in public television, because not only was team-building a by-product, but WEDU saw viewership increased by 27 percent, underwriting by 30 percent, and membership dollars by 11 percent.

Pledge Drive Reinforcements

PBS supplies local stations with print ads and on-air promos carrying program-specific message points, particularly during pledge drives. These pledge messages, designed to reinforce core station messages, have been drawn from research on why people give to public television. Stations can develop **pledge scripts** (what station spokespeople say on the air during program breaks for fundraising), as well as on-air and print campaigns stressing how voluntary contributions underscore the value people place on public television. The paragraph in 9.2 illustrates a pledge script.

Individual stations continue to develop their own materials for signaling value, sometimes sharing them with other stations and with PBS. Several stations,

9.2 Pledge Script

Public television is made possible by the financial support of viewers like you. Viewer contributions represent public television's single greatest source of funding. In partnership with government, corporations, and foundations, viewers have made public television an essential educational institution within their communities. When you join WXXX, you are joining more than 5 million families nationwide in saying that public television makes a difference in your life.

for example, use filmed viewer **testimonials**, letting viewers themselves signal the value of the station, a strategy that is often more convincing than using station staff. Such positioning spots can also easily be tagged with messages that encourage membership.

PBS kicked off its Fall 1990 season with the first-ever Showcase Week, a tactic designed to encourage viewers to sample the full range of PBS programming. Leading into Showcase Week was a bold programming maneuver — airing Ken Burns' *The Civil War* for five consecutive evenings. PBS heavily promoted Showcase Week on the national and local level, and for the first time invested in prime-time national tune-in advertising on commercial broadcast and cable networks, a practice that continues to the extent that PBS can afford it and their commercial competitors will permit it.

BRANDING PUBLIC TELEVISION

Building public television's brand really started with its commitment to common carriage because that ensured its best programs found consistent time slots across the nation. Next, branding promotion had to capitalize on the trust viewers placed in public television programming. PBS encouraged stations to develop promotional campaigns highlighting the uniqueness of public television's programs. The national slogan, "If PBS doesn't do it, who will?" was adapted by local stations to highlight their own original, locally-produced programs. In Salt Lake City, as shown in the newspaper ad in 9.3, proof-of-performance spots for local productions and for outreach activities were consistently tagged with "If KUED doesn't do it, who will?"

Such campaigns have effectively *branded* public television stations as unique educational and cultural institutions in their markets, in contrast to the host of other program services available on the television set. Using such positioning slogans also lets stations focus on their own special roles in their respective communities. The notion of **localism** — a station's ability to provide locally-produced programs and activities — has always been extremely important to public stations. Although PBS's programs may be the engines that drive viewers to the stations, local promotion directors wanted to preserve their own individual and *local* brands in the minds of their viewers to create loyalty that translates to local financial support. Some national and local press releases included all or part of the messages in 9.4 as closing statements to reinforce the benefits of public broadcasting.

Once viewers consciously or subconsciously appreciated the greater benefits of public television, they would use it more, it was hoped, and gain more satisfaction. Over a period of years, such unified messages repositioned public television in the minds of viewers as valuable and distinctive community resources.

9.3 *"If KUED doesn't do it, who will?" Used with permission.*

9.4 Closing Statements for Press Releases

The Public Broadcasting Service, a longtime leader in advancing communications technology for public service, is a private, nonprofit media enterprise owned and operated by the nation's 349 public television stations. A trusted community resource, PBS uses the power of noncommercial television, the Internet, and other media to enrich the lives of all Americans through high-quality programs and education services that inform, inspire, and delight. Available to 99 percent of American homes with televisions and to an increasing number of digital multimedia households, PBS serves nearly 100 million people each week.

Evolving Tune-In Messages

Nonetheless, after the turn of the century, such genre channels as Discovery, A&E, The History Channel, and The Learning Channel had taken large bites from the traditional PBS audience, driving the PBS Advertising and Promotion staff to build its audience numbers by pulling viewers away from commercial — and, in some markets, other public — stations. Active **counter-promotion** against cable had become PBS's paramount goal, but first, PBS faced the problem of convincing local stations that these specialized cable channels — not local commercial stations — posed a significant threat to public television. It accomplished that by changing its positioning message.

The popular "If PBS Doesn't Do It, Who Will?" campaign became increasingly irrelevant when competing cable networks began offering the same kinds of genre programs. PBS therefore launched a new positioning campaign, called "Stay Curious," and phased out "who will?" The new campaign featured storytelling spots that captured a moment when someone satisfied his or her curiosity in a uniquely creative way (look back at 5.2, which is part of this same campaign). On-air promos integrated the new "Stay Curious" tagline. The slogan capitalized on viewers' presumed love of learning and apparently boundless curiosity. PBS referred to this target audience as "stimulation seekers," who are naturally curious. A "Stay Curious" manual distributed to all stations provided practical suggestions for incorporating the new campaign. As an **incentive**, PBS provided an "early adopters" grant to stations that used the new package's easily incorporated tagline that could fit into all station materials, from on-air spots to ads to brochures, such as in 9.5.

9.5　*KUED ad: "Stay Curious." Used with permission.*

Just as "Stay Curious" was taking root among viewers, PBS switched to yet another tagline — the "Be More" campaign. Like previous campaigns, PBS's next strategic positioning campaign included an on-air design package, a print package, and other elements, as well as new on-air spots. In a memo to stations, PBS Head of Branding and Promotion, Lesli Rotenberg, explained that PBS and its audience shared core values. "In the end, these shared values boil down to something quite simple: PBS stations inspire people to Know More, Do More and Be More," and PBS distilled the idea to "two simple words: Be More."[2] As part of the campaign, PBS distributed a set of adjectives stations could use with "Be More." Wisconsin Public TV was quick to merge the two campaigns by using "Be more curious" as its slogan.

Co-Branding Strategies

The PBS brand became Rotenberg's mantle. Research showed that the PBS brand was exceptionally strong, and that most viewers identified their local public television stations with PBS. Stations, however, were not uniformly taking advantage of associating with the PBS brand. Indeed, a few stations, particularly the large producing stations, saw their own brands as stronger than the PBS brand. Many did not consistently use the PBS logo on the air or on any of their materials. Some stations took the spots PBS fed and replaced the PBS logo with their own station logos on the end frame.

Furthermore, surveys showed that cable niche services competing with public television had so successfully branded themselves that PBS viewers were confused and actually thought that some PBS programs aired on a cable competitor. To reduce the likelihood of such confusion, PBS began following the industry practice of placing its translucent PBS logo **bug** on most programs.

At the same time, PBS began an aggressive campaign to encourage stations to **co-brand** by placing the PBS "P-head" logo alongside their own station logos in station IDs, prime-time spots, kids' spots, pledge spots, and positioning spots, as well as in print, signage, websites, educational materials, special events, and all station efforts. Extensive use of the co-branding concept was encouraged in virtually all promotional materials, and by mid-decade, PBS had persuaded most stations to adopt a **co-branded bug** to air on their programs (a bug combining the local and PBS-head logos). PBS now distributes various options for co-branding to stations, including several samples of how to combine the two logos, leaving it to stations to select the most suitable one for them. (Using the PBS logo alone as a bug is limited to PBS-distributed programs and materials.) A handful of stations have even changed their names to incorporate the PBS brand; for instance to PBS Hawaii, Rocky Mountain PBS, and as shown in the logos in 9.6, to Montana PBS and Rhode Island PBS.

9.6   *Montana PBS and Rhode Island PBS logos. Used with permission.*

Because the PBS brand continues to be one of the strongest media brands in the nation, the philosophy behind much of PBS's institutional promotion is that viewers not only expect to find much higher quality programs on public television, but more important, that these programs have a far greater impact on them and their communities than other television programs. Moreover, because PBS's on-air positioning campaigns clearly differentiate PBS member stations from competitors by emphasizing the benefits viewers derive from watching, the member stations can safely assert that they deserve the financial support of viewers.

PBS PROGRAM PROMOTION

Faced with increased competition for viewers, PBS has ratcheted up its promotional and advertising campaigns for individual programs. Based on data derived from audience testing at four pilot stations (KUAT in Tucson, Maine Public Television, WNET in New York, and WVIZ in Cleveland), PBS was determined to beat the cable channels seeking the same educational niche at their own branding game. The principle focuses of its **competitive strategies** were The History Channel and Discovery, because research indicated the greatest amount of audience confusion existed regarding which channel viewers actually were watching.

A PBS tracking study had previously revealed that some 56 percent of the study's respondents rated Discovery as their first choice for nature programs, compared to 14 percent for PBS. Discovery also got top marks for science programs, and The History Channel beat out PBS in the history program category.[3]

Yet these results failed to match standard Nielsen television ratings data showing that public television had much higher regular viewing across all three of these programming genres.

The Bundling and Scheduling Solutions

The problem, according to a PBS promotion executive, was that since cable channels have been so aggressive in promoting their genre-associated names, viewers tend to think they are watching one of the competitors when they actually are tuned to their local PBS station. PBS responded first by **bundling** its history programs so they could be labeled with a "History's Best on PBS" promotion campaign, and second by giving them *consistent scheduling positions* on Monday nights. The PBS staff then worked through the other genres in an effort to take the competition head on. Underlying its promotion was the message that PBS had the "best" of each genre, whereas the cable channels (that had to keep their respective genre programs on the air 24 hours a day) could not possibly maintain consistent quality.

Keeping viewers on track about their programming sources got more difficult as programs that once were the exclusive province of public television were later syndicated to the cable competition by program producers. For example, such popular children's shows as *Sesame Street* and *The Magic School Bus* began to appear on both cable and broadcast television stations. In 1998, Nickelodeon bought the rights to the entire output of the Children's Television Workshop (meaning the cornerstone *Sesame Street* series) for its new commercial-free network The Noggin. Additionally, episodes of *Mystery!* began to air on the A&E channel. In their effort to expand profits, program producers were compromising traditional **exclusivity**.

While the major cable competitors had ample funds to purchase programs, PBS would have to increase station dues — an unpopular move among stations — to have the resources it needed to compete more aggressively to purchase programming rights. Some station managers argued at annual meetings that self-interest should drive stations to pay slightly higher dues in order to ensure that important programs remained in their schedules. But many stations, already struggling with tight budgets, claimed they couldn't make the sacrifice.

Additionally, the commercially supported cable channels, with their massive promotion budgets, had the means to successfully convince audiences that they could find their favorite programs on cable. In response to cable's promotional spending, PBS upped its promotion budget to about 10 percent of its total budget. Even so, it still spends far less on promotion than its cable competitors. *The Newshour*'s Jim Lehrer has advocated that public television stations ideally should spend one dollar for advertising a program for every dollar they spent producing it — an ideal that continues to be unrealistic and unheard of in the public television world.

Tune-In Strategies

Audiences are rapidly adopting such new delivery technologies as DVDs, digital cable, satellite, broadband, and TiVo, and households commonly have three, four, and five television sets. More than half of viewers make their programming decisions with the remote in hand. None of this bodes well for any television stations. Furthermore, prime-time audience research conducted in 2004 showed that *the biggest competition for viewers came not from so many channel choices or from look-alike cable competitors, but from people's busy lives.*[4] People have changed the way they use television. They simply aren't watching as much television as previously, and when they do, they want escape and background noise. As pointed out in Chapter 6, television viewing across the spectrum has been declining for some years. Nonetheless, PBS is at least managing to hold steady in this environment. *No longer is public broadcasting's main goal to increase audience size; it has shifted to maintaining current audience levels.*

For PBS, the very nature of its schedule presents promotional challenges. Some 2004 research showed that the biggest barrier to watching PBS programs was not knowing when they were on. Almost two-thirds of viewers said they didn't know when programs aired on PBS, while 10 percent thought the system had no schedule at all. One cause of this difficulty is that PBS carries relatively few regular series, which viewers have come to expect from networks. Furthermore, mini-series and program stunts, including two-night specials, are common programming practices at PBS. *By far the largest segment of the PBS schedule is made up of one-time-only programs, which are not only the hardest for viewers to find, but the most difficult to promote.* Local stations offer even fewer weekly series, although a few, such as *Oregon Art Beat, Tennessee Crossroads,* and *Greater Boston,* have gained loyal local audiences. Additionally, PBS interrupts its schedule during its pledge drives, which adds to viewer confusion.

Because of their regular presence, **series** *are the easiest programs to promote, but PBS does not emphasize series as much as* **specials** *in its program lineup.* Given a large number of programs to promote and limited resources, as a solution, PBS borrowed the strategy of selective monthly program promotion from premium cable practices, calling it **KEY** program promotion. PBS began giving priority to two or three common carriage programs each month, tagging them for high viewer and press attention at the local and network levels. A formula for each station for generating gross rating points (**GRP**s; based on three exposures per viewer) spells out a station's target for audience impressions. PBS also provides each station with suggested spot rotations, including the most effective placements of spots for these KEY programs.

At the station level, effective promotion of KEY programs needs to begin one month in advance of the airdate to achieve assigned GRP levels. In addition to a package of 10-second teasers and 30-second spots — often of the behind-the-scenes variety—PBS's materials for each KEY program include press releases, 30-second radio spots, feature stories, talent bios, photos, and ad slicks that can be tailored to the station's advertising needs. If this is beginning to sound a lot like the long-time practices of commercial television, it is no coincidence.

At the national level, PBS buys ads for KEY programs in *TV Guide* magazine and newspaper inserts such as *TV Week*, incorporating station logos for each market (**co-branding**). The ads mention PBS's airdate, but not airtime to allow for variations in scheduling by multiple stations in the region the publication serves. As another incentive for stations, PBS negotiated a contract with *TV Guide* that enables stations to place ads at a discount in order to advertise specials and series beyond the targeted KEY programs of the month. This strategy has resulted in impressive increases in ratings.[5] Higher ratings for KEY programs have been consistent, firmly embedding the KEY strategy in public television's promotional armament.

Increasing Time-Spent-Viewing

The next strategy devised to compliment the promotion of KEY programs is what the network advertising and promotion departments call **pop-outs**. The pop-out promotional strategy gives two to four programs in a season — those best at branding public television as unique — a heightened promotional push. This push includes augmented paid media, ad grants to local stations, special events, and features via PBS Online, the network's in-house website. The goal of identifying and providing support for pop-outs is to maintain current viewing levels through on-air promotion, publicity efforts, and station program guides and to attract new and occasional viewers through paid advertising. Like the KEY program promotion, the pop-outs have been judged highly successful.

To build on its national efforts, PBS also offers incentives to stations in the form of advertising grants for additional promotion of the programs it deems important pop-outs. KERA in Dallas, for instance, supplemented PBS's extensive national advertising and promotion campaign for *Jack Johnson* by using advertising and publicity off-air to draw KERA audiences to the show. By giving an added push to what PBS had identified as one of the shows best at brand definition (a pop-out), KERA scored a record-breaking 5.2 rating and a 7 percent share.

Leap-Frog Promotion

Of course, once viewers tune in to pop-out programs, PBS embeds a preview for the next "best" coming attraction of the same type. This encourages viewers to stay tuned longer and "leap" from one show to the next and the next, such as from *Deep Jungle* to *NOVA Science Now* to *Scientific America Frontiers* to *National Geographic*. As a result of this **leap-frogging** strategy, pop-outs perform about 75 percent above the prime-time average.

In the 2005 season, PBS designated four programs — *American Masters: Bob Dylan; Rx for Survival; Frontline: Country Boys;* and *Texas Ranch House* — as pop-outs. They also designated related programs for viewers to jump to as part of a leapfrog package. Unfortunately, these pop-outs represent only a small percentage of the total PBS programming schedule. Because PBS's advertising budget can't support adding more pop-outs, having a few of these super promotional events each year isn't enough to increase overall audience size.

Consequently, PBS focuses on its own airtime by using leap-frogging packages. Nationally, PBS has the opportunity to reach an average of 2.3 million people with **lower-third messages** embedded inside its prime-time content. In the marketplace, it would cost $25 million dollars to buy access to this audience over the course of a year. PBS now embeds promotion for about three or four dozen programs per month, and modest but consistent ratings demonstrate the value of this strategy. It is an approach that not only delivers more viewers to programs, but delivers more viewers to station breaks carrying "next-on" promotional information (**advance titling**).

LOCAL PTV PROMOTION

The advertising and promotion departments at public stations operate with a sophistication usually comparable to that of their immediate commercial competitors. Budgets and staffs, however, vary greatly from one public station to another, leaving some stations with only their own air and program guides for promotion and other stations operating with substantial external advertising budgets. Despite the disparities in market size and budget, several local promotion strategies characterize virtually all local stations.

On-Air Breaks

On-air promotion time is a valuable commodity at all stations, and the amount of time available for on-air promotion is a major difference between public and commercial television. *In commercial programs, about 14 minutes of every half-hour are eaten up by breaks, but because public television airs programs without interruption, its break time comes only at the ends of programs.* Because PBS carries few 30-minute programs, breaks typically occur at hourly intervals, although some PBS programs run 90 minutes or as long as two hours. Occasionally, some programs, such as a *Great Performances* or *Live From Lincoln Center* offering, run as long as three hours, in which case PBS often adds a built-in "intermission" break — which it fills with positioning spots and promos for upcoming specials.

Public television stations not only have less time in which to promote their own programs and services, but their breaks must be shared with other station business such as underwriting credits, development messages, institutional spots, and event announcements, as well as **station IDs**. Therefore, in a two-and-a-half minute break, often only two 30-second spots can be devoted to program promotion.

Without question, *on-air time remains television's most valuable resource for communicating with its audience*, and when it comes to leveraging on-air breaks for promotional purposes, cable and commercial stations clearly outperform PBS stations. For instance, the annual promo value of PBS breaks runs about $84 million, while look-alike cable station Discovery has an annual break value of over $373 million, and A&E's breaks are worth over $228 million. Commercial network affiliate breaks, however, are estimated at an average value of $2.1 billion.[6]

Almost all stations construct their own breaks between programs. The length of these breaks can vary greatly depending on the running time of the before and after programs. Some prime-time breaks are 3½ minutes, while others are as long as 12 minutes. At local stations on-air producers create promos by tagging PBS-created spots or by developing original spots from program video when none have been made or when programs come from another program provider (such as programs from American Public Television, many of which come from Britain). The breaks themselves are scheduled by station traffic departments, with input from promotion departments on effective placement strategies.

Although public television breaks can be as short as 2½ minutes, viewers perceive the breaks as longer. When the local station break is combined with the non-programming material built into the end of the PBS program, the "perceived" break time seems longer than the comparable break on commercial television.[7] A public television break with closing production credits, book offers, national underwriting credits, local underwriting credits, website spots, and a couple of program promos makes the viewers feel that public television breaks are as cluttered as the commercial television landscape.

Based on research that closing credits with simply a voice-over are far less likely to lead to viewer departure than text-only credits, stations often begin their local breaks with **voice-overs** that reach targeted audiences before the actual break begins. These placements are valuable promotional tools not only for the related programs but more specifically for maintaining audience flow to what is coming up next. Because public TV breaks obviously do not include elements that sell products, they are devoted to four other things:

- Selling shows — horizontally, vertically, by genre, and for appointment viewing
- Increasing viewer and corporate funding

- Building the brand
- Maintaining audience flow

Ideally, because the majority of programming choices are made by channel surfing, public stations try to capture viewers who are avoiding commercials and who pause at video that most resembles actual programming by creating spots that are less frantic than those found on commercial television. Typically, after local underwriting credits, station breaks start with a program tune-in promo that is attractive to the viewers of the previous program. They then may move to a promo of contrasting tone and content. This may promote a weekly series or may be a station or PBS positioning spot. Preferably, it will not be another tune-in spot because that might confuse the viewer by adding an airdate and time to the one to be remembered from the previous promo. The next element may be a longer program promo, perhaps bundling several programs like the next night's lineup (**multiple spot**), which can be remembered as a group with no need for specific recall. Along the way, there may be a membership promotion for something like **planned giving** (for example, for donors to bequeath their estates) or even a website promo. The final element often is combined with the station identifier.

PBS has two disadvantages concerning station breaks: Not only do they have fewer breaks, but they have the worst place to speak to audiences because viewers are free to change channels at the ends of programs — the only place PBS has breaks. Moreover, *underwriting elements are by necessity the first item in a break, another reason viewers tune out.* PBS urges stations to put promos first in the break, but this is not possible for many local stations that must take care of business first. PBS also urges stations to be ruthless about what they allow in their breaks and to wipe out boring elements. PBS has also toyed with split-screen credits and with embedded promotion, common practices on commercial networks. While commercial networks have had success with **seamless transitions** between programs, PBS has no such flexibility, although some stations have experimented with collapsing breaks to hold audience. For instance, KUED collapsed breaks between its Saturday morning How-To programs, airing shows back-to-back in packages branded as "Fix It Up" or "Cook It Up." The station saw ratings jump during its Saturday dayparts as a result.

Program Guides

Since the founding of public television in the early 1950s, stations have promoted their own unique identities and program services by offering monthly *program* or *viewing guides* to members who contribute financially to the station. The guides are a staple for attracting viewers to become members ("friends") of the station through a basic membership gift usually in the range of $35 to $50. A guide normally contains the monthly program listings, weekday schedule, and feature stories about upcoming specials and series, both national and local. It also may include station highlights, articles on and photos of special events, donor salutes, underwriter lists, advertising, and a general manager's letter.

Viewing guide surveys consistently show that readers want the program information the guide delivers — what is on and when — and all else is peripheral. As television schedules in most newspapers provide less and less program information beyond program titles, PTV viewers rely on their station guides for program content information. The guide is also a major outlet for delivering the station's "message points," through regular features on its broadcast and nonbroadcast services to its community. Both public radio and television stations create local guides for their members, as in the example in 9.7 featuring Guns, Germs and Steel. Because of the cost of printed guides, however, more stations are beginning to explore online program guides.

9.7 *KUED program guide cover. Used with permission.*

Stations that **tradeout** advertising with local businesses and cultural organizations (symphony, theater guild, opera company, art museum, and so on) frequently offer a member card in conjunction with the program guide subscription. In return for on-air underwriting announcements and mention in the program guide, these businesses and organizations will provide free tickets, meals, or services during the station's pledge drives and also two-for-the-price-of-one benefits to member cardholders. Beyond the promotional advantages for emphasizing educational, cultural, and corporate partnerships with the community, program guides have enormous value to the station because listings often employ graphic layouts that emphasize locally produced programs, major program genres, and repeat program schedules, plus **tie-ins** to other station services.

Websites

The PBS website, which has won numerous awards for its rich content, is home to comprehensive companion websites for more than 1,000 PBS programs and specials, with more than 150,000 pages of easily searchable content. PBS promotes its website in on-air promotion, publicity, and paid advertising, touting its online services and links to local stations and other educational outlets. PBS pioneered the use of the Internet — way before many commercial networks got the point — to extend its content and provide supplementary value to its viewers. Today, local public stations have embraced websites for three reasons:

- They provide program and station information to viewers
- They supplement program content with resource materials
- They promote station services and activities

PBS provides web guidelines to stations, as well as content, graphics, and promotional materials for use on the web to local stations. The majority of public stations have developed their own websites that also link back to the PBS site. The quality, depth, and extent of station sites vary widely; some stations simply link to the customizable PBS site, but many have developed robust, content-rich sites that offer extensive sub-sites for local productions as well as material for educators, and some offer video and audio streaming. Some stations employ a dedicated web master, and others add web duties to the activities of other staff. A major producing station like WGBH in Boston has an extensive, content-rich site with an entire department devoted to interactive content (see *www.wgbh.org*).

Direct Mail/E-mail

Public stations have been using **direct mail** to solicit contributions and communicate with viewers for many years. Targeting community organizations and demographic groups to receive special communications about upcoming programs is a regular promotional strategy at stations. To save money and better use technology, however, stations are increasingly replacing postal mailings with targeted e-mails to viewers. *Having a wide variety of databases, keyed to specific program genres, is an extremely effective way of promoting upcoming programs, series, and events.* Local stations also have replaced postal distribution of news releases with electronic releases. In addition to media outlets, station promotion staffs typically maintain distribution lists for special interest groups and donors. Some even provide e-mail notification services to individual viewers who want to know about program schedule changes or program repeats. Promoters can readily expand and refine their e-mail lists by gathering information from attendees at station events and taking information from callers during pledge drives.

At both commercial and public stations, e-mail addressed to a local station's account typically goes to the station's promotion staff. It is the staff's responsibility to answer viewer inquiries or pass the messages on to appropriate departments for handling. *The timely handling of incoming e-mail has become as important to a station's public relations efforts as prompt and efficient handling of telephone calls.*

Like cable networks and web services, as illustrated in Chapter 8, PBS uses **electronic newsletters**, generally sent out on a weekly basis. These e-letters have become another promotional tool for most public stations. Typically, e-news is used to highlight upcoming programs, share station news, and announce upcoming events. Brief items in the e-news are linked to pages with more information. Just as the monthly program guide serves as a periodic reminder of the station's appreciation of the member's support, electronic forms of communication serve to signal the bond that exists between a public TV station and the audience it serves. It reinforces the concept that viewers are the "public" in public television.

Advertising Trades

Regardless of its size, a local station's promotion budget is never enough, and **tradeouts** are a means for bartering airtime for merchandise and services. In public television, trades often include a mix of cash and in-kind support or complimentary advertising in return for on-air underwriting credits. Interpretations as to what constitutes appropriate underwriting recognition vary widely from station to station, but even the most conservative guidelines include use of corporate logos, slogans, and product lines.

Stations make trade agreements with daily newspapers, weekly newspapers, magazines, radio stations, play bills for the performing arts, radio stations, and even on occasion have secured trade with local cable systems. Many stations double the reach of their advertising budgets using tradeouts, while some stations are totally dependent on trades alone for any advertising they do. Stations also use tradeouts for public relations and advertising consultants, photography, design and graphic services, and printing — all of which help make promotional activities possible.

One of the most effective in-kind advertising venues for local public television is local public radio, and virtually all public television stations take advantage of cross-promotional opportunities with local public radio stations. Because their audiences don't always have similar demographics, promotion must be carefully targeted to appeal to a desired audience.

Public television and radio are used very differently. *Public television has greater reach, but people tend to "sample," using it for a shorter period of time (an hour or two), while public radio is used by fewer people for longer amounts of time (all morning, all evening).* Consequently, television usually provides radio with fewer exposures in exchange for many radio exposures that provide the repetition so essential for behavioral change.

PUBLIC RADIO PROMOTION

The promotional strategies used by public radio more closely parallel those of commercial radio than those of public television. First, as suggested above, the radio medium is used differently than television, thus dictating different acquisitive and retentive strategies. Second, the programming strategies differ considerably: Public radio stations tend to have at least as many local programs as national or syndicated offerings, and public radio stations generally have a strong local presence *within* national programs. For example, public radio stations commonly insert local newscasts and features in National Public Radio's *Morning Edition*, sometimes occupying as much as one-third of the total program.

While many of the rules that apply to commercial radio apply equally to public radio, contrasting missions and means of support add a unique dimension to promoting public radio programs. Simply put, the role of commercial radio is to deliver an audience to advertisers. In contrast, for public radio to survive, each station must develop an audience so *loyal* that it will send money to keep the station on the air and so *distinctive* that it will attract businesses that will pay to reach these listeners with their program underwriting and sponsorship messages. *Public radio's strategy must include the usual goals of acquiring and retaining listeners, with the added goal of converting some of those listeners into paying members.*

Listeners become members because they believe the station, or more accurately the programming, is *personally* important. One promotion objective, therefore, is to get the listener to use the station more often. But, unlike commercial stations, public stations cannot buy loyalty with forced-listening promotions such as contests and giveaways. Indeed, the process of turning a listener into a member can take years. Although increasing the number of people that listen (**cume audience**) and their time-spent-listening (**TSL**) are both important, the critical objective is to attract listeners and lead them to become contributing members.

Actual listening, as opposed to *reported* listening, becomes crucial to promoting public radio, and the spectrum of listeners includes those who are not aware of public radio and those who are shareholders in their local public radio station. Promotion and advertising must speak to both groups, as well as to those people quite aware of the service but not donors, often because of small incomes.

Meanwhile, marketing's **20/80 rule** applies to public radio. The rule suggests that 20 percent of some audience or readership will be active and responsive, while 80 percent will be passive. For public radio, this means that about 20 percent of listeners contribute the bulk of pledges, and the other 80 percent remain only listeners. Therefore, *concentrating on upgrading membership levels and satisfying large donors* (called "supersizing the core") *usually results in more revenue for the station than focusing on small donors*. In other words, stations must cater to the program preferences and interests of the **core audience** that is responsible for the bulk of the financial contributions. This ever-increasing fund-raising/programming dilemma has generated considerable criticism from scholars who argue that targeting the affluent audience members, who are largely white, violates the service mission of serving a diverse population — the very public for whom *public* broadcasting was created. However, the reality of generating adequate financial resources to keep the stations on the air forces this too-familiar practice.

Hard to Promote Programming

Public stations also differ from their commercial counterparts in programming strategy. While most commercial stations air the same formats throughout the broadcast day, most public stations air two or more formats, such as public affairs and music (usually classical and jazz), with blocks of diverse programming. *Having multiple formats not only tends to give public stations an inconsistent on-air sound, it also makes it harder to promote the stations.* Listeners don't know when to tune in to hear their favorite format and will tune out when the program format changes.

Research consultants have also suggested that classical listeners as a subset of the total audience were not paying their fair share, were growing older, and were disrupting the flow of programming for public affairs listeners attracted by such highly acclaimed NPR programs as *Morning Edition* and *All Things Considered*. Despite the outcry from loyal classical fans and the rallying of community fine arts groups such as local symphony and opera companies, the trend toward eliminating the daytime classical music has spread among public stations across the nation. In cities with major music schools, however, music may remain the top program favorite, and program guides can be used to keep listeners aware of regular and special programs. The cover of WTIU's monthly radio guide, *Directions in Sound* in 9.8, illustrates the high level of much of public radio music programming where it still persists.

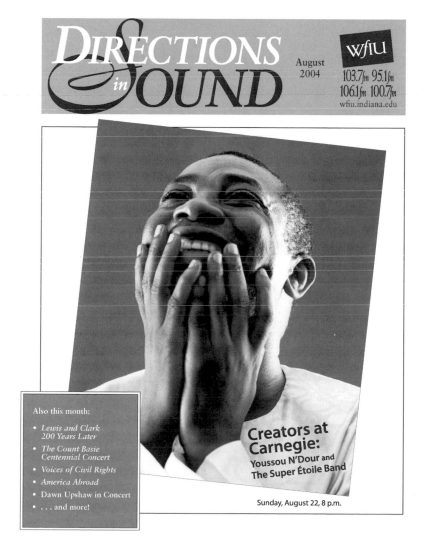

9.8 *WFIU's program guide, showing Youssou N'Dour at Carnegie Hall. Used with permission.*

Some observers suggest that the September 11, 2001, terrorist attacks on the World Trade Center were at least partly responsible for the general trend away from music. Following the attacks, a new audience of listeners hungry for serious, in-depth coverage of news events was attracted to public radio as never before. This influx of listeners wanting a steady diet of public affairs programming forced many stations to recognize that they could no longer risk losing those important audience members. Keeping a public affairs format during the daytime with jazz or classical in the evening or late night has resulted in a growing dependence on news/talk offerings from National Public Radio, Public Radio International, and American Public Media, along with a variety of other program syndicators. Although more than 300 public radio stations still report that classical music is an important part of their broadcast schedules, the mainstay of the public radio industry has become news and public affairs.

Setting Goals

Whether for public television or radio, a promotional strategy requires measurable goals. One standard might be the station's cume or average quarter-hour (AQH) audience; another might be the level of listener contributions. Either of these measures can be influenced by effective promotion. The precise goal will determine how messages are crafted and which media are used.

If a station's goal is to increase the audience for a certain program or in a certain daypart, the promotion director must first decide from where the audience should come. *As a general rule, most promotion and advertising affects* **which station** *a person listens to at a particular time, not* **whether** *a person listens.* Hence, the promotion director's objective is to get people to listen to a specific public station when they would otherwise be listening to a competitor. The audience targeted for the station's promotional appeals consists of two groups: people who already listen to the station but not at the desired time, and people who never listen to the public station (parallel to **formers** and **nevers** in cable). Formers can be reached through on-air and off-air (**external**) promotion strategies, but the nevers can be reached only off the air and are much more difficult to influence.

It seems only natural that the audience-building process would start with acquiring then retaining listeners. But in public radio, the process usually works in reverse. Many stations have established firm program schedules and try only to increase TSL by existing audiences. Retaining listeners for longer periods of time is especially important given public radio's reliance on listener contributions. *The promotion director's main objective, then, is to get current listeners to use the station more often and to listen for longer periods.* This strategy builds TSL and AQH, which are leading indicators of whether a listener is likely to become a contributor.

NPR adopted a positioning campaign called "Voices of NPR" to create an image that served multiple functions. First, the poster put faces with the familiar voices heard on NPR (see 9.9) and brought those faces to the communities where NPR stations were heard. Second, the poster created a connection between local station staff and NPR personalities by making the poster a regular decorative item in public radio offices and studios across the country. Third, the poster brought the program and fundraising functions together by creating a gift that could be distributed to major donors, given away at special events, and offered as a "Thank You" gift to fund-drive volunteers.

And finally, the collective images of national NPR radio voices served as an incentive for local stations to create ads, posters, and other visuals that celebrated and promoted local station personalities. The RadioWest Voices poster in 9.10 adapts the national campaign to Salt Lake City.

Promo Scheduling

Public radio stations commonly use tactics of *forward, cross*, and *horizontal* promotion to change or reinforce listener behavior. **Forward promotion** is a variant of the teaser that attempts to increase the duration of each tune-in. It gives the current listener a reason to stay tuned for what is to follow. Copy that begins "Stay tuned for . . ." is forward promotion. Always program-specific, forward promotion touts the immediately upcoming program.

Cross-promotion, on the other hand, attempts to increase how often an individual tunes in. Cross-promotion encourages the listener to sample similar programs at another time of the day. Generic or specific, it should promote programs having demographics or psychographics matching those of the program in which the promo is inserted. **Horizontal promotion**, the third tactic, attempts to increase the number of tune-ins by an individual. It encourages a listener to sample the next installment of a stripped program (on at the same time the next day or week) or the next segment of a mini-documentary that has been spread across multiple news days. Copy that reads "Tune in again tomorrow for Part 3 of . . ." is an example of horizontal promotion. The copy for forward, cross, and horizontal promotion strategies often is similar, but their placement differs. Consider this fictitious copy for NPR's *Weekend Edition*:

> Saturday on *Weekend Edition,* the Secretary of State tells her version of why U.S. troops remain in Iraq. This and much more when NPR correspondent John Smith holds a Washington newsmaker's feet to the fire on *Weekend Edition*, this Saturday morning, beginning at 8 o'clock here on WXXX, FM 90.

9.9 *Voices of NPR poster. Used with permission.*

9.10 *KUER RadioWest Voices poster. Used with permission.*

If the copy is read within Friday's *Morning Edition*, the promotion is horizontal; its purpose is to remind listeners that they can get the news at the same time on the next day. If this same promo runs on Friday afternoon during *All Things Considered*, this cross-promotion is now intended to get listeners to sample a different program with similar appeal at a quite different time of day. Finally, when the announcer reads the same promo for *Weekend Edition* very early Saturday morning before the program goes on the air, it becomes forward promotion, intended to keep listeners from tuning out.

Increasingly, local stations have been guided in their scheduling of on-air promos by adhering to concepts gleaned from research data. One of the most popular approaches to promotion spot placement is called **optimum effective scheduling** (OES), which calculates the number of times in a week a message needs to air to reach a particular station's entire audience. The first step is to calculate the turnover ratio by dividing the station's cumulative (cume) audience by the average quarter-hour audience (AQH). Then multiply that number (turnover ratio) by the OES spot factor of 3.29. The resulting figure is the number of times a promo needs to run each week to achieve total audience saturation.

Research Findings for Public Radio

A CPB study found that no two public radio stations promoted programming the same way, and that the majority of the stations in the system were not following the standards suggested by earlier research studies.[8] The recommendations called for stations to adhere to the three R's of program promotion: *reduction, repetition,* and *real content.*

The report argued that in order to air program promos often enough for listeners to remember their essential information, there needed to be a *reduction in the number of different promos being aired simultaneously*. In other words, stations should do away with the practice of trying to promote every program during the week and focus promos on two or three promotional priorities. By doing this, a far greater opportunity occurs for the *repetition of the selected promos*. Stations reported airing a promo an average of eight times a week, which is roughly one-seventh of the recommendation suggested by OES. The final "R" — *real content* — refers to the writing, production, and aesthetics of the promo itself. Far too many promos fail to be written in response to a *specific promotional objective that has measurable criteria*. Station staff members are often unable to talk about a promotional objective in terms that can be translated into the creative process of writing and producing the promo. Such abstract statements as "increase audience awareness," "develop listener appreciation," or "build the number of listeners" offer little guidance for the creation of effective promotional messages. The CPB-supported project called for greater coordination at the national and local levels, and NPR has responded to the challenge.

National Promotional Support

From an historical standpoint, many of the promotional initiatives of the 21st century linking NPR with its member stations can be traced to two decisions made by network executives in 1998. First, after target audience testing of the network's "radio waves" logo, NPR executives conceded what stations had been saying about NPR's corporate logo for many months — it was confusing, difficult to read, and did not lend itself to co-branding in print ads. The result was a new "clean" logo, designed by an identity consulting firm, that shows the NPR letters on three individual blocks. Unlike the radio waves, the block logo permits a reverse image of the letters for black-and-white print ads. The previous and current NPR logos are compared in 9.11.

Within months, public radio stations from coast to coast were redesigning their station logos and experimenting with more effective co-branding. Stations

9.11 *Old wave and new block NPR logos. Used with permission.*

kuer
FM90

kuerFM90

kuer
FM90

9.12   *KUER logos: The new local block style. Used with permission.*

such as KUER redesigned their own logos (see 9.12) to complement but not necessarily incorporate the NPR logo.

Second, the network mounted a high-visibility national branding campaign called "NPR takes you there" launched nationally with ad placements in *Newsweek, National Journal,* and *The Atlantic Monthly.* The campaign earned immediate response with a burst of people calling the toll-free telephone number listed in the ads to request information about NPR member stations in their area or to find the *NPR.org* website. Immediately following the adoption of the new logo and the mounting of the national campaign, NPR encouraged local stations to use the national ads acquisitively in their own markets after customizing them with their own station logos and dial positions. Not only did the ads help attract new listeners, they built awareness for stations and drew attention to their high-quality programs.

NPR and its member stations followed the path previously cleared by PBS and public television stations. And while the NPR logo may never be as readily recognized as that of PBS, awareness studies show that the network's recognition is growing. Public awareness also has been aided by NPR's success in acquiring multimillion-dollar private donations that have generated high visibility in the popular press.

National Public Radio and Public Radio International, the two leading sources of nationally-distributed public radio programs, have benefited from PBS's more aggressive promotional leadership. Both NPR and PRI maintain constantly updated websites that are designed to give member stations access to promotional materials and provide guidance for individual station initiatives. For example, the NPR website offers an impressive menu to member stations with such headings as Program Information and Support, Listener Services, On-air Promotions and Fundraising, Development, and Research, among others. Included in the promotion support materials are "customizable" promo scripts that run the gamut from individual programs, branding, and generic spots to promos for on-air fundraising and local special events. Promotion workshops to train station personnel also are scheduled periodically. NPR also publishes *Scoop,* a monthly newsletter that provides program updates, promotion suggestions, and marketing news. NPR stations also receive electronic postings that can be customized for local station websites and incorporated into e-newsletters that are sent to financial supporters.

LOOKING BACK AND AHEAD

In recent years, PBS, NPR, and their member stations have adopted the aggressive competitive strategies of commercial broadcasting, adapting them to the unique mission of noncommercial educational radio and television and the special needs of their audiences. Public broadcasting has succeeded in carving out its own unique niche as the nation's source of the highest-quality educational and cultural programming.

But public broadcasting faces far more than competition from commercial media: The fact is that life today is so hectic that people simply have less time and many more options from which to choose. The environment has become increasingly challenging for public broadcasting. As stated at the outset of this chapter, public broadcasting continues to be attacked by the White House and members of Congress for news programs that include critical coverage of the administration and are deemed to have a liberal bias. The political climate at the time of this writing was perhaps best captured in a popular cartoon (in 9.13) that called attention to the attempts of CPB Chairman Kenneth Tomlinson at increasing politically conservative content on public broadcasting.

The future of public television and radio in America remains a matter of continued debate within academic, professional, public, and policy-maker circles. While those working within the promotion departments of public television and

Kenneth Tomlinson was here

9.13 *John Sheffius's Tomlinson cartoon. Used with permission.*

radio stations are more knowledgeable and using more sophisticated promotional strategies than ever before, the multiple challenges facing public broadcasting suggest that the long-term success of their efforts remains problematic.

SELECTED READINGS AND WEBSITES

Public Broadcasting Service. *www.pbs.org*

National Public Radio. *www.npr.org*

Corporation for Public Broadcasting. *www.cpb.org*

Current Newspaper — Public Broadcasting's news. *www.current.org*

Public Radio International. *www.pri.org*

America's Public Television Stations. *www.apts.org*

Aufderheide, P. (1999). *Communications Policy and the Public Interest*. New York: The Guilford Press.

Avery, R. K., and Stavitsky, A. G. (2000). *A History of Public Broadcasting: Mission v. Market*. Washington, DC: Current Publishing.

Balas, G. (2003). *Recovering a Public Vision for Public Television*. Boulder, CO: Rowman & Littlefield Publishers.

McCauley, M., Peterson, E., Artz, B., and Halleck, D. (Eds.) (2003). *Public Broadcasting and the Public Interest*. New York: M. E. Sharpe.

Stavitsky, A. G. (1995). Guys with suits and charts: Audience research in U.S. public radio. *Journal of Broadcasting & Electronic Media*, 39, 177–189.

NOTES

1. Elements of NPR's 2004 campaign made available by Jacques Coughlin, Director of Creative Services, NPR Communications, May 26, 2005.
2. Memo from PBS to station promotion managers, June 14, 2002.
3. These findings were presented to PBS stations at the 1996 annual summer meeting.
4. PBS Public Opinion Poll prepared by PKS Research Partners, 2004.
5. In 1996, PBS reported that 100 percent participation among eligible stations resulted in overnight ratings increases of 38 percent for programs advertised in *TV Guide*.
6. Estimated based on a 1996 survey by Hal Riney & Partners adjusted for a 5 percent per annum increase until the year 2000. In the first half-decade of the 21st century, values did not keep pace with a 5 percent annum increase.
7. 1993 study for the Corporation for Public Broadcasting conducted by Norman Hecht Research Company.
8. In 2003, the Corporation for Public Broadcasting commissioned a study to determine the existing program promotional practices of the various public radio stations across the United States. The project report, released in April of 2004, titled "On-Air Program Promotion Insight Study" by Eric Nuzum, revealed some disturbing findings.

CHAPTER 10

Global Promotion and Marketing of Television

Robert V. Bellamy, Jr., and James B. Chabin

Previous chapters have shown that the television industry is in the midst of radical changes that range from the proliferation of channels and viewing options to the new ways in which television content is received and used by viewers. **Globalization** — defined as the connection of economic interests of corporations and, in some cases, nations with one another into an interrelated worldwide system of commerce — is yet another of the realities of the television industry in the early 21st century.

In the last few years, the distribution and production of programming has expanded around the globe through the introduction of new services and channels, the formation of co-ventures, and the expansion of licensing arrangements with existing content providers. The trend toward globalization is accelerating as television content providers seek newly available audiences, especially in China and other populous countries in the east. Promotion is a key element in this process, as it is the primary if not exclusive means of differentiating programming in a multichannel environment and of making a program or service locally and personally relevant.

GLOBAL PROMOTION PRACTICES

Understanding the global activities of U.S.-based corporations is crucial to functioning in today's media environment. Despite the lessening of world trade barriers via the World Trade Organization (WTO) and such regional alliances as the European Union (EU) and the North American Free Trade Agreement

(NAFTA), the United States remains the primary source of global television pro-motion and marketing. Although not as dominant as in the past, American programming remains a major economic and cultural export and a key source of television programming throughout the world. *True* television globalization, implying a relatively free and fair exchange of programming, has yet to develop for long-standing political and economic reasons.

The American Model

The highly developed, successful, and popular U.S. television industry remains the strongest force in television globalization, while also a barrier to the success of programming imported into the United States. Box 10.1 gives examples of the international operations of four of America's major media corporations.

The Global Model

Despite the expansion of American networks abroad, however, a major compo-nent of globalization is the de-linking of corporations from nation-states. One debatable question is whether Americans are forcing the media businesses in other countries to become American clones or whether U.S. companies them-selves change so drastically when they extend into other countries that they become something new. As market-oriented economic systems have gained increasing credence and market share in most of the world, the idea of a com-pany being purely "American" or "British" or "Japanese" has faded. Corporations in all industries, including television and media, now routinely shift operations across international borders primarily for economic reasons rather than any sense of "belonging" to one nation or the other. Global companies may be tied to their countries of origin as a loose matter of tradition rather than strategy or actual practice.

One indicator of the emergence of a more global television industry is the continued growth and international expansion of PROMAX/BDA, the trade asso-ciations for electronic media promotion, design, and marketing executives (part of its brochure was shown in 3.1). The organizations now have members from over 60 nations and sponsor separate meetings in Asia, Europe, the Middle East (Arabia), Japan, China, India, and other nations. In addition, the organization's awards for excellence increasingly are going to non-U.S. promotional spots or campaigns.

News Corp. also provides an example of television industry globalization. This once-Australian firm is headed by a naturalized American (Rupert Murdoch), who had to become a U.S. citizen in order to legally create the Fox Broadcasting Company. News Corp. now has operations in almost every part of the globe and

10.1   Globalization or Americanization?

Selected International Operations [as of March 2005]

Disney	
Disney Channel	Australia, Italy, Middle East, Taiwan
ESPN	Brazil, Israel, Pacific Rim, International
News Corp.	
FX	Mexico, Latin America
Star	India, China, Japan, Asia
Sky	Brazil, Ireland, Italy, Latin America, U.K.
Viacom	
MTV	Asia, Mandarin (China), Philippines, Korea, Japan, Brazil, Europe (to Middle East), Italy, Latin America, Russia, Base (Africa)
Nickelodeon	Australia, CIS and Baltic Republics, Hungary, Latin America, Nordic Region, Philippines, U.K., Middle East
Showtime	Spain, Turkey
Time Warner	
Cartoon Network	Asia Pacific, Latin America, Europe, Japan
CNN	Spain, International, Turkey
TNT	Latin America
TCM	Asia Pacific
HBO	Asia, Brazil, Czech, Hungary, India, Poland, Romania
A&E	Mundo Latin America
E!	Latin America
The History Channel	International, Latin America
NBC Universal	
CNBC	Europe, Middle East, Africa, Asia Pacific
NBC	Europe
Telemundo	Latin America
Sci-Fi	Europe, Latin America
USA	Europe, Latin America

controls such international brand names as Fox, Sky, and Star. Another example is Viacom's MTV Networks division, which reaches more than 331 million homes outside the United States (in 18 languages and in 164 nations). Its domestic U.S. operation reaches only 87.6 million homes, and although its American operation still contributes the vast majority of revenue, MTV International is growing at a much faster pace. As MTV Networks' CEO Judy McGrath puts it, "We just finished another plan . . . and international is in the DNA of every sentence."[1]

The Commonalities

The basics of promotion (content, brand, image, time, date) in global television *do not differ substantially* from domestic promotion in the United States. The fundamental rules of promotion are not owned by any country or culture, even though the rules were developed primarily in the United States. Successful and unsuccessful promotion and marketing practices, while taking into account cultural differences, apply both to domestic *and* global promotion. Consider, for example, contemporary sports images in the advertising of the TeleFutura network (owned by Univision), which carries large quantities of international soccer. The ads can be published in trade magazines to target foreign systems. It is easy to imagine a few words about soccer translated into almost any language with the same style of soccer illustration and text addressing advertisers and potential affiliates in European, Asian, African, and Hispanic countries as well as to television viewers irrespective of nationality. Much of worldwide program promotion is driven by sports — a kind of content that easily crosses linguistic and cultural barriers — and the same tools and methods of communicating to audiences (and affiliates and advertisers) are used around the world.

The dichotomy of global television is the coexistence of an increasing amount of global (or at least U.S.) programming combined with *local* promotion and marketing. Although domestic television promotion and marketing is increasing everywhere, the role of promotion and marketing is even more important in global efforts, where it must fulfill its basic functions of generating interest and action while often being the only local bridge from programming to viewer.

THE GLOBAL IMPERATIVE

The ongoing globalization of the television industry is part of a trend in virtually all kinds of businesses, fueled by the privatization of once state-owned firms in many parts of the world, the consequent deregulation of markets, the diffusion of new technology, and rising living standards in some parts of the world.

Globalization has been identified as one of the six "imperatives of marketing" of the present era, as important as productivity, innovation, distribution, alliances, and quality.

As in the case of many other industries, television globalization is an enhancement of long-existing business practices rather than a new practice. The U.S. television industry has distributed programming abroad for many decades, a practice that began in radio with the formation of CBS and NBC Latin American radio networks in the 1930s. As far back as the 1970s, critics decried the standardization of global television and the U.S. domination of substantial portions of the world television market. Two things are new: the enormous importance assigned to globalization by the industry, scholars, trade press, and the popular media beginning in the mid-1990s, and the increased focus on both programming and content providers in worldwide recognition of brand names and images. Several interrelated factors led to these changed emphases.

Political Change and Deregulation

The final decade of the last century was a time of enormous global political change, by far the most far-reaching since the establishment of commercial broadcasting in the 1920s. The replacement of communist governments in the former Soviet Union and Eastern Europe led to the ascendancy of a capitalistic market system in most parts of the globe. Enormous markets that before had been all but closed to Western media companies were opened, as the former statist nations generally welcomed foreign investment to build new market economies.

The 1990s also saw a liberalization of the once closed economy of the world's largest nation (and market), China. These trends have continued into this millennium, with the expansion of the European Union and the further economic (if not political) liberalization in China, Russia, India, and other nations.

Even before the political shift, the United States and certain other Western European and Asian nations had begun relying on market mechanisms rather than regulation as a matter of national policy in many areas of their economies. The result of this "deregulatory" philosophy in the United States was government-fueled structural changes that altered the conduct and performance of the television industry — changes that actually were set in motion decades earlier in an age often perceived to be one of the most heavily regulated eras in U.S. telecommunications. Beginning with the first "definitive" cable rules and the partial deregulation of domestic satellites in 1972, the Federal Communications Commission (FCC) provided the impetus for entrepreneurs and investors to challenge the dominance of the ABC/CBS/NBC oligopoly. The emergence of an increasingly powerful cable television industry led to that industry's subsequent argument for more open markets and access to viewers. This argument was echoed by the Big 3, which wanted to enter new businesses. Such arguments were accepted and acted on by the FCC and Congress, which have been increasingly predisposed to equating the poorly defined "public-interest doctrine" in broadcasting with whatever the market would provide.

Competition and Technological Diffusion

With regulatory protection weakened in many areas, the television industry had to cope with previously unknown levels of competition. Globalization is one of the two major ways of coping because it offers the possibility of extending image, product, and revenue generation to previously unavailable markets, a process perceived as a necessity in a competitive domestic and global market. The second way of coping has been the continuing consolidation of the television industry both domestically and globally. Such combinations as Time Warner/Turner (and AOL) and Disney/ABC/ESPN, as well as the continuing expansion of Murdoch's Fox/Sky/Star empire are indicators of the ongoing formation of what can be labeled the *new oligopoly*. As pointed out in Chapter 1, the combining of well-known media companies across once disparate media boundaries is a means both of gaining competitive edge and of ensuring a role in the developing global structure of media corporations.

The global shift to reliance on market mechanisms had a direct effect on promotion in that promotion always is a by-product of competition. The amount and importance of promotion increases in direct proportion to the amount of competition for the time of the television viewer or user.

The videocassette recorder (VCR), the remote control device (RCD), the digital video disc (DVD), and the digital video recorder (DVR) are four technological items that have had a significant impact on the evolving global television industry. The VCR and RCD gave viewers of television control over the time element of programming and created a new market for theatrical motion pictures and other off-air programming that provided more competition for the attention of the viewer. They also permitted zipping past and jumping away from the all-important commercials. DVDs in combination with DVRs "upped the ante" for viewer choice with more storage capacity, better picture and audio quality, ease of use and storage, and automatic recording capability. Because of these technologies, *in order to capture and hold viewers, promotion for programs needs to be exciting and involve television.* That rule applies around the world because the Internet and export of American programming have raised the level of expectations worldwide for content, while the diffusion of user technologies have raised the ease of rejection of unacceptable or plain uninteresting content.

NEW MARKETING EMPHASES

As viewers demonstrated less and less loyalty to specific channels or services and seemed "up for grabs," the role of effective promotion increased exponentially in several ways. First, advertisers shifted increasing portions of their budgets to promotional and other non-spot marketing activities. For example, sponsors began to lend their names to sporting events rather than buy one or two commercial messages in them. Then, as already noted, **integrated marketing**, the combination of the once relatively disparate practices of advertising, public relations, and promotion, became a key concept in sales, and **branding** became the means for unifying promotional messages. Meanwhile, an emphasis on promotion of television *content* became a primary strategic element within the television industry.

The present consensus is that "on hand and on demand" will become one of the major mantras of the audience. Younger viewers/users of television, wherever they live, increasingly will expect the medium to provide a great variety of product whenever they wish to view it. The viewing platforms will be not just television receivers but portable devices that go with the user. Indeed, just as cellular technology leapfrogged inadequate ground-wire telephones in many parts of the world, portable media are likely to bypass traditional reception processes. Already, video services are widely available on the Internet and increasingly on cell phones. Live video broadcasting to cell phones is being tested in both Europe and Asia. In the home, video-on-demand (VOD) is becoming a standard component of digital cable systems.

Three trends seem likely to accelerate. First, *purely advertiser-supported television will become a smaller component of the television mix for most viewers.* Young people are conditioned to paying for (or in some cases pirating) electronic media content in a way their parents and grandparents were not. As long as the content is appealing and "on-hand and on-demand," paying for services is less and less a barrier to diffusion.

Second, *advertising and program promotion will become even more intrusive than is already the case.* The key word here is integration, meaning that more and more advertising messages will become part of the programming in order to keep from being avoided or "zapped" by the viewer/user. The Coke cups on *American Idol* and Home Depot packages on *Survivor*, as well as the ubiquitous product and promotional messages on sports telecasts are but the beginning of an ever-growing trend.

Third, *branding will become an enlarged emphasis in the promotional strategy of television services and program distributors.* Channel and service branding is vital in a crowded television environment, because research indicates that most people, even those who graze, pay attention to only a limited number of channels, which then become part of the individual or family *channel repertoire.* A highly targeted service with a strongly recognizable brand image has a much better chance of becoming part of the channel repertoire of the intended viewer.

Obviously programs and accompanying advertising on a repertoire channel have a much greater chance of being consumed by the viewer.

Promotion, however, does have certain advantages over product advertising: On-air promos are informational components of the very product being consumed. In this way they are similar to the motion picture "trailers" or previews that are not only accepted but often desired by consumers. The informational and entertainment nature of promotional messages will only increase as the television universe becomes ever more cluttered and difficult to navigate. Crucial differences between advertising and promotion have been located by industry researchers. For example, TiVo research found that while 70 percent or more of users skip advertising, only about 30 percent skip promos.[2]

GLOBAL TELEVISION MARKETING

Global television has three major forms. First are the global television channels and services that compete with a variety of domestic and other international channels for viewers, affiliates, and advertisers. Examples include Fox Sports Americas (Latin America) and MTV Base. The second form consists of the long-existing businesses of selling (syndicating) individual programs to a variety of channels. Third is the **franchising** of successful programs. The many international versions of *Pop Idol, Wheel of Fortune, Who Wants to Be a Millionaire?*, and *Big Brother* are examples of franchised programs. For all approaches, the major concerns related to promotion and marketing globally are establishing an effective brand image, establishing effective local partnerships, and understanding cultural differences and demonstrating sensitivity to them.

Brand Identity and Image Building

Although branding is "no miracle cure," it is essential to cutting through the clutter of advertising messages. Effective branding campaigns begin with settling on one key message because multiple messages confuse the viewer and dilute the value of brand equity. The various global versions of the Hallmark Channel, for example, all promote themselves as the place "Where Great Stories Come to Life," a message that channel research found was **culturally transcendent** — both understood by and relevant to audiences around the globe.

The Walt Disney Company has been hugely successful in extending its brand into a wide range of products and building their popularity around the world. The images in 10.2 will be readily recognized virtually anywhere, especially by children. These five frames came from an award-winning promo broadcast in Latin America to promote the Disney Latino website.

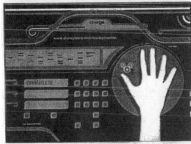

10.2   *Frames from a promo for* www.DisneyLatino.com. *Used with permission.*

Also culturally transcendent is CityTV's key message to "reflect the contemporary urban lifestyle." Originally only in Vancouver and Toronto (*www.citytv.com*), CityTV's potential appeal is broad, and its approach was readily converted to more market-specific versions by parent Chum Television International, a division of the Canadian media conglomerate that includes such brands as CityTV and MuchMusic. Chum has "extended the mother ship" by entering into partnerships (including either equity or financial option considerations) where consultation and expertise are offered to program services operated by locals. Branding in these scenarios becomes the primary responsibility of locals, who use many of the materials, media, and on-air tools discussed in earlier chapters. This approach has led to the establishment of such networks as CityTV in Barcelona and Bogota and MuchMusic in Buenos Aires and Mexico City.

Local Partnerships

Chum provides a good example of the necessity of developing local partners. Programs that seek to cross national borders need a promotional strategy that fosters joint creative goals. However, partnerships are just as important, if not more important, for full-service television services seeking to expand globally than they are for the relative "loose" structures employed globally by Chum.

As illustrated in Box 10.3, Nickelodeon Latin America (Nick LA) spent considerable time after its 1996 launch convincing television exhibitors to consider themselves partners responsible for the network's success. This concept was quite elusive in countries with little history of competition and subsequent promotion. Nick LA wanted system operators and exhibitors to think of themselves more as a software (programming) provider, rather than simply as a supplier of hardware for campaigns and the sales effort. Local marketing campaigns serve local audiences with custom messages targeted to local needs.

In addition, exactly because they are on the spot, local partners can provide timely information on local events, thus creating off-air marketing opportunities that would not otherwise be known to distant networks. Nick LA found out about Peru's major consumer products trade show and Panama's Holiday Parade, major events for marketing efforts, by speaking with and listening to distributors in those two nations. Clearly, maintaining open lines of communication with distributors and exhibitors is essential to learning about the local market and in "educating" the operator as to contemporary promotional campaigns.

10.3 Nickelodeon Latin America

Viacom's Nickelodeon (Nick) is one of the most valuable brand names to emerge in the cable-multichannel age. Established in 1979, Nick is now available in 70 million U.S. households and consistently is one of the highest-rated basic cable networks. It reaches over 55 percent of all U.S. children between ages 2 and 11.[1] In addition to its core mission of reaching children (which Nickelodeon always refers to as *kids*), Nick has developed a successful nighttime programming block ("Nick at Nite") consisting of old family-oriented television series that reaches young adults. The success of "Nick at Nite" has led to the establishment of a separate "TV Land" basic service.

Nickelodeon entered the global television market through dedicated channels, programming blocks, and individual program syndication. As of early 1999, Nickelodeon programming had a potential reach of approximately 100 million households in about 100 countries. Dedicated channels are in operation or in the planning stages in Australia, Japan, Hungary, Italy, Latin America, the Nordic Countries, the Philippines, Turkey, and the United Kingdom, in addition to the United States.[2]

The key operational philosophy of Nickelodeon is that it "Puts Kids First," a culturally transcendent premise that applies to operations anywhere in the world. Extensive research is conducted to identify the interests of the children in each market. This information then is used to develop program schedules and promotional or marketing campaigns.[3]

Nickelodeon Latin America (Nick LA) provides a good example of the operational philosophy in action. The Miami-based Nick LA was launched in late December 1996 and, by early 1998, could boast of being Latin America's "fastest growing multichannel program service," reaching 6.5 million homes in 20 Central and South American countries.[4] The distribution breakdown is approximately 41 percent in the "Southern Cone" (Argentina, Bolivia, Chile, Paraguay, Uruguay), 43 percent in the "Northern Cone" (Colombia, Ecuador, Mexico, Peru, Venezuela, and Central America), and 16 percent in Brazil. Nick LA was conceived as a pan-regional (versus a national) service after research showed that Central and South American nations are more homogenous in language (Spanish and Portuguese [Brazil] with a substantial English-speaking minority—the three languages of Nick LA) and other cultural variables than Europe or Asia. Latin America also was seen as a desirable market due to the long attraction of U.S. television and popular culture in most of the area,

(Continued)

the high percentage of children in the population, and the relatively nonrestrictive entry policies.

Operationalizing the message of "Put[ting] Kids First" into local terms was a vital step in effective branding. Nick LA used extensive focus group interviewing of children in Argentina, Brazil, and Mexico to discover similarities among children in quite distinct nations. The main finding was that children had a "real interest in learning about kids in other places." This led to the adoption of "Nickelodeon Te Conecta a Tu Mundo" ["Nickelodeon Connects You to Your World"] as the channel's major promotional slogan and the use of footage showing children in many Latin American nations in on-air promotions.

Nickelodeon Latin America relies heavily on research of various types, from telephone surveys to focus groups to "photo surveys" that involve the analysis of subject-submitted photographs of areas of interest and personal importance. In addition, every letter, e-mail, and contest entry is entered into a database. The result is a service that attempts to be "in touch" with the desires and concerns of children in the region.[5]

Although 75 percent of Nickelodeon Latin America's programming is original for the Latin American market, most of it was produced in the United States. Nick LA acquired some "local" programming and has long-term plans to develop programs with local or regional television providers. An interesting global effort of Nickelodeon is the "Global Character Lab," described as an attempt to "break up the New York–Los Angeles–London creative axis" by presenting short videos, and perhaps longer form programming over time, developed in the countries where Nickelodeon operates.[6]

Despite these efforts, ways other than program acquisition have been the keys to localizing the service. Many of these efforts are related to cultural differences. For example, the program schedule of Nick LA differs considerably from the U.S. service to adapt to local school times, to parental content concerns that are often greater than in the United States, and to the fact that children in Latin America tend to stay up later at night than their U.S. counter-parts. In addition such U.S. broadcast network programs as *Sabrina, the Teenage Witch* and *Clueless* are scheduled in the evening rather than Nick at Nite's tongue-in-cheek presentation of "Classic TV."[7]

As explained by Steve Grieder, vice president and creative director, "Localization is not specifically a programming acquisitions issue. We don't feel we have to buy shows from the region; we look for the best stuff to serve the audience from everywhere. Our responsibility is to make it local through very high quality dubbing and adaptation."[8] The main burden of localizing Nickelodeon Latin America falls on promotion and marketing, with most of the

(Continued)

campaigns localized versions of campaigns that have been successful in the United States. Key examples include:

1. "Nickelodeon En Vivo" ["Nickelodeon Live"], a traveling live theatrical show with interactive games based on such popular programs as *Rugrats* and *Clarissa*.
2. "Ayuda a Tu Mundo" ["Help Your World"], a "pro-social initiative" that encourages children to get involved in volunteer helping activities. "Ayuda a Tu Mundo" provides a good example of corporate "synergy" or integrated marketing as Viacom-owned corporate siblings Blockbuster Video (as information center) and Simon & Schuster (through educational material designed for Mexican teachers) were employed to support the effort.
3. "Director por un Dia" ["Director for a Day"], a regional sweepstakes.

Nickelodeon Latin America. Used with permission.

Cultural differences had to be accounted for in these and other campaigns. For example, "Ayuda a Tu Mundo," based on "The Big Help" initiative in the United States, had to be carefully positioned in Latin America because, while "helping" others is understood, volunteerism is a relatively vague concept. The "Super Toy Run" promotion that was popular in the United States was not attempted in Latin America due to the general absence of toy superstores. References to "milk and cookies" as a common snack were changed because few children in Latin America drink milk after infancy.

(Continued)

Merchandising is an important component of Nickelodeon in the United States and increasingly in other countries. Magazines, books, videos, videogames, clothing, toys, and other licensed merchandise follows the service to new markets. Theme park attractions and retail stores are likely to be added to the Nickelodeon presence in Latin America in the near future, as they have been elsewhere.

Nickelodeon Latin America provides a good example of the importance of knowledge of and sensitivity to market conditions and cultural factors in building a brand. In addition, Nick LA is an example of how continuing research and canny promotion and marketing campaigns can make a service "local," even if most of the programming is from outside the region.

Sources

1. "Nickelodeon Latin America Fact Sheet," press release. Miami: Nickelodeon Latin America, February 1998.
2. Donna Friedman, vice president of marketing and associate creative director, Nickelodeon Latin America. Telephone interview, August 24, 1998.
3. Jimena Fridman, "The U.S. Invasion of Latin American Kids' TV," *The Big Blue Box* (Fall 1997 [reprint]); Donna Friedman, vice president of marketing and associate creative director, and Valerie G. McCarty, vice president, Marketing and Communications, Nickelodeon Latin America, joint telephone interview, March 4, 1998.
4. Friedman; "Nickelodeon Latin America Fact Sheet."
5. "Nickelodeon Latin America Fact Sheet."
6. Steven Grieder, vice president and creative director, Nickelodeon Latin America, telephone interview, March 30, 1998; "Nickelodeon Worldwide Development Group Announces Creation of Nickelodeon's Global Character Lab," press release. Miami: Nickelodeon Latin America, July 29, 1997.
7. "Nickelodeon Latin America Celebrates the New Year by Premiering Two New Acquisitions," press release. Miami: Nickelodeon Latin America, December 23, 1997.
8. Grieder; Ed Kirchdoerffer, "Courting Latin America," *KidScreen* (January 1998 [reprint]).

The effectiveness of Nickelodeon Latin America's local partnerships is evident because the network is touted as "the fastest growing cable and satellite network in Latin America." It has two feeds (North and South), a separate Nickelodeon Brazil service, and programming blocks that reach about 65 million homes. The model used for Nick LA also has been replicated throughout the world with such Nick event and promotional staples as the "Kids' Choice

Awards" and "The Big Help," among others, being introduced everywhere from Malaysia to the UK and from China to Brazil.

Strategic media partnerships also are common among content providers. Nickelodeon programming blocks, for example, are parts of CNBC Europe in Turkey and MTV in Belgium, as well as on such national broadcast services as Globo (Brazil) and CCTV (China).

CULTURAL SENSIBILITIES

There is general consensus in the industry that local people at stations and net-works must be involved in designing and implementing promotional campaigns because only they truly know and understand local conditions, issues, and gen-eral culture. Cultural ignorance is by definition insensitive and often perceived as arrogance, a very bad position for a channel attempting to carve out a niche in a crowded marketplace.

Exported programming, to a limited degree, can be "localized" through careful editing and state-of-the-art dubbing. However, *promotion generally is the key to local-izing*. The first step in creative localizing is for non-native people working on the campaign to avoid cultural errors by immersion in the culture or, optimally, empowering natives to make creative decisions.

Any discussion of cultural differences is certain to be incomplete and in some ways stereotypical because the differences often are regional, rather than national, and because they often are the opinion of a small number of people. Nonetheless, some reporting of observed differences will be instructive of the types of issues that can arise when developing promotion for international markets.

Asia is a very culturally complex area of the world because of the dozens of separate cultures that make up the continent. As learned by Murdoch's Star TV and other pan-Asian services, facial images usually are to be avoided on-air and in print materials because of the many different people in Asia who do not iden-tify with each other. Instead, commonalities of culture used in promotional campaigns are natural imagery such as the sky, clouds, water, or trees. Other observed differences are the Pan-Asian disdain for the word *disaster*, the "taboo" on showing a father putting his arm around his daughter in several parts of the continent, the preference in Hong Kong for long promos and trailers, and the avoidance in China of promotion that demonstrates disrespect for elders (such as *Dennis the Menace*).

Despite these limitations, American firms also provide much of the design for on-air promotion in other parts of the world, including Asia. In India, Hungama TV was the first 24-hour children's channel in the Hindi language. It targets 8- to 14-year-olds with multigenre programming. Although the frame in

10.4 comes from a promo by T.A.G. for Hungama TV's 2004 launch, it could be recognized by children anywhere.

Disrespect for elders and more specifically monarchs, also is a problem in much of the Middle East, where *Archie* is not shown because of the crownlike hat worn by the "Jughead" character. Motion pictures and television programs featuring female lead characters traditionally have been a tough sell in many Middle Eastern and African nations.

Europe includes some of the most difficult markets to enter by non-native program suppliers because of the highly developed television and film industries in many nations and EU restrictions on imported content. In addition, in much of Europe, a neon or electric style of design is not well liked, especially among the older population. Older Europeans, whose television viewing experience has been defined by limited and often noncommercial channels, have a tendency to regard most modern design imagery as too brash, "too American." Disliked in most of Europe (with the exception of the United Kingdom) is the use of fire or flames in marketing material. Two other national differences are the need to avoid purple in Italy, the color of death, and the dislike of the British for program recaps in promotion.

Obviously, these differences are dissipating, as younger people show no such tendencies. Such leveling influences as exposure to MTV-like programming and

10.4   *A frame from a promo for Hungama TV. Used with permission.*

10.5   *SIC TV's studios and control room. Used with permission.*

more provocative media content (in terms of nudity and sexuality), while lacking the plentiful media choices of Americans, have made European youth more likely than Americans to use their cell phones as a media center via ringtones and other downloads. At the same time, they have become receptive to cutting-edge design in media. Television broadcast studios around the world are being redesigned by top American designers in order to become stronger parts of contemporary-looking visual identities of stations and networks. The three frames in 10.5 show the studios (designed by Devlin Design) and control room of SIC, Lisbon's leading broadcast television station.

GETTING AUDIENCES

Despite television's enormous contribution to cultural commonalities and its demonstrated power to affect politics, economics, and most other areas of life, there are powerful limits to television's ability to impose cultural domination over viewers. There are impediments to getting viewers to try out new channels and to building loyalty to them.

Local programming, for example, almost always is preferred over imported material. The Sony Corporation, for example, regards local programming as the "passport to success offshore." This viewer preference does not necessarily reduce American and other program imports because of the cost advantage of imports over domestic programs in many nations. India, for example, exports its movies all over the Far East and parts of Africa and South America. However, as most countries now experience a proliferation of television channels, the U.S. television program suppliers and other out-of-country suppliers find themselves in a situation where they have to *creatively localize* their product to gain a spot in viewer repertoires. American television providers cannot simply make deals for the transmission of a domestic feed into other markets. Dubbing has proved less than satisfactory when most programs face serious competition.

POSITIONING NEW SERVICES

New services can be branded as local or regional even if much of the programming is not. Viacom's Nickelodeon and MTV localize their various international services by incorporating local talent in all phases of production, as explained in 10.3. These networks also schedule differently than in the United States due to variations in meal, sleep, or work/school times. MTV also attempts to be aware of and sensitive to local cultural conditions. For example, MTV Indonesia televises Muslim prayer calls on a regular basis.

Disney concentrates on using cartoon images (such as mouse ears) that have become internationally recognized. Like sports, animated characters, in particular, seem to speak clearly to children across language barriers and have a universal sort of culture of their own. Animated global image campaigns are conducted by most international program promoters because logo design elements can easily be altered depending on the markets reached and targeted. Again, MTV provides a good example of this as it merges its standard logo with different color and design schemes for different international markets (see *www.msnbc.msn.com/id/8008262/site/newsweek/*).

Another common approach to localizing content is to replicate existing ideas (**franchises**) with alterations to match local culture and tastes in promotional messages. For example, MTV's U.S. series *Pimp My Ride* is refashioned as *Pimp My Bicycle* in Germany. Cartoon Network UK partners with post-graduate art and design students to produce promotional messages and station IDs ("idents" in Britain) that are seen throughout Europe.

EFFECTIVE GLOBAL PROMOTION

The list in 10.6 summarizes effective marketing today beyond the U.S. borders. For the most part, these principles should be regarded as general guidelines as our understanding of global television promotion is still in its infancy. One key consideration is that *television promotion, whether domestic or global, remains both a blend of science and art, of both a quantitative and qualitative nature.* Research on both demographic and psychographic (lifestyle) variables has never been more important in a time when the number of television and other media options continue to exponentially increase. This proliferation of options has made each viewer/user/subscriber (at least the ones valued by advertisers) more important. She or he now has the tools to design individual media menus and channel repertoires that present ever-increasing challenges to media promotion professionals that can only be met by intensive research on all dimensions of the media usage process.

10.6   Keys to Effective Global Television Promotion

1. *Promotion and marketing basics need not be reinvented for nondomestic markets.* The basics of time, date, content, image, and brand are essentially the same everywhere in the world.
2. *The importance of branding increases with the number of television and media program and platform offerings.* Global branding is particularly problematic because of the need to balance a brand identity across the world: A brand identity can be too generic or *vanilla* to appeal to viewers, or it can be too specific to a given set of cultural understandings. MTV International's approach of "mixing universal youth sensibilities with local tastes" is an example of how a brand can encompass both the global and the local. The Hallmark Channel's "Where Great Stories Come to Life" has also been successful because the connection of stories to life is a truly global message.
3. *Residents of the host country should be key members of promotion and marketing teams.* These individuals can help avoid embarrassing or more serious mistakes resulting from cultural insensitivity or ignorance. Local residents also are likely to be knowledgeable of and sensitive to domestic cultural indicators.
4. *Optimally, non-natives working on campaigns should have lived in the nation(s) in which the programs or services are being marketed and speak the local language(s).* Operating constantly at second-hand via translators is neither practical nor sufficiently sensitive to nuance.

5. *Promotional campaigns should be congruent with the entire program chain and not just the program service or channel* (the typical primary client). Particularly important is the local exhibitor. A local exhibitor's role as gatekeeper can be essential to the success of the program or promotion and so deserves attention from any canny marketer. A local manager also often is knowledgeable about local events that present off-air marketing opportunities.

6. *Local political and economic conditions should be well understood.* Limitations on nondomestic content or lack of exhibitor capacity can determine the form and level of television globalization (full channel, shared channel, program blocs, or individual programs) both in terms of programming and promotion.

7. *Promotional campaigns should reflect an understanding of what global television programming actually is and is not.* With a few exceptions, it is not about globally popular programs, because individual differences among viewers and the proliferation of channels shrinks the chance of any one program becoming popular all over the world. Beyond certain children's programs and news and sports events, global television programming operates on the macro-level of economic globalization, a level usually not relevant to viewers. Standardization of promotional materials, as part of the globalization of marketing television programming, works only with the generic functions of promotion and when both product usage and culture are similar — a rare circumstance.

8. *While culturally transcendent meanings should be part of any effective promotional campaign, the most important fact of global television is that the viewer or user consumes television* locally, *regardless of the source of the programming.* Promotion and marketing campaigns, which often carry the burden of making nonlocal programming creatively local, must themselves reflect local conditions over superficial global similarities. As articulated by CityTV founder Moses Znaimer and increasingly obvious, the expansion of television worldwide means the demand for localism in media increases.

9. *The "rules" of promotion both internationally and domestically are being challenged by the rapid diffusion of personal media technologies.* "On-hand and on-demand" is increasingly the mantra of television viewers and other media users. Although new distribution means do not signal the abandonment of marketing basics, they do signal the need for media promotion professionals and media scholars to adapt to the latest in traditional television platforms (such as to HDTV) as well as such rapidly changing distribution platforms as cell/media phones, PDA, and the Internet.

The problem is that, in many respects, the relatively sterile social-scientific research of the past has proved unworkable in many countries because of such limits as lack of timely transportation (to survey), the absence of widespread communications (to telephone), or other privacy barriers (such as restriction of access to women). In South Africa, for example, where 11 different languages are spoken and there is great disparity in income and living conditions, research into media usage uses a 29-variable segmentation process — involving degree of urbanization, ownership of cars and household appliances, languages spoken, access to such basic services as water, electricity, telephones, and so on — that is far different from the usual gender and age classifications of most ratings. The difficulties of random sampling in an era of global expansion and proliferation of cell phones casts doubts on the usefulness of the methodologies well-established in the United States and Europe. At the same time, small or nonrandom samples or other qualitative methods such as interviewing, while important, lack the validity and predictability needed to draw conclusions that involve spending huge amounts of money. Research on media usage and promotional effectiveness has had to move toward a triangulation of methods, and media producers must acknowledge that usage findings for many countries probably apply only to some specified subgroup and cannot be generalized.

Regardless of methods, research in and of itself is insufficient to achieve effective global promotion at this time. "Living and breathing and feeling" a culture without preconceived notions is probably the key to effective marketing. The nature of television is also changing in ways that would have been con-sidered unimaginable a generation ago. Media practitioners will probably have to live with multiple *definitions* depending on geographical location or political/economic status. For many countries, however, researchers are only beginning to formulate the proper questions to ask of the audience/users. For the producers of promotional materials, "living the culture" is coming to include both the cul-tures of location and of television/media usage. Ultimately, these are the keys to formulating proper and effective questions and beginning to get useful answers.

DIRECTIONS AHEAD

Discussing television marketing is necessarily bound to the way television oper-ated in the past and operates at present. Digital web transmission has the poten-tial to substantially alter the viewer–content provider relationship. Nonetheless, the major parameters affecting promotion are likely to remain essentially unchanged regardless of how the industry evolves. Although the traditional *date and time* (the *when* function) will not be as important in an on-demand television situation, the *content, brand*, and *image* functions of promotion — versions of the *what* and *who*, as well as the *where* and *call-to-action* functions — will become increasingly more significant. The basic fact remains that, as long as advertisers use television (however distributed or delivered) to reach desirable target audiences, the traditional functions of promotion will be essential to content providers in producing those audiences. Acquiring and retaining viewers will continue to be essential even if much of advertising moves away from separate commercial spots and is buried inside the program content.

Global television, along with other media, is the great "leveler" of cultural differences. As more people from diverse cultural environments watch the same television content and find positions in the television and advertising industries and as the television industry becomes more structurally integrated across international boundaries, the more the "rules" of television programming, promotion, and marketing become standardized. While the recognition of and reaction to cultural differences is an integral component of international television promotion and marketing, the components and fundamentals of the promotion process are rapidly becoming an understood common language among industry professionals.

Globalization is both here and now as well as the future of the television industry. Economic consolidation and technological convergence will continue to fuel global expansion by major television providers, as will the eventual maximization of domestic growth in the world's most developed television markets. Global consolidation is leading to a new oligopoly, whereby a limited number of giant media companies will control much of the world's access to and content of television, with U.S. firms in a privileged, if not dominant, position. However, the operational parameters of this oligopoly are still in flux and subject to both political action within individual nations or regions and local competitive circumstances.

As viewers become exposed to and comfortable with multichannel and mobile television, they become increasingly difficult to capture. Consolidation will not necessarily lead to the generic sameness of product usually found in oligopoly structures. In an increasingly cluttered television universe, localism remains the most important way for a program or a program provider to differentiate itself from other programs or delivery channels. Also crucial will be the increasing sophistication of both quantitative and qualitative lifestyle research to enable programming and promotion professionals to better target viewers culturally, ethnically, and personally in a variety of countries. Promotion and marketing that can persuade the viewers that a specific program or channel is worth their investment of time and attention (and perhaps money) are fundamental to the success of global and domestic television providers. The one thing that it is quite safe to predict is that for the practice of global marketing, the Road Runner in 10.7 is entirely right!

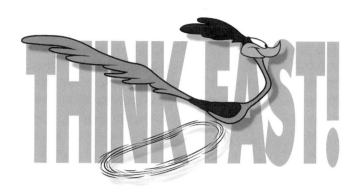

10.7 *Road Runner "Think Fast." Used with permission.*

SELECTED READINGS AND WEBSITES

Chum Television International. www.chumlimited.com/television/international.asp.

Danielson, M., Vice President of Marketing, Hearst-Argyle Television. Telephone interview, March 11, 2005.

Disney Corp. *www. corporate.disney.go.com/index.html.*

Eastman, S. T. (ed.). (2000). *Research in Media Promotion.* Mahwah, NJ: Erlbaum.

Hallmark Channel. *www.hallmarkchannel.com/us_framework.jsp?CNTRY=US.*

Moseley, C., Executive Vice President, Worldwide Marketing and Brand Strategy, Hallmark Channel. Telephone interview, March 28, 2005.

News Corporation. *www.newscorp.com/index2.html.*

Nick International. *www.nick.com/all_nick/everything_nick/intl_home.jhtml.*

PROMAX & BDA. *www.promax.org/main.asp.*

Roberts, J. L. (2005, June 6). World Tour. *Newsweek,* Internet Edition. *www.msnbc. msn.com/id/8017001/site/newsweek/.*

Viacom. *www.viacom.com/.*

WorldScreen.com. *www.worldscreen.com/index.php.*

NOTES

1. Roberts, J. L. (2005). World Tour, *Newsweek,* June 6, p. 34.
2. As pointed out in previous chapters, industry research studies have found that people use promotion more than previewing the actual program to make decisions about whether or not to attend to the entire program. Promotional spots have been described as the road signs on a very fast moving highway of entertainment options. In fact, conventional promotional wisdom, supported by several research studies, supports "The Big Bang" theory, which says that *a spot has 3 seconds to attract and hold the attention of viewers before they zap to another channel.*

About the Contributing Authors

William Jenson Adams (Chapter 3) is Professor of Communication in the School of Journalism & Mass Communication at Kansas State University. His primary research interests lie in motion pictures and network television programming for prime time. He has written chapters for several textbooks, including multiple editions of *Media Programming: Strategies and Practices* (2006), and published his research in such periodicals as the *Journal of Broadcasting & Electronic Media, Journal of Communication*, and the *Journal of Media Economics*. He also writes for the popular press. Professor Adams can be reached at *wadams@ksu.edu*.

Robert K. Avery (Chapter 9) is Professor of Communication at the University of Utah. A former public radio and television administrator, he was directly involved in public broadcasting's early promotional efforts as chair of the Board of Directors of the National Association of Educational Broadcasters, and continued his connection by serving as academic liaison with KUER-FM and KUED-TV in Salt Lake City. Professor Avery has authored four books, including *Public Service Broadcasting in a Multichannel Environment* (1993), contributed to three editions of this book, and published numerous articles on the subject of public broadcasting. In addition, he was founding editor of *Critical Studies in Mass Communication* and serves on the editorial boards of *Journal of Broadcasting & Electronic Media* and the *Journal of Radio Studies*. He can be reached at *rka@utah.edu*.

Robert V. Bellamy, Jr. (Chapter 10) is Associate Professor of Media Studies at Duquesne University in Pittsburgh. His research interests include media and sports, television programming, and the impact of technological change on industry structure, conduct, and performance. His work has appeared in several edited books and in such publications as the *Journal of Broadcasting & Electronic Media, Journal of Communication, Journalism Quarterly*, and the *Journal of Sport & Social Issues*. He co-authored *Television and the Remote Control: Grazing on a Vast Wasteland* (1996) and co-edited *The Remote Control in the New Age of Television* (1993). He can be reached at *robellusc@yahoo.com*.

James B. Chabin (Chapter 10) is President and CEO of PROMAX and the Broadcast Designers Association (BDA). PROMAX is the international trade association of the promotion and marketing executives in electronic media, and BDA serves designers of

303

promotion and marketing materials. At one time, he was vice president of national promotion at E! Entertainment and more recently served as president of the Academy of Television Arts and Sciences, the organization that awards the Emmys. His career in radio, television, and cable marketing, sales, and management included positions with Chabin Communications (owner of KKIS AM/FM in Walnut Creek/Concord, CA), CBS Television Stations, CBS Radio Sport Sales, CBS Television National Sales, and KVMT-TV (Vail, Colorado). He can be reached at *jim@promax.tv*.

Mary L. Dickson (Chapter 9) is Director of Creative Services at KUED-TV, Channel 7, in Salt Lake City, a PBS affiliate. Dickson is a former newspaper reporter whose articles, commentary, criticism, and essays won many awards. In addition, under her leadership, KUED won an Emmy and other major recognitions from the New York Film Festival, PBS, and the Utah Broadcasters Association. She wrote and produced *No Safe Place: Violence Against Women* (PBS, 1998) and is a columnist for *Salt Lake Weekly* and contributor to the *Salt Lake Tribune* and other western newspapers. She has served on the PBS Communications Advisory Council and currently serves on the Communication Council of the National Educational Telecommunicators Association and is an advisor for the National Center for Outreach. A Distinguished Alumnus, she teaches an honors course on media literacy at the University of Utah. She can be reached at *mdickson@kued.org*.

Susan Tyler Eastman (Chapters 1 and 5) is Professor Emerita of Telecommunications at Indiana University. Before coming to Indiana, she taught at Temple University in Philadelphia. In addition to editing and authoring five editions of this book, she is senior editor/author of seven editions of *Media Programming: Strategies and Practices* (2006) and edited *Research in Media Promotion* (2000). As well as contributing to many other books, she has published more than 100 articles in professional journals. Her studies of on-air promotion have reached wide audiences through such journals as *Journal of Applied Communication Research, Journal of Broadcasting & Electronic Media, Journal of Communication, Communication, Ecquid Novi, Journal of Sport & Social Issues,* and *Television and New Media*. She can be reached at *eastman@indiana.edu*.

Douglas A. Ferguson (Chapters 1, 3, and 6) is Professor and former Chair of Communication at the College of Charleston, South Carolina. Early in his professional life he was program director of NBC-affiliated WLIO-TV, a station manager, local cable program director, and later chair of the Department of Telecommunications at Bowling Green State University. He co-authored *The Broadcast Television Industry* (1998) and co-edited three editions of *Media Programming: Strategies and Practices* (2006) and three editions of this book. His scholarly work his been published in the *Journal of Broadcasting & Electronic Media, Communication Research, Journalism Quarterly*, and *Communication Research Reports*, and he is the current editor of *Journal of Radio Studies*. He can be reached at *fergusond@cofc.edu*.

Robert A. Klein (Chapters 1, 7, and 8) is President and CEO of Klein &, a Los Angeles firm that creates and produces media branding concepts. This award-winning company initiates and oversees strategic marketing; design, audio, and visual production; copy; and music for new media services. He is currently active in developing interactive television services and helping to design "life after TiVo." Over the years, Klein & has developed promotion for major television networks and station groups, cable networks and operators, and Internet services in the United States, Europe, and Asia. In addition to guest lecturing at many universities, he served on the board of directors of PROMAX and the Pacifica Foundation. He can be reached at *kleinand@earthlink.net*.

Stephen Masiclat (Chapter 8) is Assistant Professor of Visual & Interactive Communication at the S. I. Newhouse School of Public Communication at Syracuse University. He is also Director of the Graduate Program in New Media and Co-Director of the Center for Digital Convergence at Syracuse University. Prior to joining the Newhouse faculty, he was an interface designer and research assistant at the Interactive Multimedia Group at Cornell University. He currently serves as a multimedia design consultant to the NEC Corporation, and has a professional background in interface design, MACINTOSH programming, graphic design, and art direction. In addition to contributing to two editions of this book, he conducts research about audience online usage and preferences. He can be reached at *masiclat@syr.edu*.

Gregory D. Newton (Chapter 2) is Assistant Professor of Telecommunications at Ohio University, after a stint at the University of Oklahoma. Before climbing into the ivory tower, he served as operations manager, program director, and production director, as well as air talent at several radio stations where he accumulated a wealth of stories about stupid promotion tricks with which he now bores (or entertains) students. He authored a chapter in *Media Programming: Strategies and Practices* (2006) and has published in such journals as the *Journal of Applied Communication Research, Journal of Broadcasting & Electronic Media, Journal of Communication*, and the *Journal of Radio Studies*. He can be reached at *newtong@ohio.edu*.

Ronald J. Rizzuto (Chapter 4) is Professor of Finance at the Daniels College of Business at the University of Denver. In addition to teaching about capital expenditure analysis, mergers and acquisitions, and cable finance, he has conducted numerous workshops and conferences for professional managers in the cable telecommunications industry. He also co-directs the Bob Magness Institute at the National Cable Television Center and Museum. He co-authored *Costs, Benefits, and Long-Term Sustainability of Municipal Overbuilds* (1998), contributed to two editions of this book, and has authored numerous case studies of cable communications. He can be reached at *rrizzuto@du.edu*.

Michael O. Wirth (Chapter 4) is Director of the School of Communication and Professor and Chair of Mass Communications and Journalism Studies at the University of Denver. He is also a senior fellow of the Magness Institute for cable telecommunications, and has been a visiting professor at Renmin University in Beijing, Zhejiang University in Hangzhou, and Curtin University of Technology in Perth, Australia. In addition to consulting and research, he hosted a public affairs program on KWGN-TV for many years. He participated in two editions of this book and has contributed to many scholarly books. He co-edited *Media Management and Economics Handbook (2006)* and coauthored *Costs, Benefits, and Long-Term Sustainability of Municipal Overbuilds* (1998). His research has been published in the *Journal of Broadcasting & Electronic Media, Journal of Regulatory Economics, Journal of Media Economics, Quarterly Review of Economics and Business*, and *Telecommunications Policy*. He can be reached at *mwirth@du.edu*.

Glossary

*This selective glossary consists of media-related terms that were **boldfaced** in the text. The definitions focus on meanings as applied to promotion and marketing of media. For other terminology, consult other reference books or an online thesaurus. Italicized items in definitions are themselves defined elsewhere in this alphabetical glossary.*

Access The early evening period immediately preceding network prime time, generally 7 to 8 p.m.

Accountability Responsibility for activities.

Acquisitive goal Media promotion that is intended to gain new viewers, listeners, or subscribers.

Advance titling On-screen notices for the next program, appearing as *pop-ups* in the lower-third of television screens.

Affiliation The contractual relationship between an individual station and one of the national television or radio networks or between an individual local cable system and one of the national or regional cable networks.

Appointment TV Programs that draw viewers to adjust their lives (even turn on their television sets) specifically to watch them, including the most popular prime-time series, annual big-budget specials, and classic public television series.

Aspect ratio Proportions of television screens, magazine ads and pages, billboards, signs, and newspaper ads; an item's width and height.

Automated advance tilting See *advance tilting.*

Avails (availabilities) Unsold airtime.

Backstory Overall plot of a program, especially what preceded the current episode.

Banners Static sections on a television or computer screen used for sequenced text messages on television screens, such as sports score *banners*; also refers to horizontal elements such as page headlines on websites.

Barter Trading; in programming, trading airtime to get programs; in promotion, trading on-air mentions for prizes and other giveaways; for print or outdoor advertising space for the station; or for useful commodities, such as lunches for guests, station vehicles, and maintenance services. See also *Tradeouts.*

Basic tier Lowest level of analog cable service.

Benchmark research Studies establishing the audience's level of consumption (or interest) or delineating the audience's attitude or image for a station or talent prior to a promotional campaign, providing a basis for comparison and evidence of positive or negative change in audience consumption or image.

Benefit That which a viewer, listener, or advertiser gains from watching, listening, or advertising; the advantage or profit.

Billboard A large outdoor sign or an on-air listing of upcoming programs by title and time.

Bill stuffers Marketing messages enclosed with monthly cable bills.

Blogs Online logs or other personal journals written by individuals for general consumption; may include video or audio.

Boilerplate statements General forms of promotional messages that can be customized by individual stations.

Bookend promos Spots at the beginning and end of commercial *pods* used to promote the network's or station's programs.

Brandable A product or service that is differentiated from other products or services and thus can be effectively marketed.

Brand awareness Audience recognition of and familiarity with a particular brand name.

Brand management Protection of brands and other copyrights from look-alikes and competing companies.

Brand positioning Promotional messages that convey particular images or sets of associations with specific media companies and their *logos*, usually conceived as large-scale all-media campaigns.

Branding Giving something an identifiable and unique image.

Breakthroughs (also **break-out spots**) The condition of standing out, or exceptional *promos* or advertising spots that attract an unusual amount of audience (and industry) attention and generally influence future design practices.

Broadband network Digital cable network, especially with the capacity to deliver Internet access and telephony as well as standard and high-definition television.

Budget A plan of the costs for future activities.

Bugs Miniature *logos* superimposed on programming, usually — but not always — in the lower right corner, serving to identify the source of the currently-viewed program.

Bumpers Brief video titling sequences between programs or in breaks that invite viewers to watch the upcoming program (usually 2 to 3 seconds long).

Bundling Grouping as a one-price package or promoting as a group under a single label (*umbrella* theme); especially packaging several cable channels for one price, as in offers of "expanded basic," sets of digital video or audio channels, and incorporating high-speed Internet access and phone service.

Buzz Publicity or the process of generating audience (and advertiser) interest in a program or new service by means of publicity, promotion, and advertising.

CAB (Cable Advertising Bureau) A nonprofit support organization, supporting cable advertising; *www.cab.org*.

Calls Short for **call letters**, the letters beginning with W or K assigned by the FCC in the United States (X in Mexico, C in Canada, and so on for all the countries of the world).

Campaign Planned approach to promotion over a substantial period of time, usually involving multiple media and possibly sequenced messages.

Cause marketing Public service campaigns that are intended to improve the public's health or help with social problems.

Churn Turnover in subscribers.

Click-throughs Online icons that take users to another site, generally to view advertising messages; useful for measuring audience interest in an advertising or promotional message.

Clips Small segments of video used in promotional spots.

Clones Close copies of other programs or visual/auditory materials with roughly the same plots but using different actors.

Co-branded bugs Using on-screen bugs with both the network and station logos, as in PBS profile bug and a local PTV station's bug identifier.

Co-branded event (also **double-sponsored**) An activity with two or more sponsors, one being the station.

Co-branding Having two sponsors for a local event, such as the station and an advertiser; also, linking a local station with its network, as in the case of PBS *affiliates*.

Combination promos Network on-air spots with space for a station's local access program, intended to link local and network evening programs to produce audience flow.

Combined ID A *logo* or *bug* that combines a graphic image and a *wordmark*.

Common carriage The schedule of PBS programs carried by most public stations in prime time.

Compensation Payment by a network for use of a station's airtime.

Competitive positioning Finding an image that distinguishes one service from others.

Competitive promotion Promotional messages that identify a specific competitor's product (or program) as lesser in some way to the detriment of the competitor; activities that mimic a competitor's game or contest for the purpose of undermining its impact, usually in radio.

Concept research The testing of ideas for formats, slogans, and campaign elements.

Congruence Matching, closely akin, as in different pieces of promotion.

Contesting Offering games of chance and skill to win prizes on radio, websites, cable, and occasionally broadcast television.

Co-ops Joint advertising offered by networks to affiliated stations; also, retail co-ops which are joint advertising between retail stores and a media company.

Cooperative advertising See *co-ops*.

Cooperative ventures Joint production deals by two or more companies.

Copyright Legal protection from use by other parties without agreement (usually payment).

Core audience In PTV, donors responsible for the very largest donations.

Corporation for Public Broadcasting (CPB) The government-funded financial and administrative unit of national public broadcasting since 1968.

Counter-promotion Spots or ads that seek to capture part of a competitor's audience.

Crawls Text messages that scroll across the bottom of television screens, traditionally used for sports or business information, and also now for promotional messages.

Cross-channel promotion Spots promoting one cable channel scheduled on another channel.

Cross-platform Promotion of a program or event in another medium, such as at retail stores and in movie theaters and at a theme park.

Cross-plugs Verbally or visually mentioning an upcoming person or program in a preceding program; see also *bumpers*.

Cross-promote Advertising one program in a preceding show or one channel on another channel.

Cross-property promotion Touting programs across media platforms, such as from newsletters to television.

CTAM (Cable and Telecommunications Association for Marketing) A nonprofit trade association supporting marketing; *www.ctam.org*.

Cume (audience) Short for cumulative audience, meaning total number of unduplicated listeners or viewers.

Cushioning rate increases Incremental increases in rates rather than all at once, or offers of new services as a screen for rate increases.

Customization Putting identifying source and maybe time or location information on materials.

Cyberspace style Multifaceted screens consisting of vertically and horizontally divided screens, multiple scrolls, inserted boxes, and moving design elements, resembling the nonlinear, information-rich environment of websites.

Database marketing Sales of subscriptions and upgrades using in-house residential subscription lists to target telemarketing and direct mail.

Demographics In ratings, data on the audience's age and gender; in program research, sometimes includes such quantitative information as income and education.

Differentiate Distinguish, as in unique positioning of a cable channel's image

Direct mailers Marketing messages sent by postal mail or e-mail to consumers.

Doorhangers Plastic bags of promotional materials left on doorsteps (or hung on doorknobs where people have doorknobs) by cable operators.

Doubles Usually refers to promos that tout two programs, such as two sequential comedies

Downgrading Reducing cable services, such as by canceling pay channels.

Duopoly Rules FCC regulations regarding the number and types of stations that one company can own, much relaxed in recent years.

DVRs (digital video recorders) Ancillary television equipment for recording, delaying, and manipulating television programming signals, such as *TiVo*.

Economies of scale Efficiencies (with monetary benefits) that come from combining purchasing, billing, promotion, and/or production and distribution so that all operate on large rather than small scales.

Edge effect The visual phenomenon of making the human eye move off a page or away from a screen when items are placed too close to the frame's edge.

E-forwarding Viral distribution of a message to a wider and wider group of people.

Electronic newsletters (e-news) E-mailed instead of printed newsletters to consumers and press.

Episodic A *tune-in* promo for a series.

EPKs (electronic press kits) Video and print materials delivered by satellite for incorporation in local promotion and publicity.

Equity Partial ownership.

Event marketing Promotion of a concert, performance, or other public event, generally sponsored in part by a station and some other entity.

Event promotion Advertising and publicity for special events to be aired, usually on a larger scale than the amount normally given to other programs.

Exclusivity Sole or limited participation, as in a program licensed to just one station in a market, or a special event sponsored by just one of each type of sponsor (one car, one cola, and so on) or a small group of selected sponsors.

External promotion Advertising and other promotion not on the station's own air.

Fall campaign Elaborate promotional efforts to introduce and arouse interest in the coming season's new and ongoing programs.

FCC (Federal Communications Commission). The government agency that regulates the electronic airwaves, including television and radio stations, microwave, satellite, and common carriers (wired telephone); *www.fcc.gov.*

Feedback Audience responses.

First-run series Syndicated series that did not previously appear on a network.

Fixed positions In promotion, airtime in certain time periods reserved for promotional messages.

Flash Animated short programs using Macromedia's Flash animation software.

Flash series Short parodies or humorous animation in video downloaded from the Internet, originally from JibJab.

Flight A modest number of commercial spots or promos covering a short period of time.

Forecasting Predicting events that will require promotional activity.

Format The pattern of a program or *promo*; its type or structure, as in sitcoms or long-form promos.

Formers People who used to subscribe to cable, but moved or canceled.

Forward promotion Promoting the next program in the schedule.

Franchising Contracted use of a brand name by another party, such as variations of *Who Wants to Be a Millionaire?* sold in other countries.

FVOD (free video-on-demand) A limited selection of no-charge programs available alongside for-pay *VOD*.

Generic promotion General promotion for an entire program series rather than a specific night, or for a station or network; see also *Identity* and *Image* promotion.

Giveaways Merchandise or tickets given to a radio caller or website visitor just for being "the seventh caller" or "one millionth visitor."

Global branding Establishing a brand name in many countries.

Globalization The connection of economic interests of corporations and, in some cases, nations with one another into an interrelated worldwide system of commerce.

Graphic vectors Lines within artwork or screens that cause a directional thrust (weak or strong) that affects how the viewer's eye travels within the image.

GRPs (Gross Rating Points) Calculating the size of the delivered or anticipated audience by summing the rating points for all airings of a promo (or commercial spot).

Horizontal promotion Promos that are scheduled across the week or promos that encourage viewing of the next episode of a series.

Horizontal recycling Promoting for the purpose of getting listeners (or viewers) to return to the same channel the next day at the same time (or on television, the next week at the same time).

HUTs (Homes Using Television) The number of households tuning in to television generally at a given time, a subset of which are watching any given channel.

Hybrid stations Television stations affiliates with a network that provides only a small amount of daily programming, thus partly independent, partly affiliated.

Hyperlink Direct connection from e-mail to a website.

Hypoing Artificial and excessive inflating of ratings by using prohibited on-air or printed station activities, such as mentioning diaries or ratings on-air during a ratings period.

ID Short for identity or identification.

Identifier In promotion, the essential information about the source of a program, generally the television channel number and show time, but slightly different for radio, cable, and networks.

Identity The true nature of a media company, meaning a network's or station's programming.

Identity promotion Spots or a campaign to establish a particular image for a station, network, or service in the audience's mind; spots that reinforce a particular image.

Incentives Rewards for certain behavior, such as purchasing advertising or cable subscriptions.

Index vectors Arrows or other direction-suggesting graphic elements that strongly invite the human eye to move in certain directions.

Insertion capability The technical ability to inject local advertising and promotional spots into positions in network programming intended for inserts.

Institutional positioning *Positioning* of companies as a group, as in PBS and public television stations marketing to viewers as a unit rather than a network separate from stations; required *unified branding*.

Institutional promotion Nationwide promotional efforts on behalf of stations and/or networks.

IM (Integrated Marketing) A unified approach to all of a company's marketing, including advertising, promotion, publicity, and community involvement, under a single overarching strategy and using closely congruent tactics.

Image The manufactured and marketed perception of a product or person.

Instant messaging Form of simultaneous e-mail from cell phones or computers.

Interconnects Wired and/or microwave links among many cable systems for the purpose of simultaneous distribution of advertising and promotional messages.

Jingles Bars of music with call letters/identifier or a slogan sung over them.

KEYs In public television, programs selected monthly for network and station promotion.

Keys In station program promotion, the where (channel) and when (time) information essential to effective promotion; in network promotion, the what (title), who (stars), and when (time) messages for effective promotion of prime-time programs.

KISS (Keep it simple, Stupid) Directive to keep promotional message clear under the worst exposure circumstances.

Launch Start of distribution of a new program or new cable or Internet channel.

Glossary **313**

Leap-frogging Advance tune-in promotion for the next program of the same type, as opposed to the upcoming program.

Leave-behind Folder holding a quantity of promotional items mailed or given to advertisers and other appropriate individuals, usually containing selected ratings information, photographs of stars, talent bios, and information about advertising availabilities.

Line extensions Creating new networks using an existing brand name and logo, such as the many Disney companies or many HBO channels.

Liners Voiced transitional devices, prerecorded or live, used on radio between songs or other scheduled elements.

Live shoots Transmitting events by video or audio as they happen, as opposed to prerecorded.

Localism The attitude and FCC policy that much of television and radio programming should be produced in or near a station's city of license, should involve community members, and should be concerned with community problems, activities, and interests.

Logging Recording, as in the official records of what a station airs.

Logos Unique graphic images of a company's name or identity that are protected as trademarks.

Lost cume Smaller ratings as a by-product of inaccurate diary completion.

Lotteries Games and contests that involve all three elements of chance, effort or pay (consideration), and prizes, which are illegal under some conditions.

Lower-third graphics/messages Promotional, advertising, or informational text and graphics superimposed on the lower-third of television screens, covering program content; includes supplementary information (*banners, tickers*), channel now being watched (*bugs*), and what is coming up next (*snipes*).

Machinima Video programs created by taping computer games as players play them.

Made-for-online Original programs produced for online distribution.

Maintenance promotion Goal of retaining listeners; same as *retentive goal.*

MediaPCs Computers connected to cable TV with software that permits e-mailing of digital content.

Merchandising In media, the distribution and sale of customized network or station-related products, such as hats, totes, or games with logos, or related to program content (dolls, toys, DVDs).

Message What the promotion person wants to convey.

Message points Brief positioning statements.

Mobisodes One-minute TV programs intended for mobile media recipients.

Motion vectors Aspects of video, such as actors or cameras moving, that attract viewers' eyes.

MSOs (Multiple System Operators) Owners of many local cable franchises.

Multiple spots Promos that mention several upcoming programs, commonly two or three or more in one 30-second spot.

NAB (National Association of Broadcasters). The powerful trade association representing the entire media industry; *www.nab.org.*

NCTA (National Cable Television Association) The trade group for cable systems and networks; *www.ncta.org.*

Netvertising Using a range of sensory inputs and graphics on the Internet to sell products (or possibly programs).

Nevers People who have not previously subscribed to cable service.

New builds Recently developed residential areas, ripe for marketing cable subscriptions.

News co-ops Extra money for stations for promoting network newscasts, usually adjacent to local newscasts, in print media or radio.

Next-up promotion Titles or video that spells out the name of the immediately following program; includes automatic advance titling as in *snipes* and *bumpers*.

NTR (nontraditional revenue) Income from sources other than advertising spot sales.

OES (Optimum Effective Scheduling) Number of times per week needed to reach the station's entire audience at least once.

On-air campaign A planned sequence of promotional spots.

On-air promotion Promotion via *promos, signatures, IDs*, and so on that is broadcast or placed in and between programs on television, cable, or radio, as opposed to appearing in print or signage.

Online mini-movies Typically, short musical parodies distributed via the Internet.

OPM (Other people's money and other people's media) Shorthand for *tradeouts* and gaining donations.

Over-credits promo A promotional message that may be read aurally while credits are rolling or that is visually superimposed over or sharing a split screen with the end credits.

Overlay graphics Promotional messages placed briefly on top of ongoing program contents, usually promoting the upcoming network program.

Overmarketing Selling customers on more cable services than they can readily afford.

Participatory empowerment The sense of control over one's environment gained from participation.

Pay-for-play The practice of record companies paying stations (legally) to play their songs in a certain time period with a certain frequency.

Payola Bribes or kickbacks for promoting songs on the air.

PDAs (Personal Digital Assistants) Hand-held electronic gadgets including calendars, calculators, phone lists, and note-taking space, intended to take the place of rolodexes and appointment diaries.

Peoplemeter An electronic meter attached to a TV set requiring all viewers to log themselves in and out of viewing (via buttons).

Personality appearances Public activities by a station's *talent* as hosts or guests.

Photo ops Opportunities arranged for the taking of photographs or video by the media.

Planned giving Arranging for bequests in wills.

Platforms Complex levels of digital media technology encompassing bandwidth, types of compression, computerized memory, and other technical requirements in production and distribution; commonly distinguishes among types of over-the-air broadcasting, wired and microwave cablecasting, and wired and wireless Internet distribution.

Pledge scripts Written guidelines (in actual sentences) for fundraising breaks in programs to be used by station spokespeople.

Plug An on-air mention.

Plugola Bribes or kickbacks for covert promotion of products or places on the air.

Podcasting Short episodes (5 minutes or less) of long-form commercials on the Internet, generally live and not stored.

Pod A group of commercials, promos, and public service announcements in one break inside or between programs.

Point-of-purchase displays Signs in such places where products or services may be purchased, such as signs about HBO offerings for cable operators' lobbies.

Pooling A group of stations or other companies sharing costs and profits, or in the case of pooling contest resources in radio, co-owned stations contributing their available prize money to offer one gigantic prize so that they can air (and promote) a single big contest.

Pop-outs In PTV, extra promotion for a few shows in a season to make them stand out to viewers.

Pop-ups Promotional (or advertising) messages that briefly overlay program content on the screen and then disappear; having a program graphic and start-time suddenly superimposed on top of program content for a few seconds, an attention-getting *tune-in* device.

Portals Entrances to the World Wide Web or other major parts of the Internet, especially AOL, MSN, and others such as Google that lead to many sites.

Positioning Establishing a unique location for a media company's (or program's) recognizable image in the minds of viewers, listeners, and advertisers.

PPMs (portable peoplemeters) Experimental hand-held methods of capturing media usage information.

PPV (pay-per-view) Type of premium *VOD* in which the subscriber pays only when a program (usually a movie) is viewed.

Press releases Written notices of newsworthy events, usually relating to a station (or network) personality, music, or staff, delivered to media and selected community groups in person, by mail, or increasingly, by e-mail.

Prestige branding spots Image spots produced by acknowledged industry leaders who do not need to raise their *brand awareness* but may need to deliver "proof of performance," that is, spots which demonstrate the program source is living up to its promises.

Primary research Studies conducted by the user, such as surveys or focus groups implemented by a network or station itself.

PROMAX An acronym made from parts of "promotion," "marketing," and "executives" that names the nonprofit international trade association representing and informing the marketing managers for the electronic media, predominantly in broadcast television around the world; *www.promax.org*.

Promos On-air messages about programs and media services that try to motivate viewers, listeners, and users to watch or listen to specific programs or particular channels.

Promotion In media, enticing audiences to view television programs, listen to radio stations, or use websites, as well as the selling of programs and services and the marketing of company and program images.

Proof of benefit Promos that remind viewers of a particular gain they received from viewing or listening.

PSAs (public service announcements) Preproduced or live messages about community events and concerns that are carried by stations as a public service obligation (for example, messages from the National Cancer Society or announcements about the local county fair).

PSPs (Play Station Portable) Sony's newest contribution to video Play Station hardware.

Psychographics Information about audience's preferences, likings, recognition, and other non-demographic data.

Publicity build-up Public relations and promotional activities prior to an event, such as a launching a new season or a new cable or online channel.

Pull Promotion to stimulate viewers' desire for a cable channel.

Push Promotion to stimulate cable operators' desire to carry a cable channel.

RADAR An arm of the Arbitron Company that conducts audience size research for the national radio networks.

Recycling In radio, the effort to lure listeners to return at some later time.

Reinforcement Repetitions that increase impact along with promotional *congruence* among messages.

Remarketing Reselling cable services to households that failed to subscribe previously or selling *upgrades* to current subscribers.

Remotes On-location live broadcasting and personality appearances.

Reps (representatives) Sales agents handling time sales for a station or system.

Repurposing Replaying a program on another co-owned platform, such as scheduling a broadcast program on a cable network or a website, or in another time period, such as rerunning prime-time shows in daytime; also refers to reuse of a program idea in merchandise sales, theme parks, computer games, video games, and so on.

Reruns Repeats of programs on the same or different stations or networks; usually syndicated or repurposed.

Retentive goal Aiming to motivate viewers or listeners to return loyally to a channel or to convince them to watch or listen to one channel for long periods of time.

Revenue Dollar income that is usually a gross amount unless identified as net, meaning after subtracting expenses.

Reversal Print ads (or on-screen messages) that have the writing in white instead of the usual black or color.

Sales promotion The process (and materials) for selling advertising in television and radio programs to advertisers; in radio, often connected to listener contests and games.

Satellite (media tours) Allow stations to bring well-known personalities to local programs.

Satellite (talent interviews) Stars of network series and specials are available for local interviews.

Schmoozing Interacting with clients, stars, or *talent*, with the intent of keeping them happy.

Seamless programming Shifting from program to program without intervening end-credits, commercials, promotional spots, or start-credits.

Segmentation Audience research analyses which are subdivided by findings for small demographic groups of interest to advertisers or particular radio stations.

Series A regularly-scheduled program with many episodes.

Shared IDs On-air screens split between identification of the station (its logo) and promotion for a program.

Shell A printed heading or border on stationary that can be filled in with sales messages.

Signaling value Telling viewers (and underwriters) why public broadcasting is important; positioning messages that stress the gains for individuals or society.

Signature The combination of visuals, graphics, and audio by which a station wants to be recognized.

Singles Promos that tout just one program, not two or more.

Sister sites Websites of co-owned cable channels or other co-owned properties.

Slicks High-quality versions of promotional or advertising materials on shiny paper intended for reproduction in magazines or other printed materials, largely superseded by e-mailed digital files.

Snipes Very brief notices of upcoming television programs, commonly accomplished with pop-ups of program titles and other graphics during the preceding television program.

Solicited (e-mail/e-newsletters) Electronic messages that were ordered by the receiver; contrasts with *spam.*

Soundbeds Reusable background sounds comprising music and effects on which vocal announcements are superimposed.

Spam Unwanted e-mail messages.

Spam filter Junk mail blockers installed at servers or locally on personal computers.

Specials One-time-only or once-annually programs, such as the Academy Awards or Super Bowl.

Specific spot A promotional message for a program on a certain date rather than generically for the whole series, also called *topicals* and *episodics*; see also *tune-in promotion.*

Spinoffs Programs that come from other programs, most commonly taking a character or subplot from a successful series and turning it into a separate full series.

Splash page The first screen that a web user sees when accessing any site.

Split logging Dividing an on-air announcement into portions attributed to public service and portions attributed to commercial matter.

Split screen Dividing the TV screen in two segments with different content on the halves, such as end-credits on one side and news teases on the other.

Spots On-air television or radio promos or commercials.

Spreads Estimates of anticipated expenses by the month.

Stack ads Print advertising for programs that promotes several programs, usually all network prime-time shows or a co-op combining network and local evening programs, commonly appearing in guides and newspapers.

Station buy-in Voluntary agreement with a practice advocated the network.

Station IDs Legally, on-air identification of call letters and city of license required only at sign-on/sign-off (or once at 6:00 a.m.); more informally, any identification of the station on the air, such as a logo or signature.

Stickiness A quality of promotional (or advertising) messages that compels viewers to stay to experience the entire message.

Strategic goal Overarching aim that spells out the purpose for a service or a campaign, usually incorporating the method of producing revenue.

Studios The major Hollywood movie studios, especially Columbia TriStar, Paramount, 20th Century Fox, and NBC Universal.

Subniche channels Second and third cable networks multiplexed with the established signal to capture more of the viewing audience; often used to time-shift pay movies.

Super bugs Pop-up messages combining animation and sound effects to capture viewers' attention.

Supersizing the core Greatly emphasizing the needs of the donating audience at the expense of serving nondonors.

Sweeps The quarterly nationwide ratings periods in November, February, April, and July, in which ratings are collected for all local television stations.

Sweepers In radio, short, highly-produced imaging spots consisting of station identifiers, slogans, and/or air talent's names used to transition from one song to the next while identifying the station.

Syndicated research Also called secondary research, meaning that a company purchases research data and analyses from another company who actually did the primary research, such as a network or station purchasing Nielsen or Arbitron ratings.

Syndication The business of marketing old and some new *series* to individual stations or to networks outside the United States.

Syndicators Distributors of programs that prepare promotional material to aid in the selling of movies and programs to potential affiliates in broadcasting or cable.

System promotion Advertising of customer services and program *tune-in* spots.

Tactical approach Ways of implementing a strategy, such as choosing a specific medium and level of repetition to reach teenage viewers or some other group.

Tag (tagline) Copy for superimposed audio telling where and when something will occur; also, a theme line placed under a logo, defining the service's offerings.

Talent On-air personnel of a station, including news anchors, weather and sports reporters, and video and disk jockeys.

Target group In promotion, the demographically- or psychographically-defined audience group that an item of promotion or a campaign aims at reaching.

Teases Brief live spots intended to lure viewers to a newscast or talk program, such as when newscasters stand in front of cameras and lure viewers by telling them that the upcoming newscast will tell them a sporting event's outcome and tomorrow's weather.

Testimonials Brief video (or audio) expressions of support from celebrities or the general public.

Themes Ways of tying together several programs or movies, as in Western Night or Fright Night, or that creates an umbrella image for a station.

Tickers Listings of stock and bond prices or other numeric data that scroll across the bottom of television or computer screens; also, digital (or analog) clocks that count down until the next program or some other event starts.

Tie-ins Packages from a network of materials for assembling local station promos using network themes, graphics, and music; also, campaigns that are joint operations of an advertiser and a network or station.

TiVo Brand name for the first and most widely known digital video recorder.

Topical A *tune-in* promo for a series.

Tradeouts Agreements to trade on-air mentions of a company for merchandise or services.

TSLs (time-spent-listening) The measure of continued exposure to a radio station.

TSOs (time-spent-online) The measure of continued use of a website.

TSVs (time-spent-viewing) The measure of continued exposure to a television station or cable network.

Tune-in promotion On-air *promos* or print advertising that entice viewers or listeners to watch or listen to a specific episode of a series or a one-time-only airing of a special program; has a brief shelf-life — only until that episode or program is aired.

Turnkey arrangements Use of specialist companies to handle a portion of a company's business, such as an advertising agency to sell the time on a cable system or a billing company to handle monthly subscription payments.

TVB (Television Bureau of Advertising). Nonprofit trade association supporting television advertising; *www.tvb.org.*

Umbrella Overarching theme or label for many programs or elements of promotion.

Underwriters Companies that fund the production (and concomitant promotion) of public television and public radio programs.

Unified branding Using the same logos, themes, and graphics in all promotion, publicity, and advertising.

Upgrading Adding more channels or services, such as pay channels, digital service, or Internet access.

USP (unique selling point) A phrase capturing that which is special about a service or program.

Variance report Informally, notes about differences between predicted and actual expenses, to be summarized in a formal report.

Vectors In two-dimensional design, the lines of force or visual pressures that make the human eye move in fixed patterns, such as vertically, horizontally, or diagonally.

Vertical integration Ownership of the means of production and distribution by the same company, as when one media company produces the programs it airs on its network; distributes them to stations it owns, as well as its affiliated stations; and later syndicates the programs to other stations, and markets the videos or DVDS.

Vertical recycling Promoting with the aim of getting listeners (or viewers) to return to the channel later in the same day.

Viral marketing Using consumers to spread promotional (or advertising) messages by forwarding, generally occurring when the messages are especially funny and clever or exceptionally useful.

VOD (video-on-demand) Programs (usually movies) that can be called up for viewing when desired; may be for pay (or not).

Voice-overs Promotional tags or next-ups delivered by announcers in audio over unrelated video, such as closing credits.

VoIP (Voice over Internet Protocol) Telephone service relaying calls over an Internet relay rather than beginning on a traditional wire carrier (a phone company), although the calls may connect to a traditional telephone or cell receiver.

Webcasts Amateur or professional video content placed online as programming.

Webisodes Brief episodes (5 minutes or less) of series-like programs on the Internet; also, video *blogs.*

Wild lines Clips out of context, requiring permission from clip distributors.

Wordmarks Trademarked ways of writing a media company's name.

Selected Bibliography

This bibliography lists books and articles focusing on promotion and marketing by media companies that have been published since 2000. Some items cited in individual chapters are also included here, as well as periodicals that carry frequent and substantial articles about media company practices and the marketing of television and radio programs and services. Videos and websites of interest to students of promotion appear at the end of each chapter. For books and articles published before 2000, consult the bibliographies of preceding editions of this book.

Albarran, A. B. *Management of Electronic Media, 2ⁿᵈ ed.* Belmont, CA: Wadsworth, 2002.

Albarran, A. B. *Media Economics: Understanding Markets, Industries and Concepts, 2ⁿᵈ ed.* Ames, IA: Blackwell, 2002.

Austerberry, D. *Technology of Video and Audio Streaming.* Boston, MA: Focal Press, 2002.

Avery, R. K., and Stavitsky, A. G. *A History of Public Broadcasting: Mission v. Market.* Washington, D.C.: Current Publishing, 2000.

Balas, G. *Recovering a Public Vision for Public Television.* Boulder, CO: Rowman & Littlefield, 2003.

Billboard: The International Weekly of Music and Home Entertainment. New York, 1894 to date.

Bland, M., Theaker, A., and Wragg, D. *Effective Media Relations: How to Get Results, 3ʳᵈ ed.* Herndon, VA: Kogan Page, 2005.

Boyle, R., Flood, P., and Kevin, D. *Sport and the Media.* Mahwah, NJ: Erlbaum, 2004.

CableFax Daily. Online publication. Potomac, MD: Access Intelligence Cable Group, 1989 to date.

CableFax Magazine. Biannual. Potomac, MD: Access Intelligence Cable Group, 1989 to date.

Cooper-Chen, A. (Ed.). *Global Entertainment Media: Content, Audiences, and Issues.* Mahwah, NJ: Erlbaum, 2005.

Current. Weekly Washington newspaper about public broadcasting, 1981 to date. *www.current.org.*

Eastman, S. T. (Ed.) *Research in Media Promotion.* Mahwah, NJ: Erlbaum, 2000.

Eastman, S. T., and Billings, A. C. (2004). Promotion's Limited Impact in the 2000 Sydney Olympics. *Television and New Media, 5*(4), 339–358.

Eastman, S. T., and Ferguson, D. A. (Eds.) *Media Programming: Strategies and Practices, 7ᵗʰ ed.* Belmont, CA: Wadsworth, 2006.

Eastman, S. T., Newton, G. D., and Bolls, P. (2003). How Promotional Content Changes Ratings: The Impact of Appeals, Humor, and Presentation. *Journal of Applied Communication Research, 31*(3), 238–259.

Eastman, S. T., Schwartz, N. C., and Cai, X. (2002). Children and Promoted Television Movies: Unwanted and Inescapable Content. *Communication, 28*(1), 3–15.

Eastman, S. T., Schwartz, N. C., and Cai, X. (2005). Promoting Movies on Television. *Journal of Applied Communication Research, 33*(2), 139–158.

Eastman, S. T., and Walker, J. R. (2005, Apr.). Who Gets Promoted: Character Portrayals in Network Promotional Messages. Paper presented at the Broadcast Education Association Conference, Las Vegas, NV.

Hamilton, S. *Entertainment Content Protection: Technology, Rights Management, and Legal Constraints*. Boston, MA: Focal Press, 2004.

Hamula, S. R., and Williams, W. (2003). The Internet as a Small-Market Radio Station Promotional Tool. *Journal of Radio Studies, 10*(2), 262–269.

Hoch, M., and Rayburn, D. *The Business of Streaming and Digital Media*. Boston, MA: Focal Press, 2004.

The Journal of Broadcasting & Electronic Media. Broadcast Education Association, 1955 to date.

The Journal of Radio Studies. Broadcast Education Association, 1991 to date.

Kapferer, J.-N. *The New Strategic Brand Management: Creating and Sustaining Brand Equity Long Term, 3rd ed.* New York: Kogan Page, 2004.

Keith, M. C. *The Radio Station, 6th ed.* Boston, NY: Focal Press, 2003.

McCauley, M., Peterson, E., Artz, B., and Halleck, D. *Public Broadcasting and the Public Interest*. New York: M. E. Sharpe, 2003.

Miller, P. *Media Law for Producers, 4th ed.* Boston, MA: Focal Press, 2003.

Moody, A., Greer, J., and Linn, T. (2003). Public Radio Station Web Sites and Their Users. *Journal of Radio Studies, 10*(2), 255–261.

Mueller, B. *Dynamics of International Advertising: Theoretical and Practical Perspectives*. New York: P. Lang, 2004.

Multichannel News. Weekly trade magazine. New York: Reed Business Information, 1979 to date.

Noam, E., Groebel, J., and Gerbarg, D. (Eds.). *Internet Television*. Mahwah, NJ: Erlbaum, 2004.

Pitts, M. J., and Harms, R. (2003). Radio Websites as a Promotional Tool. *Journal of Radio Studies, 10*(2), 270–282.

Potter, R. F. (2002). Give the People What They Want: A Content Analysis of Radio Station Home Pages. *Journal of Broadcasting & Electronic Media, 46*(3), 369–384.

Potter, R. F., Williams, G. C., and Newton, G. D. (2003). Juggling Brands: The Pressures and Perks of Radio Promotion Directors in the Age of Acquisition. *Journal of the Northwest Communication Association, 32*(2), 78–95.

PROMO Magazine. New York: Primedia Business Magazines and Media, 1987 to date.

Rosen, E. *The Anatomy of Buzz: How to Create Word of Mouth Marketing*. New York: Doubleday/Currency, 2002.

Smith, P. R., and Taylor, J. *Marketing Communications: An Integrated Approach, 4th ed.* New York: Kogan Page, 2004.

Stafford, M. R., and Faber, R. J. (Eds.). *Advertising, Promotion, and New Media*. Armonk, NY: M. E. Sharpe, 2005.

Swann, P. (2000). *TV Dot Com: The Future of Interactive Television*. New York: TV Books.

Szwarc, P. *Researching Customer Satisfaction and Loyalty*. New York: Kogan Page, 2005.

Television Week. Chicago, 1982 to date. *www.tvweek.com*.

Trout, J., and Rifkin, S. *Differentiate or Die: Survival in Our Era of Killer Competition*. New York: John Wiley, 2000.

Van Gelder, S. *Global Brand Strategy: Unlocking Brand Potential Across Cultures*. New York: Kogan Page, 2004.

Variety: Weekly Trade Newspaper of Stage and Film, Television, and the Recording Industries. New York and Hollywood, 1925 to date.

Waisbord, S. (2004). McTV: Understanding the Global Popularity of Television Formats. *Television & New Media, 5*(4), 359–383.

Walker, J. R., and Eastman, S. T. (2003). On-Air Promotion Effectiveness for Programs of Different Genres, Familiarity, and Audience Demographics. *Journal of Broadcasting & Electronic Media, 47*(4), 618–637.

Ward, D. (2004). *Public Service Broadcasting: Change and Continuity*. A Special Issue of *Trends in Communication, 12*(1).

Webster, J. G., Phalen, P. F., and Lichty, L. W. *Ratings Analysis: The Theory and Practice of Audience Research, 3rd ed.* Mahwah, NJ: Erlbaum, 2006.

Werner, C., and Buchman, J. G. *Media Selling: Broadcast, Cable, Print, and Interactive, 3rd ed.* Ames, IO: Blackwell, 2004.

Wimmer, R. D., and Dominick, J. R. *Mass Media Research: An Introduction, 7th ed.* Belmont, CA: Wadsworth, 2006.

Wirth, M. O. (Ed.). *The Economics of the Multichannel Video Program Distribution Industry: A Special Issue of the Journal of Media Economics*. Mahwah, NJ: Erlbaum, 2002.

Zettl, H. *Sight Sound Motion: Applied Media Aesthetics, 4th ed.* Belmont, CA: Wadsworth, 2005.

Index